Sustainability And
The Small And Medium Enterprise (SME):
Becoming More Professional

Sustainability And
The Small And Medium Enterprise (SME):
Becoming More Professional

Michael J Sheehan

Copyright © 2013 by Michael J Sheehan.

Library of Congress Control Number:		2013902604
ISBN:	Hardcover	978-1-4797-6239-2
	Softcover	978-1-4797-6238-5
	Ebook	978-1-4797-6240-8

All rights reserved. No part of this book may be reproduced or transmitted in any form or by any means, electronic or mechanical, including photocopying, recording, or by any information storage and retrieval system, without permission in writing from the copyright owner.

To order additional copies of this book, contact:
Xlibris Corporation
1-800-618-969
www.xlibris.com.au
Orders@xlibris.com.au
502610

Contents

Preface 13
Acknowledgements 17

Chapter 1. Introduction 19

    Introduction 19
    Setting the scene 20

        Economic drivers 21
        Global financial crisis 22
        Australasian region 23
        Prospects for SMEs 24

    Reasons for the focus on staff skills and performance 26
    Economic recovery 27
    Environment 29

Chapter 2. Sustainability 30

    Introduction 30
    Sustainability and sustainable development 30
    Creating a sustainable future 31
    Key characteristics of sustainability 33
    Strategy for sustainability 34
    A role for the SME 35
    Encouraging sustainability in an SME 35
    Engaging employees in building a sustainable SME 37
    Minimum requirements for SMEs 39

Cost 39
Quality 39
Time 40
Absence of customer complaints 40
One further requirement 40

Chapter 3. The Small and Medium Enterprise (SME) 42

Introduction 42
Background 42
The small and medium business (SME) 43
SME Defined 45

>Social Entity 45
>Strategy 46
>Structure 46
>Culture 46

An SME owner/manager defined 47
The SME as a learning organisation 48

>Mental models 48
>Personal mastery 49
>Shared vision 49
>Team learning 50
>Systems thinking 50

Chapter 4. Mental Models 52

Introduction 52
Mental models 52
Complex adaptive systems (CASs) 55

>1. Relationship creation and networking 58
>2. Responsibility and empowerment 58
>3. Agility 59
>4. Equality and diversity 60
>5. Sensemaking 60
>6. Embrace learning 61
>7. Improvising 62
>8. Emergent thinking 63

Chapter 5. Professionalism 65

   Introduction 65
   About professions 65
   About professionalism 67
   Principles of professionalism 69
   Consequences of professionalism 70

      Values 71
      Attitudes 72
      Behaviour 73

   Summary 74

Chapter 6. Qualities for Professionalism in SMEs 75

   Introduction 75
   A set of qualities for professionalism in SMEs 75

      Commitment to excellence 76
      Honesty 76
      Integrity 77
      Respect for others 78
      Compassion 79
      Transparency 79
      Fairness 80
      Professional responsibility 81
      Social responsibility 81
      Altruism 82

   A set of requirements for being a professional 83
   Summary 84

Chapter 7. Self-Awareness 85

   Introduction 85
   Becoming professional 86
   Recognising a lack of self-awareness 87

      The 'know it all' 87
      The 'whinger' 88
      The 'egotist' 88

The 'manipulator' 89
The 'chopper' 90
The 'criticiser' 90
The 'irrationalist' 91
The 'bullocky' 91
The 'despot' 91

Becoming self-aware 92

The self 92
The importance of self-awareness 94

Johari window 95

Johari quadrant 1—open/free area 97
Johari quadrant 2—blind area 98
Johari quadrant 3—hidden area 98
Johari quadrant 4—unknown area 99
Johari window example—increasing open area
through feedback solicitation and disclosure 101

Transactional analysis 102

The script 102

Ego states 103

Parent 103
Adult 104
Child 105

Contracting 105
Contemporary transactional analysis theory 106

Parent 106
Adult 106
Child 106

Effective modes 107
Ineffective modes 108
Summary 108

Chapter 8. Mindfulness 109

Introduction 109
Mindfulness 110
Development and use of the concept within a Western framework 110
Becoming mindful... 112
Inhibitors of mindfulness 114
Different from self-awareness 114
Recognising mindfulness 115

    The 'self-assured' 115
    The 'acceptor' 116
    The 'individualist' 117
    The 'inspirationalist' 117
    The 'valuer' 118
    The 'supporter' 118
    The 'rationalist' 119
    The 'humanitarian' 119
    The 'democrat' 119

What being mindful will do 120
Using mindfulness in the workplace 122
Summary.. 122

Chapter 9. Adult Learning 124

Introduction 124
Learning 125

    Context for learning and continuous improvement.................... 125

The Importance of considering change as a learning process........... 127
How those notions inform adult learning in the
   transition to a professional SME 129
Approaches to learning in organisations 130
Definition of learning.. 130
The scientific approach to learning in organisations 131

    1. Behaviourist theories... 131
    2. Cognitive theories.. 132
    3. Social learning theory.. 133

Progressive-humanist approaches to learning in organisations 134

    1. John Dewey, Carl Rogers, Paulo Freire,
       and Malcolm Knowles 135
    2. Jack Mezirow 137
    3. Stephen Brookfield 138
    4. Reg Revans 139
    5. David Kolb 141
    6. Peter Honey and Alan Mumford 143

Definition of reflection and critical reflection 145
The Importance of critical reflection as a tool for understanding 145

Chapter 10. Leadership 147

Introduction 147
General understanding of leadership 148
Overview of major leadership theories 149

    Trait theories 150
    Contingency or situational theories 151
    Transactional leadership theories 151
    Transformational leadership theories 152
    Authentic leadership theory 153
    Developing leaders and leadership 154
    What I mean by leadership development 155

Summary 157

Chapter 11. Team Learning 158

Introduction 158
What team learning entails 159
Meaningful conversations 160
How to hold a meaningful conversation 165
Roles for team learning 166
Roles for SME team learning 167
Identifying that team learning is occurring 168
Summary 169

Chapter 12. Systems Thinking 170

    Introduction 170
    Systems thinking explained 171
    How you will know systems thinking is occurring 172
    Summary 173

Chapter 13. SME Change and Its Consequences 174

    Introduction 174
    Theories of organisational change (and their application for SMEs) 175
    Organisational change assumptions 176
    The importance of considering change as a learning process 177
    The centrality of the conceptualisation of the learning experience ... 178
    The difficulty of reconstructing relationships 179
    The experience of unfulfilled expectations 180
    The importance of a heightened tolerance of others 181
    A heightened understanding of self 182
    Conclusion 183

References 185
Further Reading 201
Index 203

Preface

The early years of the twenty-first century appear to be perplexing to many of us who can recall *the good old days*. There were, of course, no such days. Life is relative to our spatial and temporal experiences. Nonetheless, working in some contemporary organisations, and in small and medium enterprises (SMEs) in particular, is turning out to be an almost daily struggle to survive. Some of the confusion inherent in that struggle may be attributed to a perceived lack of government support for SMEs and the need to adapt rapidly in the face of ever-emerging uncertainty. Such uncertainty also may partly be attributed to factors such as globalisation and its consequences, an ever-changing social, economic, and environmental climate, institutional failures, and to acts or threats of acts of terrorism. An ever-changing labour market and increasing customer and supplier expectations may be added to the mix.

There is, therefore, a broad realisation that we need to create a sustainable future. Such a future means the creation of sustainable societies and SMEs within an environment that is resilient. We need innovative products and ideas, the creation of new markets, resolution of age-old business problems, and improved public understanding and strengthening of sustainable Australian brands worldwide. There needs to be a combined effort from business, governments, and non-government organisations to do so more holistically than currently is the case.

SMEs are faced with the seemingly impossible task of responding to inescapable changes as a result of the aforementioned factors. The result for some SMEs has been loss of business and/or bankruptcy and closure. As SMEs attempt to cope with the changing conditions in an effort to become sustainable, they also face attitudinal and behavioural shifts by their employees. Concepts such as loyalty, commitment, and service have morphed over time such that there appears to be a growing mistrust of management and their motives and increased employee anxiety. Customers tend to experience the outcomes of these changes as poor goods or service.

Now is not the time to resist; rather, it is the time for change. To keep pace with the demands of change, SMEs have to develop new ways of thinking about, and dealing with, their customers, suppliers, stakeholders, and employees. Such development requires a great deal of introspection. The use of new technology, such as the Internet, iPads, and iPhones, serves as a laudable beginning, but technology can only go so far. There are other ways in which SMEs might continuously improve so that they become more sustainable. One way is for SME owners and managers to become more professional in all that they do, which may require self-development and the development of their employees.

I am a small business owner. But I also have worked as a staff development consultant and a human resource consultant in a large public sector organisation, followed by almost twenty years as a tertiary academic (but do not hold that against me). In that part of my life, I have been exposed to a number of personal development programmes in groups of various sizes. I also have worked as a consultant, mainly in a learning and development capacity, to many small, medium, and large public and private sector organisations in Australia and the United Kingdom. I have attended many conferences and other fora as a keynote speaker, a presenter of papers, a workshop convenor, an advisor, a consultant, or in some similar capacity. I also have been involved in the establishment and development of two associations and a research centre relating to inappropriate workplace behaviours.

In those fora, I have participated in discussions with many clients, client groups, colleagues, and students in which the problems and dilemmas that people surfaced during the discussions raised my curiosity about the challenges that they faced, particularly from a SME perspective. Initially I began to satisfy my curiosity by reading and watching media reports about SMEs. I then turned to social media sites for further insight before engaging with the academic literature. The information so gleaned germinated the ideas and focus for this book.

Some curiosity was aroused, for example, by a number of Australian surveys seeming to suggest that SMEs, while initially optimistic, have become increasingly pessimistic about Australia's economic recovery and lacking in confidence for their future. The October 2012 Consumer Price Index shows price increases across a number of commodities. Fears about the implications of the carbon tax and mining taxes often are expressed. Natural disasters, such as those seen throughout the eastern states of Australia, particularly in Queensland in 2010 and 2011, also impact SMEs. Together, these factors suggest that SME concerns are well grounded.

Interestingly, the main reasons SMEs give for the drop in confidence are that people are not spending, there is a general decrease in business, and they have concerns with the general economic outlook and, in particular, the impact of the carbon tax. By contrast, those who remain confident do so because they feel that they are established businesses, experienced in their business relations, and have good customer relations.

Moreover, many of the respondents to the surveys are dissatisfied with the federal government and feel that government shows a lack of respect. The reasons proffered for such thinking include lack of incentives for small businesses, unhelpful government policies, the level of bureaucracy, and the cost of doing business.

While generally supportive of what small business is saying, I also think that it is too easy to blame others. Some level of responsibility has to be accepted, particularly when there is ample evidence to suggest that SMEs are not meeting customer expectations and that they need to become more sustainable. This thinking led me to explore the literature in an attempt to conceptualise and further understand some of the problems facing SMEs and I drew a conclusion that to become more sustainable, SMEs need to become more professional. To become more professional, more investment in learning and development is required. Thus my focus in this book is on a staff development and performance approach for three reasons.

First, issues such as economic recovery and the environment are in many ways beyond the scope of an SME owner/manager in their daily routines. They are constrained in what they can do in the short term as they struggle for survival in a rapidly changing world. Second, issues such as accounting and economics are beyond my expertise, other than in a general sense. Third, it is a fundamental belief that if people working in SMEs have the knowledge, skills, and abilities to do their job, from a human relations and personal development perspective, or from a *soft skills* approach, then the more technical aspects of their roles will be more easily achieved. Those roles will be enhanced because people have a better understanding of themselves and others as they go about their day-to-day tasks. People do make it possible.

Learning *soft skills* is an important way for people to grow and develop. It allows people to discover meaning and to express themselves within the cultural and social context of their SME. It allows them to develop intimate and meaningful relationships with their colleagues, customers, suppliers, and other stakeholders. These relationships can only be beneficial for the SME and for the individual.

The aim of this book, therefore, is to help SMEs become sustainable and more professional through the development of all staff working in the SME. Some strategies for how they might do so are offered.

The reader of course must be the final arbiter of this book. What you as the reader choose to accept, and perhaps even utilise from this book, will reflect your own philosophy of doing business. At this stage, therefore, it is appropriate for me to state my philosophy and how that philosophy has helped me conceptualise and develop my professional practice.

Essentially, I believe that people in organisations, and here the particular focus is on SMEs, have a right to be treated with respect, dignity, and honesty, requiring me as a researcher, author, and facilitator of learning to take an ethical stance in terms of my professional practice. One way for me to do so is to be open about why I wrote this book and what I hope it will achieve.

The learning from my research, and the situations offered to me as a result of the research process, have helped me to understand the dilemmas and uncertainties with which many SMEs are faced. I do not pretend to know it all. Rather, I have sought to understand the problems from the distinct perspective of the individual as evidenced in secondary research and by talking to SME colleagues. The strength to be drawn from that experience comes from an understanding of the realities SMEs face as they attempt to cope with change. I relay in this book my challenge to SME owners, managers, and employees.

I have endeavoured to preserve the story of my journey for future generations. I would like to do so collaboratively and co-operatively with you, the reader. I welcome your feedback.

Acknowledgements

My parents were small business owners for a good part of their working lives. They owned a small menswear business and later were licensees of small hotels. They raised me with an ethos of service to the customer and a philosophy of *the customer is always right*. I was also raised to *value add*. When my father owned the menswear store, I was seconded after school and on Saturdays to help out. I was taught that if a customer came in to buy a piece of clothing, then I should also attempt to sell the customer something extra. So if an adult male came in to buy a pair of trousers, he should leave with a matching shirt, belt, socks, and tie. This approach well and truly predated the 'Would you like fries with that?' request from fast-food chain staff that emerged many years later. My first acknowledgement, therefore, is to my late parents, Brian and Ann.

Although most of my adult life has been spent working in large public and private sector organisations, a few places would fit the definition of a small and medium enterprise. I also had a career as an academic before moving into my own small business. I have been fascinated by the workings of small business, for what seems a lifetime, and so I acknowledge the people I have met and worked with on that journey.

My academic career has helped me to understand the fascinations and machinations of working with people and to those researchers and writers from whom I have drawn inspiration in this book, I say thank you.

I have been encouraged and supported in the production of this book by the team at Xlibris. I give particular thanks to Lloyd Griffith, Peter Lewis, Vincent Morre, and Yanie Cortes. Thanks also to all staff behind the scenes who worked so hard to bring my work to fruition.

My final thanks go to my extended family, and in particular, my wife Rosie, and my sons, Adam and Timothy, for all your love, support, and inspiration.

Chapter 1

Introduction

Introduction

Small and medium enterprises (SMEs) play a vital role in the Australian economy. It is a role that seemingly often goes unrecognised and unrewarded by the government. In part, the lack of recognition may be attributed to the nature and size of SMEs in that they do not have the political clout or lobbying ability of larger enterprises. Being unrewarded may similarly be ascribed.

But SMEs also need to shoulder some of the responsibilities for their own performance. It is not enough to blame the government, economic conditions, environmental uncertainty, rapid technological change, labour supply, education systems, or the weather for their ability to perform to the expectations placed upon them by customers, suppliers, and significant others. It is time to turn inward and to consider ways in which SMEs may improve their performance and become more sustainable. Approaches by which they might do so are offered in this book.

This chapter commences by setting the scene for the arguments to follow. It is shown that there are many drivers of change impacting SMEs and that customer expectations form a key factor for change. Economic drivers, and in particular, the global financial crisis of 2008-2009, and continuing global financial uncertainty, also are outlined as key factors. Then follows contextual information relating to the Australasian region, including a positive prognosis for the region and a discussion of a changing outlook as further evidence emerges.

Some of the reasons for the focus on staff skills and performance that are offered in the book are then outlined. The chapter concludes with further contextual information relating to economic recovery and the environment.

Setting the scene

There are many drivers for change impacting contemporary SMEs. They include increased competition locally, nationally, and for some, internationally. Increasing trade between nations, particularly in the Asia-Pacific rim, has been enabled by reduced tariffs and trade barriers. Improved financial flows between nations, the growth of foreign direct investment, and the increase in daily foreign exchange turnover in many nation-states adds pressure to demands led by increasing customer expectations, technological change, and environmental concerns (Sheehan, 2010).

Customer expectations can have a massive impact on SME performance and viability. If a customer's expectations are not met, the availability of online feedback sites soon means that those unfilled expectations are made known to a wide public. The Australian economy has shifted from the one based traditionally on agriculture and manufacturing to a more contemporary alignment with mining and a service economy. But the concept of a service economy may be found wanting because we seem to have lost sight of what we mean by service. Horror stories abound.

A recent American Express survey (The American Express Global Customer Service Barometer, 2012) sounds a chilling warning. The online random sample survey was conducted during February and March 2012 with consumers aged eighteen and over, and across ten countries, including one thousand respondents in Australia.

The survey found that, compared to the other nine countries in the survey, 36% of the Australian respondents considered that in the present economy, companies were 'paying less attention to customer service' (p. 3). While they found companies helpful, 42% of Australian respondents believed that companies did not make any extra effort to retain their business and 25% believed that companies took their business for granted. By contrast, 72% of Australian respondents said that they would spend more with a company that provided good customer service and that they would be willing to pay up to an average of 12% more. While the survey appeared to target all businesses, there nonetheless is a warning here for small businesses and that warning is, *ignore your customers at your peril.*

Customers do relate their stories about the service they have received to others. The same American Express survey indicated that 48% tell others about their good customer service experiences all the time and 47% share their experience sometimes. By contrast, 64% tell others about their poor customer service experiences all the time and 31% do so sometimes. The message is clear. While customers may not necessarily give praise or complain at the point of service, they do relate their experiences to others after the event.

The response in Australia, at least from many SMEs, seems to be *let's find someone to blame*. That someone may be in the guise of the prime minister, a state premier, assorted politicians, online sales outlets, the banks, the weather, the state of the Australian dollar, or the price of labour. The other explanation seems to be *you get what you pay for*. What you pay for may be cheap imports, mass manufactured goods from Asian countries, and longer queues because staff numbers have declined.

But the mantra of good customer service seems to elude many businesses, whether large or small. Customers are hitting back on online feedback sites such as http://www.tradecritic.com.au/[1] and http://www.notgoodenough.org/index.php[2] to name but two, so it appears timely that business ought to respond.

SMEs in particular are vulnerable because they often do not have the luxury of good relationships with banks, the luxury of shareholdings to draw upon for expansion or revitalisation of the business, or a skilled public relations person or dedicated customer service representative to address the complaint.

Economic drivers

The growth in East Asian and Southeast Asian economies, particularly those of China and India, for example, has dramatically impacted the world economy (Sheehan, 2010). In Australia, the impact has been driven by a resources boom, particularly a demand for coal. Similarly, the growth of the knowledge and digital economies because of the revolution in technology, such as computers and e-commerce, has provided new markets and increasing demand for new products.

---

[1] Tradecritic is a site designed to help people locate a tradesperson in their local area. To sign up to the site, however, tradespeople have to be prepared to open themselves up to online reviews of their work, and customers are able to rate their service from poor to excellent.

[2] NotGoodEnough (NGE) is Australia's largest and longest running online consumer community. It enables its more-than 60,000 members to discuss good and bad experiences on a range of products and services, including retailing, financial, utilities, airlines, hospitality, and telecommunications.

Growth changes the way SMEs do business. There is a need to monitor constantly what is happening in their supply chains. The cost of transportation of goods from one country to another has decreased in recent years. Low costs may be associated with improved transport systems that enable the shipment of goods to almost any part of the world within twenty-four hours. Though Australia suffers from a tyranny of distance, relatively, the speed and efficiency of transport has improved. The low costs, speed, and efficiency of transporting goods from one country to another, such as from China to the United States or the United Kingdom, are seen to be drivers of globalisation. Manufacturers now seek shorter supply chains (Sheehan, 2010).

Global financial crisis

In 2008-2009, the world economy experienced a recession considered by many economists to have been the worst financial crisis since the Great Depression of the 1930s. Indeed, there is an argument that the US and some countries in Europe experienced a depression. Many factors have been attributed to the cause of the crisis, including, easy credit fuelled by low interest rates, particularly in the housing mortgage market; fraudulent underwriting and predatory lending practices; the failure of financial regulators to keep pace with the speed of innovative financial practices; increased debt burden, particularly in US households; inappropriate risk management strategies; and a boom in commodity prices[3]. Financial scandals, such as that self-admittedly caused by Bernard Madoff, resulted in a loss of wealth (Sheehan, 2010). Smick (2008) argues that income inequality abounded. There are some signs of recovery, at least outside the major industrialised economies.

In her October 2012 address to the annual meetings of the International Monetary Fund (IMF), Christine Lagarde, the Managing Director of the IMF stated that in the almost fifty years since the meetings had last been held in Tokyo, world GDP per capita was 3½ times higher for the world and 9½ times higher in the emerging Asian region. She went on to suggest that there were three major demographic changes occurring. They were (1) a growing young population in the emerging economies, (2) an aging population in the advanced and major emerging economies whereby there will be more than a billion people aged over sixty-five by 2035, and (3) a higher participation rate by women. She also pointed out that economic power was shifting from west to east and that prosperity was shifting from north to south. Such shifts

---

[3]   See Wikipedia for a particularly useful discussion of the causes of the crisis.

were being underpinned by communications and technology innovations and, in particular, the Internet.

While Asia and Brazil were seen to be strong and dynamic, the Eurozone was being tested. Lagarde asserted that there was a need to proceed with the implementation of policy reforms and that deeper banking and fiscal integration and structural reforms still need to occur to ensure stronger economic conditions and a more robust union. She concluded by arguing that the global economy was still weak and that further growth was required to stabilise the global economy (Lagarde, 2012).

Indeed, recent worldwide events suggest slow recovery or another financial crisis. High oil prices, the effects of the Japanese tsunami, a recent weakening of US demand (Economist Intelligence Unit, 2011), unfolding events in Syria, and the debt crisis in Greece and the European Economic zone, more generally, are hurting the global economy and compounding the slowdown from last year's stimulus-dependent recovery. The Economist Intelligence Unit (2011) argues that *the latest difficulties mark a soft patch rather than a retreat towards another recession.* They further suggest that the fundamentals for sustainable growth are still in position.

Australasian region

In the Australasian region, growth in countries such as China and Japan has weakened. In their World Economy (Oct. 12) report, Gulf Oil and Gas (2012), drawing from OPEC data, suggest that a slower growth rate in Asia and Australia may be seen to reflect sluggish demand in the West. The report further suggests that the economies of China and India will decelerate and that China's slowdown, in particular, will have consequences for other countries in the region. Nonetheless, similar to Lagarde's (2012) postulation, Asia will retain its status as the world's fastest-growing region. GDP growth is expected in 2013 as stimulus in China takes effect and demand in the West improves.

There may be some net benefit to commodity exporter countries, such as Australia. The benefits to Australia also arise from early in the year policy stimulus and exports supported activity. Enhanced trade links with China have increased Australia's resilience to cyclical downturns in traditional partners, such as the United States. While the performance has been relatively impressive, a note of caution is sounded.

Any uncertainty in the external environment, such as slow recovery in the United States and the euro area, a slowdown in China, or negative spillovers from unanticipated financial shocks could impede the pace of recovery. Banking vulnerabilities remain a significant challenge amid lingering concerns about risks to the global recovery. The natural disasters experienced in Australia in late 2010 and early 2011, including floods and cyclonic activity in Queensland; floods in northern New South Wales, Victoria, and Tasmania; cyclones in the Northern Territory and Western Australia; and bushfires in Western Australia demonstrates that Mother Nature plays a crucial hand in the external environment.

At the same time, the Australian dollar has been experiencing a high against the US dollar, having pushed above parity to 100.57 US cents in early November 2010. By late-December it was back to a more moderate 0.99 US cents but rallied to close at a twenty-nine-year high of 110 US cents on 27 July 2011 (OANDA Currency Convertor, 2012). By late November 2012, it hovered around 0.96 US cents. The rate may be seen as a mixed blessing for the economy, being good news for importers and travellers to overseas destinations but less so for tax revenues, exporters, travellers to Australia, the tourism, education, and hospitality sectors, and SMEs seeking to expand their business (following Sheehan, 2011).

Prospects for SMEs

In February 2012, MYOB (2012) conducted an online business survey of 1,043 SME business operators. The sample surveyed was similar to those surveyed in September 2011.

The report of the survey concluded that SMEs had become increasingly pessimistic about Australia's economic recovery. Noting that respondents to earlier surveys had generally been optimistic, now fewer than one-fifth (19%) of respondents expected Australia's economy to improve within the following twelve months. In November 2009, 58% were optimistic about economic recovery in the following twelve months while in March 2011, 35% were similarly optimistic. The latest findings were similar to the 21% identified in the September 2011 report, which had been produced at the time of the global financial crisis.

Continuing a trend from earlier MYOB surveys, the majority of respondents were dissatisfied with the federal government and felt that government showed a lack of respect. On a more positive note, suggestions for improving business life for SMEs related to reducing the paperwork burden, such as that required for GST and BAS reporting, investing further in city transport infrastructure, abolishing the Federal Carbon Tax, providing more government funding for business innovation and R&D, and introducing a 'Buy Aussie Made' policy for central and local government procurement where possible (p. 22).

A cautionary note also may be gleaned from Consumer Price Index figures. The Australian Bureau of Statistics (2012) Consumer Price Index released on 24 October 2012 showed a rise of 1.4% in the September quarter 2012, compared with a rise of 0.5% in the June quarter 2012 and a rise of 2.0% through the year to the September quarter 2012, compared with a rise of 1.2% through the year to the June quarter 2012.

The most significant price rises were for health (+7.2%), education (+6.1%), housing (4.7%), and alcohol and tobacco (+4.3%). Further price increases for these commodities may be expected because of the impact of the carbon tax and flow on effects from mining taxes. Natural disasters, such as those seen in throughout the eastern states of Australia, particularly in Queensland in 2010 and 2011, may also impact. Many of the products supplied within most of the aforementioned categories are provided by SMEs.

Clearly, the recent global financial crisis and natural disasters have an impact on SMEs. Following the natural disasters of 2010 and 2011, many small businesses were forced to close, albeit temporarily in most cases. Many incurred significant restart costs. Some may have been covered by insurance, but some insurers refused to pay out on flood policies or at least stalled for a considerable amount of time. Consumers were slow to return to their local shops as they focused on their own rebuilding efforts.

Similar findings to the aforementioned surveys may be seen in the November 2012 ACCI Small Business Survey and the September 2012 Sensis Business Index (SBI). Both surveys identified a strong fall in SME confidence levels, with the latter report continuing a trend evident in previous SBI reports.

For the SBI survey, about 1,800 small—and medium-business proprietors were interviewed by telephone. The sample size included about 1,400 small businesses and 400 medium businesses. The way small—and medium-sized businesses were defined accorded with ABS definitions. Participants were drawn from metropolitan and major non-metropolitan regions within Australia, with quotas set for geographical location and type of business in order to approximate the standard sample structure. Interviews were conducted from 29 July to 16 August 2012. The report explored the experiences of small—and medium-business proprietors for the months of May to July 2012. It also sought to ascertain the expectations for both the current quarter of August to October 2012, and for the twelve months ending July 2013.

The report found that current perceptions of the economy remained weak and that SMEs were also concerned about future economic conditions. Accompanying the drop in confidence were falls in the key performance indicators of sales, the economic climate, and cash flow. While sales performance had increased in the quarter, that increase 'had partially come at the expense of margins, with a fall in profitability, as well as falls in employment, and capital expenditure' (Sensis® Business Index, 2012: 3).

Interestingly, the main reasons SMEs gave for the drop in confidence were that people were not spending, there was a general decrease in business, and they had concerns with the general economic outlook and, in particular, the impact of the carbon tax. By contrast, those who remained confident did so because they felt that they were established businesses, experienced in their business relations, and had good customer relations (Sensis® Business Index, 2012).

The abovementioned dissatisfaction for the federal government continued unabated in 2012 and was at its lowest level since February 1996. The Sensis® Business Index (2012) advised that 55% of the SMEs considered that federal government policy actively worked against small business. The main reasons offered for thinking that the federal government's policies worked against them included the following:

- No incentives for small businesses
- Government policies were making it harder for businesses
- The level of bureaucracy
- The cost of doing business
- Carbon trading policies,

By contrast, 6% considered that the government was supportive of small businesses.

Reasons for the focus on staff skills and performance

There are three reasons why a staff development and performance approach is taken in this book. First, issues such as economic recovery and the environment, while briefly mentioned below, are in many ways beyond the scope of an SME owner/manager in their daily routines. They are constrained in what they can do in the short term as they struggle for survival in a rapidly changing world. Second, issues such as accounting and economics are beyond the expertise of the author, other than in a general sense. Third, it is a fundamental belief that if people working in SMEs have the knowledge, skills, and abilities to do their job, from a human relations and personal development perspective, or from a 'soft skills' approach, then the more technical aspects of their roles will be more easily achieved. Those roles will be enhanced because people have a better understanding of themselves and others as they go about their day-to-day tasks. People make it possible.

Economic recovery

Statistics appear to indicate, and many commentators seem to agree, that many advanced economies will take some years to recover from the global financial crisis. The loss of output, government attempts to reduce debt and ease spending, and the increase in unemployment have long-term ramifications.

To cope with the slowdown in economic growth, governments in the UK, US, and Australia have resorted to increased spending on infrastructure. Projects relating to the improvement of transport links, energy sources, public housing, and schools were proposed for fast-tracking in the UK, as reflected in Budget 2009, *Building Britain's Future* (HM Treasury 2009).

By contrast, the Australian economic outlook was seen to be a little brighter than for the UK and US. According to the deputy prime minister and treasurer, the honourable Wayne Swan MP and the minister for finance and deregulation, Senator the honourable Penny Wong in their 2012 Mid-Year Economic and Fiscal Outlook statement, the Australian economy was expected to grow in the next year or so. Despite the disadvantages of a high Australian dollar from late 2010 to late 2012, the projected return to surplus for 2010-13 had been maintained (MYEFO, 2012). Furthermore, real GDP was forecast to grow by 3.00% in both 2012-13 and 2013-14. Australia's unemployment rate was forecast to remain low, albeit with a slight increase 'from 5¼ per cent in the September quarter 2012 to 5½ per cent by the end of 2012-13', which was seen to be 'consistent with moderate employment growth over the forecast period' (MYEFO, 2012: 4). Growth in the emerging market economies of Asia was expected to continue despite some recent slowing in China.

From a large business perspective, business investment in mining, construction, and manufacturing sectors was expected to continue. Such investment has ramifications for the SME, many of whom provide goods and services to the larger firms.

Such optimism may need to be tempered. It may be argued that many of these forecasts will need to be revisited because of the natural disasters, particularly those that occurred in Queensland. Widespread devastation caused by the floods of December 2010 and January 2011 and the January-February 2011 cyclones impacted the Queensland and Australian economies. The floods, described as of 'biblical proportions' and as Australia's worst natural disaster, covered 75% of the state. That is an area approximately equivalent to France, Germany, and some of Poland combined (Sheehan, 2011).

Imports, unattractive such a short time ago, are again attractive because of the state of the Australian dollar. Local suppliers experienced some problems competing with imports and in rebuilding their businesses after the natural disasters. Some are still unable to respond to the changes as their capacity to produce and distribute has been affected by those disasters. Agricultural products such as sugar and cotton were devastated but are slowly recovering.

SMEs will need to adjust to the impact of the carbon tax, the higher cost of parts and labour, changing shifts in the labour market, higher interest rates, the inability to obtain credit from banks, and a downward trend in sales as people readjust. For those SMEs working in construction and manufacturing, recovery for some turned out to be favourable. There was increased demand for building materials, furniture and bedding, and clothing and footwear. Some of this demand was met by imports.

The thrust for economic activity in recent years has been towards globalisation. Globalisation, however, contains a number of paradoxes (Sheehan, 2010). Given the extent of the global financial crisis and continuing economic uncertainty, there is likely to be an increasing trend towards protectionism (following Ravi Kanth, 2009) and a strengthening of regionalisation. A recent picket line on the Gold Coast in Queensland indicates such a shift. On this occasion, about 270 workers went on strike because of the use of foreign labour, at allegedly lower rates of pay, by a development group. Concerned workers held placards demanding 'Australian Jobs for Australian Workers'. The protest was similar to one held in the UK outside the Total Lindsey oil refinery in Lincolnshire, where unemployed or concerned labour held placards demanding 'British Jobs for British Workers' (Sheehan, 2010). SMEs have to be ready for such a shift.

Furthermore, while the focus usually is on big business and large corporations, they do not always provide the answers. Indeed, many see them as the root cause of our economic and environmental problems. Many large corporations have been accused of maximising profit at the expense of labour and the natural environment. The reason for the actions taken by labour on the Gold Coast construction site serves as an example. Australian workers were concerned about losing jobs because an Asian temporary workforce was brought in by the site contractor.

Environment

Environmental concerns ought not to be underestimated. Lovelock (2009) warned of the dangers of collapsing ecosystems, the consequences of global warming, and the dangers of overpopulation. He alerted us to a likely demographic shift of populations from countries in which people can no longer live because of, for example, rising sea levels to those countries where survival may be possible Countries he suggested were Great Britain and New Zealand although I argue that they too are likely to be affected by rising sea levels.

Most Australians are well aware of the risks inherent in the natural environment. While not immune to an awareness of natural disasters or unnatural weather patterns that were occurring in other parts of the world in late 2010, many parts of Australia were experiencing severe cyclonic conditions, thunderstorms, heavy rainfall, flooding or bushfires, as mentioned earlier. The eastern state of Queensland, in particular, suffered serious damage. Many cities and towns were cut off, with roads and bridges flooded and loss of life. The total damages bill was estimated to be about $5 billion. This figure approximates a whole year's worth of economic growth.

Budgetary cutbacks to help cope with the rebuilding task, including public assets such as schools, roads, and bridges that had been destroyed, were announced. With lost revenue estimated at $2.5 billion over four years, cutbacks included a delay in construction of a major transport infrastructure project, the $8 billion cross-river rail link until at least 2015; and the loss of 3,500 public service jobs over four years. By contrast, $5 million was to be allocated to Tourism Queensland for a new marketing programme; $400 million was made available to local councils to help cover their damages bill estimated at $2 billion; and grants from a $26.5 million pool were to be made available to sporting bodies to assist their recovery efforts.

Natural disasters have economic implications, not only for large industries such as sugar and mining (see Sheehan, 2011) but also for SMEs. While the government has been supportive of industries and businesses in the environmental field, the need for fiscal restraint because of the damage from the weather may mean a change of emphasis. Those SMEs in the agriculture, biosecurity, recycling, and solar energy fields may be particularly prone to risk (see Sheehan, 2011). They will need to consider how best to address that risk.

How best they might do so is a matter of some conjecture. The next chapter advances an argument for sustainability as a means for a better future for SMEs.

Chapter 2

Sustainability

Introduction

This chapter commences with an outline of what is meant by sustainability and sustainable development as it applies to SMEs. There is a very credible argument that the time has come to change the way we do things, so the next section is entitled creating a sustainable future. Then follows what are seen to be the key characteristics of sustainability. The next section is called strategy for sustainability and is followed by sections entitled a role for the SME, encouraging sustainability in an SME, and encouraging employees in building a sustainable SME. There are seen to be some minimum requirements for SMEs, and they are listed as cost, quality, time, and absence of customer complaints. But meeting minimum requirements is not enough. There is one further requirement and that is argued to be a need for SMEs to change their definition of success from a sole focus on profitability to include their societal, individual, and environmental impact. It is this argument that concludes the chapter.

Sustainability and sustainable development

Recent natural catastrophes and disasters, and the global financial crisis suggest that our world has entered an ecological and economic phase that surpasses known experience and that may be seen to place at risk what it is we value in our daily lives. Global warming, rising energy costs, and increasing volumes of waste destined for landfill sites and incinerators (Chowdhury, 2009) contribute to an indeterminate future. In a business environment of turbulence and complexity, environmental and economic uncertainty, and rapid technological change, sustainability and sustainable development, terms that have emerged since the 1980s (EU as Global Actor, 2009), seem to be of paramount importance. Those concepts need to be clearly understood by the SME owner/manager.

If you had asked an SME owner or manager twenty or thirty years ago if they thought their business was sustainable, they would have spoken about plans for future development, the development of their customer and products bases, the challenges of obtaining capital and dealing with their bank manager, and the difficulties of finding, training, and retaining suitable labour. They may even have considered expansion into overseas markets.

If you ask the same question now, however, the response may include that they have installed a solar electricity system or rainwater tanks. More than likely, the response will relate to installing insulation, using energy-efficient light bulbs, recycling paper, and ensuring that leaking taps in the toilets are repaired.

Indeed, the Sensis® Business Index (2012) demonstrates the argument. In that report, to a question posed as to what changes have been made to their business as a result of environmental concerns and using as their baseline the 35% of all SMEs who responded to the question, the responses were as follows: 35% were trying to reduce energy usage, 29% say they had introduced recycling, 12% were reducing paper usage, 9% were trying to reduce water usage, 9% had installed energy-efficient light globes, 7% turned off the lights at night, 6% were attempting to go carbon neutral, 2% were selling or using environmentally safe products, and 4% were using solar power or thinking of going solar.

At least one Australian federal government minister takes a similar view. The minister for climate change, Greg Combet, when addressing questions relating to people's concerns about rising utility bills and a then impending carbon tax mooted to increase electricity bills, responded that people should act now to reduce consumption by, among other things, installing insulation, using energy-efficient light bulbs, and turning appliances off at the wall (Maiden, 2011). Such suggestions are of course commendable, even if a little misguided in addressing the question.

Creating a sustainable future

There is a broader realisation that we need to create a sustainable future. To do so will require the creation of sustainable societies and SMEs within an environment that is resilient (following Bourne, 2005). Bourne argues that we need innovative products and ideas, the creation of new markets, resolution of age-old business problems, and improved public understanding and strengthening of sustainable Australian brands worldwide. There needs to be a combined effort from business, governments, and non-government organisations to do so.

Helpfully the Department of Environment, Water, Heritage and the Arts (2010) has developed a sustainability curriculum framework for the primary and secondary school sectors. In that document, it is argued that education for sustainability moves beyond the acquisition of knowledge or skills about sustainability. Rather, it is argued that a more holistic approach, encompassing motivation and commitment to sustainability action for improved outcomes for a sustainable world, is paramount. Such an argument suggests that the very way we think about sustainability requires a reconsideration of our values and world views on the topic (following Jämsä et al., 2011).

Clearly, the education sector ought to be one where such initiatives take place, but they appear to have been remiss at tertiary level in some disciplines. While universities produce outstanding graduates in many disciplines, they lag behind including sustainability in their curricula, particularly within the social sciences and more specifically within business disciplines. Many business employers bemoan the lack of communication skills, an in depth understanding of teamwork and motivation to meet daily challenges, let alone any insight into sustainability of a business, including an SME.

Blewitt (2010) argues that notwithstanding progress in sustainable education development, there has been no meaningful inclusion of sustainability in curriculum in a manner similar to that for equal opportunities. He suggests that the reasons for such reluctance include lack of knowledge and a suspicion that sustainability and sustainable development are too controversial, inexact, and unscientific to be incorporated successfully. He proposes that there are theoretical and practical understandings relating to 'social, economic, cultural, ethical and spiritual dimensions' (p. 480) that may be difficult to understand. Difficulty arises because of temporal, spatial, and cultural limitations that require a cross-disciplinary, systemic and holistic approach, requiring 'value, attitudinal, affective, skill, and knowledge development' (p. 481) alien to many universities. Such an approach requires a rethinking of the way teaching and learning is conducted, including more problem orientation, dialogic, and experiential learning, and lifelong learning (following Mader, 2012; Wals and Schwarzin, 2012).

Many SME owners/managers often shun formal education or ongoing learning once an undergraduate qualification or similar has been obtained; they often argue that they are time poor.

Key characteristics of sustainability

It is worth noting that sustainable development has a number of key characteristics that may be incorporated into the business imperatives and operations of the SME reasonably easily. The key characteristics are based on the principles and values that underlie sustainable development and incorporate the three major fields or pillars of sustainability: the environment, society, and the economy (Hulspas and Maliepaard, 2011). These fields or pillars are sometimes referred to as the triple bottom line (TBL).

The Sensis® Business Index (2011) defines sustainability as 'including environmental stewardship, social advancement, and economic prosperity to support the needs of both the current and future generations' (p. 20).

While I have argued that the key characteristics of sustainable development may be easily embedded, it is worth noting a counter argument relating to the tensions existing within the three major fields. George (2007) has argued that implementing economic development, remote from social or environmental development, and vice versa, is inappropriate. An example of the development of one pillar without consideration of the concurrent development of the other two pillars may be seen in the study by Pereira et al. (2007).

The purpose of their study was to analyse the development of the Brazilian energy sector within a framework of the National Energy Outlook 2030 studies. Using energy indicators for sustainable development which take into account social, economic, and environmental pillars as their starting point, they demonstrated that Brazil had an abundance of renewable energy resources. They argued that those resources could contribute to ongoing production and use of energy. Such usage would provide Brazil with considerable advantages economically and environmentally. By contrast, the unequal distribution of income weakened the social impact and continued to be the country's principal weak point in achieving sustainable development.

Another example may be seen in a study by Bryde and Meehan (2011). They surveyed forty-four English-based UK Housing Associations (HAs) regarding their sustainable procurement practices. The HAs were responsible for the provision of social housing. The HAs had sustainability-related issues in their missions and external and internal pressures to embed sustainability. Nonetheless, such requirements had not translated into widespread establishment of sustainable procurement. Their findings supported earlier research of other sectors that suggested there was a failure to overcome inertia in relation to sustainable procurement. Bryde and Meehan noted that in the few examples where practices had been established, only the environmental element of the TBL was considered.

It may be argued, therefore, that all pillars need to be developed in concert with each other. To develop one or two without the other(s) suggests that inherent tensions are being avoided. Development is doomed to failure. George (2007) argues that major changes to national and global economic structures and governance systems are required if development is to occur equitably.

Such an argument may be extrapolated to a strategic level. Co-operation between the major powers including the major European countries, the United States of America, China, and India is paramount.

Strategy for sustainability

There is a widespread argument that contemporary organisations need to be sustainable; as do the societies in which they exist. Sustainability means different things to different people. A government may want to demonstrate sustainability by attending to the health, education, transport, and welfare needs of the population. Another agenda might be to better manage the nation's natural resources. It may develop and implement long-term policies for infrastructure development, to protect the natural environment, to address household and living costs, and to ensure equity for all.

Indeed, in his budget speech 2011-2012 delivered on the 10 May 2011 to the Lower House of the Australian Parliament, the Honourable Wayne Swan MP, deputy prime minister and treasurer of the Commonwealth of Australia, used the word *sustainable* on four occasions and the word *sustainability* on one occasion. In outlining a strategy for a sustainable future, he announced investment of $4.3 billion in regional hospitals, health care, universities, and roads. He asserted that the government wanted prosperity and opportunity for all Australians, particularly for those in the outer suburbs and regional towns. He saw such a strategy as vital for the management of population growth and the promotion sustainability across the nation (Swan, 2011).

Questions regarding sustainability may then be raised as to the type and appropriateness of infrastructure, transport systems, and dwellings required to meet the needs of a growing population (following Sheehan, 2010). Resource management will have to be balanced between maximising returns for the extractors of those resources; fair returns by way of taxation to the nation, and environmental concerns. A more sustainable and efficient use of resources, with a focus on creative and innovative urban and rural development, may be required to ease the burden on already overcrowded cities.

A role for the SME

The debate on the conditions needed for the involvement of small and medium enterprises (SMEs) in sustainable development (SD) continues in most, if not all, countries. Spence et al. (2009) report, in the French language, on a study they conducted in Tunisia. They pointed out that while there may be some difficulties with involving SMEs because of their size, their involvement in sustainable development nonetheless ought to be seen as obligatory. Such a mandate was considered to be essential so as to ensure the continuation of a worldwide sustainability movement.

Encouraging sustainability in an SME

Ways that sustainable development may be encouraged within an SME requires that any activity undertaken or embedded ought to

- be locally relevant and culturally appropriate;
- be based on local needs, perceptions, and conditions, while realising that fulfilling local needs may have global effects and consequences;
- promote life-long learning;
- engage formal and informal education;
- have the flexibility to evolve as conditions change;
- address content, context, global issues, and local priorities;
- build capacity for community-based decision making, social tolerance, environmental stewardship, and an adaptable workforce and quality of life;
- be interdisciplinary;
- promote participatory learning and higher order thinking and problem-solving skills (following Blewitt, 2010; CIPD, 2011a);
- counteract inertia by learning from the experiences of others such as in innovation management;
- introduce a small number of sustainable development indicators based on the relatively more-advanced environmental practices to show how these elements have socio-economic impacts;
- emphasise the triggers that overcome inertia and lead to changes in behaviour amongst procurement staff, such as the establishment of ethical pricing models, rather than focus on just the pressures and drivers of sustainability (as suggested in strategic models of sustainability);

- recognise that procurement has a key role in sustainability as policies and practices need to extend beyond the SMEs boundaries to incorporate their whole supply chain, including a recognition of how procurement impacts suppliers (Bryde and Meehan, 2011); and
- consider eco business development, including sustainable construction when developing a new site or enhancing an existing one.

At a more practical level, sustainable development may be achieved by

- improving staff literacy and numeracy skills including competencies in economic literacy and sustainable consumption;
- minimising rework, waste, and pollution in production processes;
- the application of traditional skills and the development of new ones to accommodate the demands of new environmental technologies;
- ensuring staff have an understanding of key sustainable concepts, principles, and values;
- operationalising an ethic of social and eco-responsibility in all staff;
- the development of team and group skills;
- improving influence, persuasion and presentation skills so that staff have the ability to explain, justify, and negotiate ideas and plans;
- promoting practical citizenship in the wider community;
- embracing new and emerging smart technologies and tools (following Fien and Wilson, 2005); and
- behavioural change (following Bryde and Meehan, 2011; CIPD, 2011a).

The abovementioned concepts ought not to be alien to the Australian SME owner/manager. The SME is a valuable sector of Australian life. The entrepreneurs who have established these businesses have done so for many reasons including the provision of service, the development of new ideas and products, and the utilisation of their creative and innovative energies. SMEs generate growth.

Equally, there is a need to attend to issues of sustainability. It makes good business sense. Miles et al. (2009) demonstrated that managers who embedded sustainability into their entrepreneurial framework provided the stimulus necessary for the discovery, evaluation, and development of further opportunities. Additionally, adoption of a sustainability framework enhanced reputation and helped to create competitive advantage.

Similarly, many of the concepts have already been implemented in other countries.

Engaging employees in building a sustainable SME

It may also be recognised that sustainability for organisations may have different meanings. In January 2011, the Chartered Institute of Personnel and Development (CIPD, 2011a) published a report entitled *Sustainable Organisation Performance: What Really Makes the Difference?* The report was supported with an online tool to help managers and human resource professionals to review the extent to which they were encouraging engagement in their organisation (CIPD, 2011b).

In the report, the authors argued that it was not enough for organisations only to perform well in the short term. The short-term was defined as a less-than-one-year timeframe and long-term as more-than-a-one-year timeframe. Rather, performance needed to be sustained over time and through periods of economic hardship. They related sustainability to the financial, societal, environmental, and people aspects of the business. Responsibility for sustainability was allocated to business and human resource leaders.

The CIPD based their argument on a longitudinal study conducted with six private and public sector case-study organisations in the UK in 2009 and 2010. While five of those organisations are large businesses, the sixth fits the definition of an SME. Each of the organisations was focusing on long-term performance through the utilisation of specific change programmes. They concluded that there were eight key themes of long-term performance, namely, alignment, shared purpose, locus of engagement, assessment and evaluation, balancing short—and long-term horizons, agility, and capability-building. Below are listed the eight themes together with an abridged version of their definitions for each of the themes.

1. Alignment—the values and behaviours of internal and external stakeholders must be aligned with, and consistent with, the organisation's purpose.
2. Shared purpose—The reason why the organisation exists needs to be understood by internal and external stakeholders. The organisation's strategy must match its purpose.
3. Leadership—Leaders need to articulate their vision in a way that not only informs decision-making but also empowers employees, guiding them to achieve organisational effectiveness. Leadership may be demonstrated at all levels in the organisation.

4. Locus of engagement—Employees may be engaged at different levels in the organisation and that engagement may be transactional or emotional.
5. Assessment and evaluation—The way qualitative and quantitative information is gathered so as to assess the impact of actions and inform decision-making.
6. Balancing short-term and long-term horizons—A clear understanding of short-term organisational issues is continued while an active focus on longer-term priorities is maintained.
7. Agility—The ability to be proactive, open to new ways, willing to assess and take risks, and ensuring that all employees are adaptable and open to change.
8. Capability building—This is a broad theme that includes the ability to equip employees with the required skills and knowledge to meet present and future challenges. It also means that current and potential capabilities are identified and available.

A more comprehensive piece of research, also applied to large organisations and carrying a similar message to that of the CIPD, is provided by Gallup Consulting (2010). In their report entitled *Employee Engagement: What's Your Engagement Ratio?* Gallup states that it maintains the world's most comprehensive historical and comparative employee engagement databases. Their historical database contains data collected from more than 17 million respondents in 175 countries. Their most recent database, covering the past three years, includes data collected from more than 6.5 million employees representing more than 815,000 workgroups in 16 major industries and more than 70 sub-industries in 170 countries. The comparative database, which is updated annually, enables their clients to benchmark their organisation's employee engagement levels against the most recently gathered data collected by Gallup.

In the report, Gallup states that engaged employees are more productive employees. As a result, the organisations in which they work are more profitable, more customer-focused, safer, and staff are more likely to stay. Employee engagement is a strategic approach for achieving improvement and coping with the demands of organisational change. Such an argument may be extrapolated to SMEs.

Minimum requirements for SMEs

While some of these themes may resonate with the larger size SMEs, they may not be applicable for smaller, say one to ten people, SMEs. Here the focus more than likely will be on the traditional business approach, whether a large business or an SME. The concern will be with cost, quality, time, and an absence of customer complaints.

Cost

A primary indicator for most businesses is cost. Budgetary requirements mean that costs must be closely monitored and controlled. Some of these costs may be in the control of the SME. A currency fluctuation or a natural disaster, however, can have unanticipated consequences.

The customer too is concerned with costs but mostly in relation to what they have to pay for the goods or service. The customer buying a hamburger in your shop will not be too concerned with how much the bun, hamburger patty, cheese, lettuce, tomato, and pickle cost you. They will be concerned with how much you are asking them to pay for that hamburger.

Your accountant or bank manager, however, will have other ideas. They will want to see that your cost performance is performance against your original budget. They also will want to see what you are doing to reduce costs. Reduction can occur through the elimination of duplication, reducing waste and the need for rework, and a commitment to health and safety.

Quality

The hamburger will have to be a pleasant and enjoyable eating experience for your customer. There ought to be no defects—a stale bun, a less than fresh tomato, lettuce with a 'friend' attached. Anything less than a perfect hamburger will not be tolerated, and the customer will be at pains to point any defects out to you, to their family and friends, and perhaps even to the media. The actions of your employees need to be driven by a commitment to quality. There may be an occasional error and the reasons why that error occurred then needs to be investigated and rectified with the intention of ensuring that it does not reoccur.

Quality may also be enhanced with a commitment to health and safety so that work sites are free of the potential for accidents. Like cost reduction, quality may also be measured in terms of waste reduction, attention to environmental concerns, and a healthy and safe working environment.

Time

Fast food has become the norm in contemporary life. Whether pre-packaged on the supermarket shelves and just needing a few minutes in a microwave or sold through the drive-through window at the local fast food chain store, customers want quick food and quicker service. Equally, your suppliers do not want to be delayed when they make a delivery. Time, then, becomes a key criterion for performance. The expectation is that people will not be kept waiting. Nobody wants a cold hamburger. What is more, they want it served even faster than your specified delivery time. If you tell a customer they will wait no more than three minutes for their hamburger and you keep them waiting longer, they will be dissatisfied. By contrast, deliver that burger in two and a half minutes and they will return. The only time variation they want is one that is in their favour.

If you are unable to deliver on time, at the very least, inform the customer that this is the case and tell them what you are doing to rectify the problem. You will save time by not having to deal with a disgruntled customer.

Absence of customer complaints

You need to have good communication processes in place. A customer may complain to you about cost, quality, or time delay. Worse still, they may complain to a number of others, or, if the situation really deteriorates, they may seek to litigate. Litigation is the last thing any SME wants. Not only will you be caught in the legal vortex, but the resulting publicity is unlikely to be to your advantage.

One further requirement

Intuitively, the requirements in the previous two sections make sense. No matter what size organisation we work in, it ought to be that we strive to meet the needs of customers and that we develop ourselves and our staff to the best of their potential to help meet those needs.

In management and organisational academic literature, it is often argued that organisations that focus solely on bottom line financial performance are more likely to fail than those that also attend to the need for motivated and engaged staff. There still appears to be a narrow focus on financial performance (CIPD, 2011a, c), the meeting of targets, the setting of minute objectives, and performance management used as a tool for administration rather than developmental purposes. There may be results in the short term, but long-term sustainability is unlikely.

SMEs will need to change their definition of success from a sole focus on profitability to include their societal, individual, and environmental impact. No doubt this will be a challenge for many as it requires a new mindset, the development of new values, and a different conceptualisation and understanding of their staff in order to ensure sustainable performance. Thus SMEs ought to focus on

- developing a sense of purpose
- making staff feel valued
- the ability to cope with change, by keeping staff informed about the reasons for change and the implications
- the willingness to learn new skills
- the ability to adapt to new ways of working (CIPD, 2011a)

But the above themes are limited in that they do not provide an underpinning foundation. That foundation is professionalism. Nor do the themes offer guidance as to how to go about implementing what is suggested. This book does so, by covering some of those themes, and others, in the depth necessary to enhance such understanding.

Furthermore, the contents are conceptualised within the context of external environmental factors that may be seen to impact on your SME, and by extension you, and makes an assumption that you want to improve continuously your practice and yourself. The contextual framework for continuous improvement is located within current concepts of organisations as learning organisations, stemming from Deming's (1986) management philosophy. Deming proposed that organisations ought to evolve as learning organisations by developing intrinsic motivators for knowledge and creativity rather than using extrinsic motivators such as punishment and reward systems.

The next chapter discusses what is meant by an SME, how it is defined and delineated, and how an SME owner/manager is defined.

Chapter 3

The Small and Medium Enterprise (SME)

Introduction

This chapter commences with some background relating to the tenet of my argument. That argument is that people who own or work in an SME constantly need to be seeking ways that they might improve their business. Improvement will help their SME become more sustainable. One way to do so is by becoming more professional.

Before moving to a discussion of professionalism, however, in this chapter, some clarification as to what is an SME is provided. First, an outline is provided of what constitutes an SME in the Australian context. Second, the SME is defined. It then is argued that an SME consists of a social entity, strategy, structure, and culture. Each of these terms is briefly explored before attention is turned to the SME owner/manager. The final section of this chapter makes the argument that SMEs ought to be seen as learning organisations. Being a learning organisation relies on an understanding of Senge's (1992) five disciplines. Those disciplines are, Mental Models, Personal Mastery, Shared Vision, Team Learning, and Systems Thinking. Each of these disciplines is mentioned briefly and then used to underpin the chapters that follow.

Background

On 2 February 2011, the retired Australian swimmer Ian Thorpe held a media conference to announce his return to competitive swimming after a four-year hiatus. Thorpe, the winner of eight Olympic medals, including five gold, is considered by many to be Australia's greatest Olympian. At the conference, he stated that his aim was to compete at the 2012 London Olympics. After explaining the thinking and rationale behind his decision, he answered questions from the assembled media. One of the first questions he was asked was whether it was true that he was returning to swimming because he was in financial difficulties. Ian carefully explained that money had never been a motivator. Rather, his sole motivator was performance.

Such clarity from a popular and respected Australian athlete ought to serve as inspiration for all people in business, whether large or small. Money ought not to be the motivator. If it is, then you are probably in business for the wrong reasons. You might make money, and you might lead a comfortable material life as a consequence. But you may be left asking yourself if you are happy; and what, if any, contribution you made to the welfare of your fellow citizens and to the betterment of your country.

Small business owners and managers often claim that they cannot attend development courses, conferences, talks by esteemed citizens, or anything else they may see as sitting on the periphery of the business because they are *too busy making* money or they are *time poor*. They often do not allow their staff to attend similar functions for similar reasons. Such a phrase often strikes me as coming from a person who may be greedy and self-centred, afraid of learning and self-development, or in absolute panic mode because their business is suffering. I understand this analysis as a generalisation. I am sure other, more positive, analogies equally apply.

Nonetheless, as stated earlier, the tenet of my argument is that people who own or work in a small—or medium-size enterprise constantly need to be seeking ways that they might improve their business, and by extension, themselves. One way to do so is by becoming more professional.

The small and medium business (SME)

According to the latest Australian Bureau of Statistics (ABS) figures, in June 2011 Australia had more than 2.13 million businesses. They comprised of 826,389 (38.8%) employing businesses and 1,306,023 (61.2%) non-employing businesses. An employing business is defined as one that has an income tax withholding (ITW) role. They encompassed the construction industry (17%), professional, scientific, and technical services (11%), and rental, hiring, and real estate services (10%).

Of the employing businesses, 739,312 (89.5%) employed less than 20 employees. This comprised 508,674 businesses with 1-4 employees and 230,638 businesses with 5-19 employees. There were also 81,006 businesses with 20-199 employees and 6,071 (<1%) businesses with 200 or more employees (ABS, 2012: Catalogue Number 8165.0). The ABS considers a small business as one that employs less than 20 employees. In 2011, there were also 83,399 (10.2%) businesses with 20-199 employees (medium-size business) and 6,349 (<1%) businesses with 200 or more employees (large business) (ABS, 2011: Catalogue Number 8165.0).

Notwithstanding these figures, the emphasis in management and organisational literature often is on the large business or organisation, particularly within the public sector. Hence, an area vital to the Australian economy, that of the small—and medium-size businesses (SME), goes largely ignored, particularly in relation to soft skills development. This book is an attempt to address those oversights.

SME covers all industry sectors, including accommodation, cafes and restaurants, agriculture, forestry and fishing, cultural and recreation activities, communication services, construction, education, electricity, gas and water supply, finance and insurance, health and community services, manufacturing, mining, property and business services, personal and other services, retail trade, transport and storage, and the wholesale trade. Specific businesses include accountants, law firms, human resource consultancies, recruitment and selection firms, and investment advisors. They also include childcare centres, new—and used-car dealerships, florists, men's and women's hairdressers, nurseries, wedding planners, electrical firms and electricians, plumbing wholesalers and retailers and plumbers, small building-and-construction firms and carpenters, painters, plasterers and tile layers, landscapers; cleaners, security firms, including security guards and door staff, freight forwarding and delivery firms and truck drivers, and information technology business programmers. They are located in all Australian states and territories and range from family businesses to owner/manager concerns.

Somewhat like large organisations, they have strategic, structural, and cultural dimensions. I say somewhat because each of those dimensions will vary considerably, depending on the size of the organisation. An SME with only a few employees is unlikely to give much consideration to its structure or culture. It ought to pay considerable heed, however, to its strategic direction and focus because like most, if not all, profit-making organisations, it is subject to market forces. I now provide further description of an SME, followed by a discussion on SMEs and the global financial crisis.

SME Defined

Any organisation is commonly conceptualised in terms of its social entity, strategy, structure, and culture. Within this conceptualisation, however, an SME is a somewhat vague entity. While the concrete components of the SME, including an employee or employees, a building, a motor vehicle, technical equipment, computers, books, files, or furniture may be visible, the SME itself is more indistinct because of their size, their workforce composition, and their physical locations in urban, rural, and remote areas.

Again like most organisations, SMEs tend to exist within chaotic social systems, globalisation and its consequences, such as the erosion of established institutions and alterations to processes of governance; the need for SMEs to adapt in the face of uncertainty to acts or threats of acts of terrorism, and financial, social, and environmental scandals all impact on the SME. These conceptual elements are variously combined and highlighted in different understandings of an SME.

Moreover, the seemingly unrelenting changes as a result of these aforementioned factors have disrupted many of the organisational dynamics familiar to many people such a short time ago. The result in some SMEs is a change to concepts such as loyalty, commitment, and service, a growing mistrust of management and their motives (following Goffee and Jones, 2005), and increased employee anxiety (Chisholme, 2009). Such outcomes suggest the need for SMEs to become more professional. To do so, a number of elements of an organisation, including SMEs, need to be considered.

Social Entity

An SME may be a one-person organisation or it may comprise of people or groups of people who interact with each other to achieve a common set of goals. The interactions are consciously developed and coordinated and tend to be premeditated. Thus, most SMEs are, in the first instance, social entities in which people interact to perform the duties and functions required by the owner or manager to achieve SME goals.

Intuitively, most people would perceive and experience an SME as more social in nature. In other words, most SMEs, particularly in the medium-size range, consist of a number of different entities with different, and even contradictory, goals. Thus, employees may experience their SME, work unit, or work colleagues differently from the way another person in the SME experiences them, especially in terms of power relationships. A social entity is considered to be the first element of an SME.

Strategy

The second element of the SME is its goal direction or goal orientation. While goal direction and goal orientation are clearly important, the concept of SME strategy also is vital. Strategy may be seen in broader terms than goals as it embraces a number of processes and forces for change, including SME competitiveness, innovation, transformation and renewal, structure, culture, leadership, and learning. It is not only about making money.

Strategy ought to be an attempt by the SME to fit its external operating environment and to exploit the planning environment so that the SMEs' capital and employees may be maximised. By understanding the processes and forces for change, and by being able to plan appropriate strategies for meeting change requirements, an SME ought to be able to determine its strategic direction.

It has been argued that structure (Chandler, 1962; 1977; Kanter, 1983) and culture (Limerick and Cunnington, 1993; Limerick et al., 1984; Peters and Waterman Jr., 1985) follows strategy.

Structure

Organisational structure is the formal system by which an organisation performs its tasks in the achievement of its goals. Depending on the size of the SME, it may be simple or complex, formal or informal, and centralised or decentralised. There may be an organisational chart provided to inform employees of reporting relationships, roles, and broad responsibilities. It also gives direction for employee behaviour and the reporting relationships may then be recognised in terms of authority and bureaucracy. It may also suggest a mechanistic or organic system of work and demonstrate control and empowerment.

Culture

Organisational culture is defined as the shared meanings, understandings, expectations, and processes that inform the actions and behaviours of the SME's employees. It is evidenced by the beliefs, values, feelings, and expectations of all SME employees and generally is influenced in the first instance by the owner or manager of the SME. It permeates throughout the SME by way of common goals, stories, myths, and legends and may be both covert and tacit in nature. It is a powerful tool for guiding behaviour and for inspiring commitment. It is infused by way of activities with meaning and significance in the achievement of organisational goals. Again, the phenomenon of culture will be dependent on the size of the SME.

Culture may also be evidenced in an SME by architecture, office layout, and dress codes.

Culture tends to crystallise and is not easily changed. If you are able to understand your culture and you are able to change it to meet rapidly changing environmental conditions, then you more than likely will prosper in the contemporary economy.

An SME owner/manager defined

Clearly, an SME owner is the person who owns the SME, the person who has invested their money in bringing to fruition an idea or interest they consider will contribute to their wealth creation. A more esoteric definition may include that as well as seeking a personal financial outcome, they are also interested in social wealth generation and the betterment of the community they serve. They are the person with authority, responsibility, and accountability for the good governance of the business.

Similarly, a manager is that person who has been deemed suitable to administer the business on behalf of the owner. This might be because the SME is arrayed over a number of sites; the owner has other interests, that means they are not able to run the business as a day-to-day proposition; or they may be a silent partner, having invested money in the SME but with no interest or intent to participate in the SME on a regular basis. A manager may have the autonomy necessary to provide good management of the business, or they may be tightly controlled by the owner. Whatever arrangement may be in place, they will have some authority and responsibility and accountability for the stewardship of the SME. They are likely to perform a number of roles and functions common to most managerial positions, including financial accounting, staff management, and customer relationship management.

In general, the occupation of manager is considered to be a profession. It does not follow, however, that a manager is a professional. The achievement of such a distinction may be subject to attitude and action. It also is difficult to generalise about the personality traits and characteristics of all SME managers. Therefore, whether or not an SME manager is professional depends on a set of parameters that guide his or her attitude towards work colleagues the SME and the wider social milieu within which the SME operates. That milieu includes customers, suppliers, lobby and pressure groups, and the community in which they operate (following Sheehan, 2000).

Depending on the size of the SME and the number of sites at which it may be located, there may be more than one manager and/or there may be a management hierarchical structure in situ.

Both owner and manager, no matter what role they play, are part of a social process. They may be required to utilise people and material resources to achieve SME objectives. They will be shaped by customer demands to achieve those objectives.

The SME as a learning organisation

The philosophy of a learning organisation has been popularised in management literature by, among others, Handy (1989), Limerick and Cunnington (1993), and Senge (1992). Senge's work is deemed to be the seminal work in the area. I draw on it to advance an argument that an SME ought to consider, if it does not already do so, being a learning organisation. Senge (1992) suggested that a learning organisation contained five disciplines. Those disciplines are as follows: Mental Models, Personal Mastery, Shared Vision, Team Learning, and Systems Thinking.

Mental models

Mental models underpin the way we think and what we do in organisations. Inherently, they are based on our assumptions about the world in which we live and about the people we need to interact with on a daily basis. They tend to be so embedded in the way we think that we are unaware of the way in which they influence our behaviour. Professionalism is suggested as a new mental model for SMEs. I consider that professionalism embraces and extends Senge's notion of mental models. Chapter 4 discusses mental models in more depth. Chapter 5 discusses professionalism. Chapter 6 outlines a set of qualities deemed appropriate for professionalism within SMEs.

Senge suggests that to better understand our mental models required a great deal of personal reflection and self-awareness so that we might better represent ourselves, and by extension our SME, to others and so that we might grow and develop. The notion of self-awareness is discussed in Chapter 6. However, self-awareness may be seen to have some limitations and so the argument is extended to include an understanding of mindfulness, which is discussed in Chapter 8.

For an SME operating in uncertain and ambiguous times, it means that change within the organisation ought to be implemented in a way that enables your staff to develop fresh ideas and attitudes and to learn new skills. Such development requires that you are willing to move beyond your current way of thinking and acting so that you are able to embrace the other disciplines (following Senge, 1992). A failure to do so may mean that you continue to do the ineffective and inappropriate things you have always done. Embedded models need to be discarded while still maintaining the good things that you do.

Personal mastery

It may seem like a statement that goes without saying, but for an organisation to learn, employees must also learn. Personal mastery requires employees to be in a continual learning mindset for the development of their skills and also of their personal vision and spirituality. It is a continual journey to an unknown destination.

Employees with an enhanced level of personal mastery will have the self-awareness and mindfulness necessary to understand where their competency level may be lacking, where their knowledge is not as proficient as it might be, and how they might overcome any perceived deficiencies. They are able to see the gap between their current reality and their personal vision, creating a tension that motivates them to address their concerns as part of their personal mastery journey.

It should be noted, however, that an individual recognising their personal development needs and working towards fulfilling those needs will not guarantee that your SME will learn. For such learning to occur, they will need your support and encouragement. Adult learners require support, guidance, and constructive feedback. Adult learning is discussed in Chapter 9.

Shared vision

A shared vision requires you to develop, with your employees, a picture of what you want your SME to look like in the future. By encouraging a shared vision, employees will feel that the SME is focussed on the future and thus be willing to be innovative and creative. They are more likely to be willing to learn and develop for themselves as opposed to having to do it as part of performance management or to follow a directive.

It also means that you ought to reshape the vision through a process of continual interaction with employees, thus growing the shared vision organically and fostering enthusiasm for the achievement of the vision as part of a nurtured process (following Mirvis et al., 2010). A shared vision requires you to be attuned to notions of leadership and to have some understanding of your leadership style, including your strengths and your frailties.

It should be noted that a shared vision ought to be kept well distanced from the vision statement that often is developed and issued by decree by senior managers in some organisations.

Leadership is discussed in Chapter 10.

Team learning

Team learning enables employees to develop the team skills that they consider necessary and appropriate for their workplace. Enabling your employees to develop their own skill set facilitates the creation of the environment necessary for them to be able to work together as a unit. Your employees need to learn as part of a team rather than just as individuals. Some learning may occur through discussion and enable the team to gain deeper insight into the problems and opportunities with which they are confronted. Senge suggests that discussion involves the implementation of solutions without an exploration of underpinning assumptions, an approach that hinders the learning process because deeper issues are not surfaced and addressed.

Team learning is discussed in Chapter 11.

Systems thinking

Senge argues that one of the problems of management is that simple solutions are often applied to complex systems problems. Solutions are implemented to address one part of a problem, rather than focussing on the organisation as a whole and examining all the tensions inherent in any system. He argues that managers tend to think that cause and effect adjoin a temporal and spatial framework.

Such thinking drives action so that when faced with a problem, the most immediate and apparent solutions are implemented, particularly in relation to short-term solutions. But short-term solutions often lead to significant long-term costs. Cutting the materials' budget, for example, can create cost savings but can also severely impede the SMEs ability to deliver in the long term (following Butcher, 2011). The consequences of the action may not be noticed until sometime after the event, making it difficult to identify the reason for the inability to deliver.

Organisations are complex and interlinked in a dynamic process of action and activity. The interaction occurs within an internal and external environment and an SME, no matter how small, is not immune to such a dynamic. Systems thinking transcends such limitations and enables more appropriate managerial action.

Systems thinking examines the interrelationships between the parts of a system, exploring all the tensions, ambiguities, and inconsistencies that underpin how we work and enables the assumptions that we make to be addressed in a holistic, rather than piecemeal, way. Systems thinking assists with the integration of the other disciplines.

Systems thinking is discussed in Chapter 12.

In the following chapter, mental models are discussed at some length.

Chapter 4

Mental Models

Introduction

People are the only sustainable source of competitive advantage. In this chapter, it is argued that if SMEs are to survive and thrive in a globally competitive environment, where uncertainty and ambiguity are the norm, it is important that they understand that new mental models are required. The development of those models requires that the core competencies within SMEs are developed and strengthened and that human capital is seen as the foundation of competitive advantage, rather than as a cost. The chapter commences with an outline of mental models. The next section places the development of such a model within the context of complex adaptive systems, and this notion is explored in some depth for the rest of the chapter.

Mental models

As mentioned earlier, SMEs have strategic, structural, and cultural dimensions. It is unlikely that those dimensions will be viewed on a scale similar to those of large organisations. Nonetheless, the requirements for operating in large organisations may serve as examples for the types of models that may be applied in SMEs, albeit on a smaller scale.

Just one example may serve to highlight this point. Large organisations often focus on strategic leadership, which implies a hierarchical organisational and management structure. Power is vested in the formal positions of authority, with people filling those positions seen to be strategic.

Strategic leaders are seen to have the attributes necessary to occupy a role that requires them to create, sustain, and enhance competitive advantage.

They are expected to be multifunctional and to manage, through others, an entire enterprise that may be globally dispersed. They are presumed to be able to anticipate, envision, create, and cope with change. They are supposed to be flexible and to empower others to create strategic change. They also are expected to influence human behaviour effectively across affective, behavioural, and cognitive elements (following Daft and Pirola-Merlo, 2009) in an endeavour to achieve competitive advantage.

The key to competitive advantage resides in their ability to create a healthy workplace environment where the intellectual capabilities of employees may be enhanced in an atmosphere of creativity, innovativeness, and expertise and where leaders or SME owner/managers improve stakeholder efficiencies and competencies (following De Wit and Meyer, 2005). SME owner/managers need to demonstrate leadership by role modelling behaviours expected of others by exhibiting the ability to reinvent themselves in a continuing cycle of action, reflection, and learning.

Strategic leadership in an SME may therefore be seen as the ability to manage the SME's operations effectively and to sustain high performance over time (following Daft and Pirola-Merlo, 2009). To do so, strategic leaders continually need to be able to change their mindset and deal with diverse and complex circumstances.

The aforementioned attributes, such as coping with change, working with complexity, and creating a healthy workplace environment may be seen to suggest that SME leaders need to display qualities of honesty, trust, and integrity to inspire employees to higher order goals and new mental models.

Many SMEs lack other prerequisites for a strategic leadership focus because of their size. They are unlikely to have people with different functional backgrounds, experience, and education and thus may lack the ability to discuss and debate different perspectives to enhance their problem-solving and decision-making capabilities. The lack of ability may result in limited competitive actions, less creative thinking, and an inability to foresee and cope with change.

If SMEs are to survive and thrive in a globally competitive environment where uncertainty and ambiguity are the norm, it is important that they understand that new mental models are required.

It is necessary, therefore, that the core competencies within SMEs are developed and strengthened and that employees are seen as the foundation of competitive advantage, rather than as a cost. People are the only sustainable source of competitive advantage.

Well-developed employees will have the ability to think quickly, act competitively, share knowledge and behave ethically. They will be familiar with product lines and have a strong knowledge of the customer base and customer requirements. They will provide exemplary customer service.

By developing your employees, you are helping to shape your SME culture, which ought to be a central task. One way to do so is by encouraging the entrepreneurial flair you have bought to your SME in your employees. Hanson et al. (2002) suggest that there are five dimensions by which you might do so. They are as follows:

1. Autonomy—allow employees to take actions free of constraints and to be self-directed
2. Innovativeness—enable employees to engage in the formulation of new ideas and support new ideas and experimentation
3. Risk taking—facilitate a willingness by employees to accept risks in the pursuit of opportunities and reward learning experiences rather than punish failed attempts
4. Proactiveness—seek to be a market leader, as opposed to a follower, by anticipating trends, determining customer needs and satisfying those needs.
5. Competitive aggressiveness—demonstrate a propensity for action and a determination to outperform rivals

The aforementioned approaches suggest that SME owner/managers need to move beyond a focus on organisational effectiveness understandings that include goal achievement, performance measures, and resource allocation because those traditional approaches to management will not be enough to help the SME cope with the ever-increasing demands with which they are faced. Rather, the SME owner/manager needs to focus on how they can respond to a rapidly changing environment in a timely way. The new environment demands adaptation to traditional methods of work in SMEs so that employees are seen as colleagues and partners rather than employees. When viewed as colleagues or partners, the owner/manager will be able to share authority and responsibility, share knowledge and understanding, jointly help give meaning to, and make sense of what is happening in the environment and what needs to be done to adapt to that environment.

In such an SME, there will be recognition that achieving successful outcomes is the responsibility of all members because they have the knowledge, skills, abilities, competencies, and attitudes to grow the business together. The focus will be on symbolism rather than on tasks and goal achievement. Symbolism provides key meanings and learnings for SME employees. Symbolism may embrace values, beliefs, attitudes, commitment, loyalty, moral fortitude, ethical behaviour, team competence, and satisfaction (following Paparone et al., 2008).

Thus, traditional mental models need to shift to embrace new ways of conceptualising SMEs, their strategies, structures and culture, and to adapt to new ways of working. This shift is an imperative for survival. But change often is accompanied by 'feelings of vulnerability, embarrassment, and fear' (Fineman, 2003: 121) as organisational members struggle to understand the reasons for change and what that change may mean for them on a personal level. Such anxieties need to be addressed openly and forthrightly within the SME, which is a role for the SME owner/manager or leader.

Paparone et al.'s (2008) article focuses on the US military. They contest the traditional hierarchical strategic leadership approach that is seen to dominate the prevailing culture. They argue that the culture has been built on a traditional military organisational approach encompassing the tasks of role definition, standardisation, simplifying, socialising, decision-making, knowing, commanding and controlling, and planning based on estimates. The military is seen as a professional bureaucracy requiring an ever-burgeoning administrative support system. A similar argument may be applied to many large organisations, such as universities and financial institutions.

Equally, the argument may be applied, again on a scaled-down basis, to SMEs. Here too some SME owner/managers seek to command and control, predict and plan, bring order from chaos, manage resources so that people will work harder with less, and manage performance, for the required outcomes. Many organisations have been formulated from a perception that the military is a well-structured, efficient machine where careful administration ensures that tasks are achieved efficiently and effectively. But rhetoric does not always match reality. Furthermore, organisations of all sizes exist within complex adaptive systems.

Complex adaptive systems (CASs)

Complex adaptive systems have been developed from a number of basic principles (Boulton and Allen, 2007). First, there is more than one possible future. We cannot with any certainty predict the future, it is mysterious and enigmatic. We may understand from past experience that some things may continue to occur, but we cannot predict with total accuracy what those things might be. Experience tells us that the sun rises each day, but we cannot say with absolute certainty that it will rise again tomorrow.

How we predict the future is influenced and socially constructed by our past experiences, our history, our expectations, our knowledge, and our social norms. We may be able to influence or guide the system, but we cannot predict the outcome. An SME owner/manager, for example, may influence or guide a staff member in how to perform a task safely, but staff ought not to be watched at all times. Even if they could be, a staff member who had been guided in safe working practices may forget or act without due care and attention with subsequent unhappy consequences. Experience may also alert us to the possibility that future uncertainty will be clouded by events that, in general, are unanticipated, unpredictable, and unwanted, such as the sudden death of a valued colleague. At these points, the system with which we are familiar could turn in any direction, destination unknown.

Second, complex systems that are comprised of political, historical, environmental, economic, technological, and sociological components may *turn* into profoundly new systems, or components of a system, with new features. The final turning point may be caused by anticipated or unanticipated events. A change of government, the introduction of a new tax, such as a carbon tax, a new competitor entering the market, a disaster caused by weather conditions, or a global financial crisis serve as examples of factors impacting on a system and that system having suddenly to brace for, and cope with, a sudden turning point. Moreover, a new manager or new key staff member in an SME may come with new ways of wanting things done. While those new ways may seem to have been developed from rational, logical thought processes, the decisions introduced and the plans implemented may have intended and unintended consequences.

Third, there is seen to be a need for interconnectivity. It has been argued that a system that is *open* rather than *closed* to its environment will be better able to respond to changes in that environment. General systems theory, the cross-disciplinary study of systems in general, tells us that all parts of a system are interconnected, that systems need to self-regulate, and that they need to be open to feedback (following von Bertalanffy, 1950). An action or activity in one part of a system will impact on other parts of the system. Thus, if a staff member does not report for duty because of illness, other colleagues may have to work longer hours to ensure customers receive the required level of service. Employees may act independently, but they are dependent on their colleagues in the system to varying degrees.

Additionally, intraconnectivity also is important. Intraconnectivity relies on SME staff participating in learning opportunities as a collective and on reflection in action (following Chisholme, 2009). People within SMEs need to be open to each other, particularly in terms of equality and diversity (following Ebie, 2011) so that innovation, creativity, and change occur. If the system elements are able to shift and change as a result of rich diversity and interconnectivity and intraconnectivity then creativity and possibilities for survival are enhanced (Boulton and Allen, 2007). Indeed, it has been argued that innovativeness is seen to be a key feature of an SME (Levy and Powell, 2005).

Fourth, the SME system is not static. Rather, it is interacting and evolving constantly, adapting to changing environmental conditions. Such evolution requires that SMEs develop ways to encourage mindsets capable of challenging the status quo so that innovation and creativity become part of a necessary mix in order to develop market share and develop new products while still conducting daily activities. Such duality suggests a paradoxical relationship within SMEs. Thus, an ability to respond to positive and negative environmental conditions, and to adapt accordingly, is a necessary attribute (following Briggs and Peat, 2000).

Paradoxically, routine business activities utilising existing competencies and attributes need to be continued. The rational, linear approach to routinisation needs to coexist with innovation, creativity, experimentation, and risk taking so as to explore and exploit opportunities. The paradox suggests that a different approach in SMEs needs to be instigated and complex adaptive systems thinking seems a useful offering.

Utilising the CAS model may enable an SME to

1. turn from trying to forecast the future to instead playing a part in designing a desired future;
2. stop searching for what is 'right', which suggests lack of imagination and rigidity and, instead, turn to being flexible and fluid;
3. make sense of the world as opposed to spending energy attempting to *know* the world; and
4. release the dynamic potential of the system rather than trying to overcome the limits of the system (adapted from Paparone et al., 2008).

Drawing from complex adaptive systems theory, Paparone et al. (2008) argue that it is time for an alternative mental model to be infused. They suggest that eight different leadership tasks are required. The eight are as follows: relationship building, loose coupling, complicating, diversifying, sensemaking, learning, improvising, and emergent thinking. These tasks are adapted here, with some renamed, because it is considered that they also may be applied to SMEs.

Such application will be challenging. Mental models form over years, become subconscious manifestations, are ingrained because of indoctrination and socialisation, become 'theory in use', and are difficult to change. It is little wonder that people are then seen as resistant to change. But organisational life, be it in large bureaucracies or in SMEs, is about change. A 'theory of action' is required, and for the purposes of this book, that theory is based on the concept of complex adaptive systems (CASs). The eight leadership tasks are here named as follows: (1) relationship creation and networking, (2) responsibility and empowerment, (3) agility, (4) equality and diversity, (5) sensemaking, (6) embrace learning, (7) improvising, and (8) emergent thinking.

1. Relationship creation and networking

SMEs are based around bureaucratic understandings of roles, role relationships, and boundaries. People have duty statements, position descriptions, or job descriptions formulated from workforce planning and task and job analysis exercises. The aim of such documents is to enable the recruitment and selection of appropriate staff, to provide clear expectations of job and role requirements, to be able to measure and control job performance, and to be able to adjust performance if required. They serve as a performance management tool. Equally, they do not encompass changes in resource allocation that may impact on agreed outcomes, unseen or unanticipated events such as changes in personnel or measure extra tasks people might complete in order to ensure that customer expectations are met.

A CAS view of an SME suggests that the time for viewing an SME in this way is past. Attention needs to turn to the creation and maintenance of relationships and networking to reinforce and strengthen existing internal and external interdependencies. Relationships may be strengthened by sharing values and expertise. Enhanced effectiveness will follow as people understand and trust each other, work together effectively and co-operatively, and work towards a community of understanding and meaning within their SME. The development of interpersonal and intrapersonal skills is imperative to enable relationship building. Such approaches could include leadership development, self-awareness and mindfulness, skill development, and methods for initiating and maintaining meaningful conversations so that problems are resolved before conflict escalates.

2. Responsibility and empowerment

It is well recognised that SMEs operate in an uncertain, ambiguous, complex, disorderly, and volatile environment. Within such an environment, the way we may have solved a problem in the past may no longer present as the best solution to a current concern. Problems tend to be multifaceted, poorly specified, and outside a common understanding. The way to solve such an issue is not by tighter controls and oversighting. Indeed, in many SMEs that are based around the professions, such as the medical, dental, legal, and financial professions, closer supervision and monitoring of professionally qualified staff may lower performance (Paparone et al., 2008). Micromanagement no longer serves a purpose.

Rather, what is required is an understanding that the SME is a CAS. Within that framework, trust and mutual obligation form the basis for addressing the self-repeating nature of the SME system. A loose coupling arrangement whereby people are empowered to perform to mutually agreed requirements is required. By drawing on peoples' expertise, adaptability, and value systems, in concert with the self-organising properties of a CAS, a degree of freedom and responsibility is offered. Co-ordination and a unified effort are achieved without the need for close control.

3. Agility

The dynamic and complex environment in which SMEs operate may tempt SMEs to seek order, to perform to established patterns and to stay with those patterns at all cost. This head-in-the-sand approach is an accident waiting to happen. Technological, economic, political, environmental, and sociological demands are such that trying to find a recipe for the correct way of doing something and then sticking with that recipe will end in disaster. The best chefs provide recipes in books and then encourage readers to be agile, to experiment, and adapt to suit personal taste. Given the SME operating environment, such an approach seems commendable.

The operating environment needs to be understood as one that is emergent, complex, ambiguous, and diverse. Simplification of tasks and responses is not the answer. Simplification conceals environmental complexity and leads to rigidity and inflexibility in staff that then becomes difficult to change.

An SME adopting a CAS approach ought to remain agile, open to opportunity, alert to clues indicating likely changes, conscious of multiple options, responsive to the changing demands, willing to take risks, and swift in their response. It is a convoluted process and needs to be treated accordingly. Value systems may serve as stabilisers.

4. Equality and diversity

Undoubtedly SMEs make a major contribution to the economy. Despite this contribution, however, Ebie and Djebarni (2010) have argued that studies focusing on the adoption of equality and diversity innovation among SMEs suggest that the adoption of equality and diversity practices in SMEs is limited. Ebie (2011) has sought to address this oversight in his study of SMEs in England and Wales.

SMEs are a microcosm of society. They depend on patterns of interactions with their environment, be it internal or external. As such, SMEs ought to look to equality and diversity as an innovative strategy for business improvement.

If an SME workforce is homogeneous, that is, they are all the same in terms of background, education, race, and culture, and even gender and religion, then there is unlikely to be a variety of opinions, insights, and ideas shared and debated. Indeed, cultural indoctrination and socialisation may mean that the same organisational stories are repeated, reducing the opportunity for new ideas and scepticism to be shared and discussed (following Paparone et al., 2008). Such a makeup does not reflect a heterogeneous society at large. Clearly, an SME ought to reflect that society and its customer base. I have previously argued that we come from different races, ethnic groups, cultures, languages, values, religious understandings, and social, economic, and political systems (Sheehan, 2010).

5. Sensemaking

Sensemaking is the process by which people give meaning to experience (Weick, 1995). It may be a strategy for SMEs and their members to create shared meaning. When systems operate in uncertain and ambiguous environments, confusion, and anxiety tend to predominate. Under these types of conditions, it is difficult to make rational, cognitive decisions as attention tends to be diverted to more pressing emotional matters. CASs are unpredictable because work life is inherently emotional and value-based (following Fineman, 2003). The way to address confusion and anxiety is through sensemaking. That is, SME members are able to resolve the needs of the SME within the parameters of their own preferences, values, attitudes, and behaviours.

Rapid changes in technology, including the growth of the Internet and social networking sites, whereby information is exchanged reasonably freely, and sometimes without substantiation, indicate that the days when SME members, and owner/managers in particular, were seen as the font of all knowledge and able to make rational and informed decisions is long past. Putnam and Mumby (1993) argued that rationality is not a dispassionate and indisputable state. Rather, they argued that knowledge is socially constructed and is only one characteristic of organisational life. Knowledge needs to be seen within a larger context of an SME's community of practice within which emotional variables ought to be considered.

Emotional variables suggest, therefore, that people need to be self-aware, able to understand, and make sense of their world, and be willing to learn and adapt. For many, such a challenge may seem an insurmountable task, but given time and patience, people can learn to do things differently.

Sensemaking can help them to do so. As Paparone et al. (2008) argue, sensemaking is a collaborative social activity that can lead to the development of a shared sense of meaning. A shared sense of meaning will enable SME members to communicate openly and honestly, learn to agree and disagree constructively, and collectively understand explanations for work-related events (following Chisholme, 2009).

6. Embrace learning

One of the key tenets proffered is that SMEs need to be learning organisations. SME owner/managers cannot predict and control what essentially is 'unknowable'. Thus, expecting that an owner/manager ought to know everything that is happening and then telling others what to do is a pointless expectation.

A case in point, although relating to a large organisation, is the mid-2011 *News of the World* scandal. Here, Rupert Murdoch, the head of a global media empire of which *News of the World* comprised about 1%, apologised for the actions of some within that organisation who had been hacking into the phone calls of members of the public. He made the point that he could not be held responsible for the actions of every employee in his organisation and that the actions of a few impugned the good reputation of the many. He could not be across every action and activity of his employees, although his managers ought to have had such a delegated responsibility. While hierarchical in structure, it is an empire that is globally dispersed. The argument here is that the days of hierarchy have passed. An SME, as a CAS, ought to operate as a learning organisation whereby knowledge sharing, individual and team competence, and ethical behaviour are seen as values to be shared.

Individual and team learning co-exists with organisational change (flowing Senge, 1992; Watkins and Marsick, 1993). Thus, SMS owner/managers need to be open to, and willing to embrace, learning (following Beer et al., 2005).

Learning and expectations of learning also can be a painful process. Anxieties may be invoked and vulnerabilities surface as people face uncertainty about learning requirements and management and team expectations (following Chisholme, 2009; Paparone et al., 2008; Sheehan, 2000). Thus, it is useful to understand some of the theories pertaining to adult learning, and these are covered in Chapter 8.

7. Improvising

Kao (1996) explored ways for managers to develop an environment in which creativity would flourish. Drawing on his experience as a jazz musician, he used an analogy of musicians in a jam session producing new musical forms and ideas by challenging the playing and imagination of each other to create new musical ideas that were then further tested and explored. The new music was seen not as a permanent advantage but as a temporary advantage in a fast-changing world.

Paparone et al. (2008) drew from a similar analogy of a jazz band to illustrate their argument for improvisation. They used a jazz band as their exemplar as such bands were seen to be the standard by which improvisation was measured. They argued innovation practice may be prevented because professional expertise and values support the interests of the status quo. They noted, however, that such expertise was crucial for improvisation because the musicians combined years of formal theoretical and practical musical training and knowledge.

Having played in rock and blues bands in my youthful years, I argue that many rock musicians may also be seen as improvisers. The band best known for improvisation from my era would have to be the Grateful Dead. Such bands improvised for many reasons. From personal experience, our improvisations often were turned into original songs. At times, we also used improvisation to suit the mood of the audience or band members. The task was to turn improvisation into something meaningful and enjoyable for all.

The actions to do so occurred in the moment rather than having been pre-planned and rehearsed at practice sessions. Feel for the music, or intuition, played a large part in the final number, and there was a high use of intuition, rather than a reliance on detailed analysis or the predictable structure worked on at rehearsal. Improvisation gave us the capacity to respond to the moment, to unanticipated situations, and to deliver something new, untried and untested.

While to some in the audience, and indeed some in the band, the situation may have seemed chaotic, that was rarely the case. Rather improvisation enabled a mix of structure and flexibility in a creative process. We were able to do so because of our shared love of music, musical genres, and musical styles; and because we spent time together, interacting socially in the pursuit of a common goal. We played to our strengths and to the strengths of each other. We developed self-confidence, confidence in each other, trust in our own and each other's abilities, and a willingness to try new things.

Those new things did not always work, but we had fun learning about what adjustments needed to be made. Our skills developed and we improved, although some music critics may tell you otherwise. We were not constrained by policies or procedures, other than venue management demands to turn down the volume, which usually was met by audience demands to turn it back up.

An SME owner/manager's task therefore, is to facilitate the creativity and innate improvisational actions of their employees. Good things will follow.

8. Emergent thinking

Formal planning based on so-called sound scientific principles of cause and effect, industry analysis, forecasting, historic trends, estimating, and rational and linear thinking processes has been an organisational norm. Strategists have been seen to be analytical, in full awareness and control of data, and able to make sound business decisions as a result (following De Wit and Meyer, 2005). Such an argument may be extrapolated to the SME owner/manager. Reality paints a different picture.

CASs are emergent and their unpredictability means that a reliance on traditional methods of thinking is unhelpful. This does not mean that SME owner/managers ought not to be future oriented; far from it, rather, they need to consider the future in ways that may overturn tradition in the search for a better future.

New mental models, based on a professional approach may help them to do so. In this model, there is space for emotions, intuition, and creativity, for shared understanding and sensemaking, and for risk-taking as a learning process. The scientific approach is still appropriate but rather than one that relies on the formulation and testing of hypotheses, sometimes known as a positivist approach, the alternative approach relies on insights that may be gleaned for an understanding of SMEs as systems of social action and interaction, or a post-positivist approach. In a post-positivist understanding of systems, more is to be gained from an interpretive (following Denzin, 1989; Sheehan, 2000) and grounded approach (following Charmaz, 2006; Corbin and Strauss, 2008; Glaser, 1998; Glaser and Strauss, 1999; Strauss and Corbin, 1998) to understanding than that of the positivist approach. The development of an appropriate SME culture and climate is a necessary precursor to embracing and inculcating new mental models. Honesty, trust, and integrity become the new norms.

It is suggested in the next chapter that a new mental model for SMEs is professionalism.

Chapter 5

Professionalism

Introduction

SMEs need to become more professional in their approach to business and by extension their customers, suppliers, and significant others. Before considering the argument further, this chapter begins with some general information about professions. A discussion about professionalism, which includes the principles of professionalism, then follows. The penultimate section, entitled consequences of professionalism, discusses values, attitudes, and behaviour. A summary concludes the chapter.

About professions

Before being able to discuss professionalism, it is first necessary to say what is meant by a profession. Mintzberg (1973) suggested that a profession may be recognised by two criteria. The first is that a profession has a universal or similar set of roles and programmes for work performance. The second is that the profession has specific knowledge, particularly within a scientific paradigm. That knowledge is considered to be specific to the organisation, the industry in which it operates, and its particular markets.

Three general research approaches have been adopted when studying professions. Such approaches have explored the trait and institutional and legalistic features of professions (Landsbury, 1978). Some professions are seen to have in common characteristics, such as specialist roles, knowledge specific to those roles, and personality traits such as altruism. Such traits are seen to distinguish a profession from other occupations.

The trait approach ought to be treated with some caution. There is a suggestion that traits are generalisable. That is, that traits found to be particular to one profession, organisation, or industry will be reflected in all similar professions, organisations, and industries. It is highly unlikely that this will be the case. The trait of altruism is more than likely to be that of an individual rather than of a profession.

The institutional approach defines a profession in terms of a process of institutional or associational development. To reach the standing of a profession, an occupation has to be able to demonstrate that it has followed a set sequence of stages in the performance of that occupation to achieve the nomenclature and recognition as a profession. These stages include, establishing a professional association, changing the name of the occupation, developing an ethical code of practice, obtaining public support through protracted campaigning, and developing learning and development facilities (Sheehan, 2000). The Australian Institute of Management (AIM) is an example of an institutional approach to developing management as a profession.

AIM is a not-for-profit body whose sole purpose is to promote the advancement of education and learning in the field of management and leadership for commerce, industry, and government. Annual surpluses are invested in the creation of education products, alternative education distribution channels, and learning-support materials for members in the network and other interested parties.

It is an Australia-wide organisation with more than 25,000 managers at every level and over 5,000 businesses belonging to their network. AIM considers that it adds value to managers by providing them with learning opportunities so that they better understand and implement practical management approaches within their organisations. They do so by means of business and management training, events and seminars, coaching, research, and publications. They offer a specialist management bookshop and library services to support management development (AIM, 2011).

The legislative approach considers that the essential feature of a profession is that its status is recognised by the state. Recognition generally occurs through registration or licensing. For example, in The Queensland Law Society Annual Report 2009/10 (2010), the Queensland Law Society states that it represents the interests of about 10,000 members. Membership comprises lawyers, future lawyers, and those with an interest in the profession. The Society is incorporated under an Act of Parliament—the *Legal Profession Act 2007* (Qld). It is an independent professional body, subject to the governance of its council who are elected by the membership. It has specific statutory responsibilities relating to the regulation of solicitors in Queensland. Moreover, it leads the profession's knowledge development and exchange through an extensive professional development offering. It guides legislation through advocacy and provides comprehensive services and support to its members and the community.

Practising solicitors must hold a law degree. They must also undertake additional legal training through either successful completion of a Practical Legal Training (PLT) course, or by serving as a supervised trainee. PLT courses are designed to equip graduates with the practical knowledge for entry into legal practice, with courses usually covering training in areas such as ethics, legal writing and drafting, interview skills, and other common practice-related skills. Supervised training occurs at a law firm and is a form of on-the-job training, which offers the opportunity to gain practical knowledge in a practice environment while earning a wage. The institutional approach includes a consistent standard of tertiary, and ongoing, education.

While education clearly is important in the professions, professionalism is not defined by a set of competencies such as how much knowledge one has, but by an attitude. Consequently, there is no one theory or definition that can provide a simple answer as to what comprises professionalism. Some common themes and approaches may be seen as a guide, while concurrently recognising that not all occupations or SMEs will fit all criteria.

About professionalism

There are two broad ways by which professionalism may be considered. The first is often connected to the way we work and the attitude we hold towards that work and relates to particular aspects of a job or profession. It has long been recognised as paramount to performance in, for example, the engineering, legal, health informatics, and medical professions. The second evolves from the first and considers that to be professional; a person ought to be seen as an expert in their field because they are well-trained and educated, competent (which may be measured through test or examination), proficient, knowledgeable, skilled, and able to demonstrate excellence in their work. They are required to adhere to a code of professional ethics and may be relied upon to act in accordance with established societal and organisational norms (following Lysons and Farrington, 2006). Expertise is attained over a period of time and is enhanced through ongoing development.

As an example, in the UK, in 2009, the Office of Government Commerce (OGC) published its definition of the procurement professional (OGC, 2009). This document identifies such an individual as adding value to the quality and cost effectiveness of the procurement function and having an impact on commercial relationships. The procurement professional was required to extract value from the goods or services procured throughout the life of the contract and to develop contracts that provided value for money and accorded with legal requirements. The procurement professional was expected to continue their professional development.

Similarly, it ought to be the case that those seeking to work in contemporary business and management organisations aspire to be a 'professional' or to work in a professionally managed organisation, including in small—and medium-sized enterprises (SMEs). While being professional may be considered to be a virtue, recent corporate scandals in Australia, the UK, and the USA attest to the lack of professionalism by some individuals and organisations.

A number of assumptions are held about becoming a professional. It is often assumed that one can become a professional simply by acquiring a degree. Some organisations work under the impression that they can claim to be professional by hiring a certain number of graduates, including MBAs. Others include a code of conduct or similar as a way to demonstrate 'professionalism'. Such perspectives, however, overlook the role of professionalism in SMEs and how many people working in those organisations might become professional.

It may be argued that if we work in a job for some length of time and if we perform the role responsibilities of that job to set requirements, then we become professional, at least to one degree or another. Therein lays a conundrum. Task repetition does not make us a professional. Most people, particularly if they have even a basic interest in what is required and in what they do, will learn a role and perform that role to the best of their knowledge, skills, and ability for a time. To remain committed in the role over a period of time, particularly in SMEs facing constant and rapid change is more problematic. We sometimes find people who have worked at a job for years but who actually have contributed very little to the organisation as a whole. They certainly cannot be called professionals, no matter what their academic qualifications.

Some may become complacent and unwilling to give the little extra effort that often indicates the qualities of what might be considered a good corporate citizen. These qualities may embrace teamwork, harmony, respect for others, transparency, honesty, integrity, accountability, and responsibility. Some become content to provide the minimal effort that is enough just to do the task. That may be because they have become disillusioned with the SME, feel alienated by constant change, or feel unappreciated.

As a customer, it is often easy to recognise, and distinguish between, good and poor customer service. If you are shopping in a department store and are unable to find a shop assistant to help you with an enquiry about the product, even when the shop appears not to be too busy, you may determine that service is poor and resolve not to shop there again. Compare this with the shop assistant who approaches you and asks if they may be of assistance or is readily to be found when you have a query. Chances are, even if you do not make a purchase that day, you will return.

Consider too, the company that provides a staff member who answers your telephone enquiry rapidly and helpfully. Compare that situation with waiting on hold or having to punch into a keypad a series of numbers in response to the impersonality of a recorded voice message. It is not hard to imagine what company we most prefer. The aforementioned are simplistic examples of professional as opposed to non-professional behaviour.

Principles of professionalism

Many organisations and professions have a code of conduct. A code of conduct is a set of rules outlining the responsibilities of or proper practices for an individual or organisation. They are sometimes called a code of ethics or an honour code. The Hippocratic Oath taken by doctors to uphold professional ethical standards arguably is the most well-known.

The Australian Public Service Commission (APSC) states that Australian Public Service (APS) employees are required to abide by a code of conduct and to uphold APS Values. The code of conduct requires that employees, in the course of their employment, behave honestly and with integrity, act with care and diligence, treat everyone with respect and courtesy, and without harassment, comply with all applicable Australian laws, comply with any lawful and reasonable direction given by someone in the employee's agency who has authority to give the direction, maintain appropriate confidentiality about dealings that the employee has with any minister or minister's member of staff, disclose and take reasonable steps to avoid any conflict of interest (real or apparent) in connection with APS employment, use Commonwealth resources in a proper manner, not provide false or misleading information in response to a request for information that is made for official purposes, not make improper use of inside information or duties, status, power or authority in order to gain, or seek to gain, a benefit or advantage for the employee or for any other person, at all times behave in a way that upholds the APS values and the integrity and good reputation of the APS, while on duty overseas, at all times behave in a way that upholds the good reputation of Australia and comply with any other conduct requirement that is prescribed by the regulations (APSC, 2011)[4].

What may be gleaned from the aforementioned codes and others is a set of guiding principles for professionalism in SMEs. These principles are not meant to be prescriptive or descriptive. Each SME will have unique needs, and you will make your choice as to what is appropriate for you and best matches your value set.

The principles include

- competence in the knowledge and skills required and the application of such;
- competence to work of the highest standards;
- lifelong learning and continued personal/professional development;
- the application of principles, values, and standards;
- responsibility and accountability;
- a national regulatory, accreditation, and registration process (where appropriate);
- a recognised career structure (where appropriate);
- the concept of service and public, rather than self-interest;
- a focus on improving practice as a means to be the best at what you do;
- ethical practice including confidentiality, transparency, openness, honesty, integrity, and the fair and reasonable treatment of others; and
- resolution of conflict in a professional, rather than personal way.

Consequences of professionalism

Being a professional means more than simply acquiring a degree, or number of degrees. It means being true to ourselves and our chosen discipline or occupation and trying to excel at what it is we do. Sometimes that simply means doing what is 'right'. For example, as Australia, as a nation, becomes even more multicultural and diverse, the staff and customers that are attracted

---

[4] Similar codes of conduct are apparent in other organisations. See the codes of conduct, for example, for the Australian Council for International Development and Australian Institute of Management listed in further reading. Sample codes of conduct may be found on the Internet.

to our respective SMEs may come from international communities of which we, as owners or managers, have little knowledge or experience. The skill set which they bring may not meet what we imagined to be that set of skills necessary for us to function as we might wish to or with which we might be most familiar. The professional provides service to their staff and to their customers beyond the normal requirements of the job. The non-professional complains about the lack of skills, the language difficulties, and the perceived unwillingness for the staff or customers to understand and purchase their product or service. A malaise tends to follow.

Often, we have to pay for this unprofessional behaviour in terms of recruitment, training and retraining, and retention. But we may also have to action those behaviours in terms of organisational policies and procedures, including performance management, counselling, and discipline. Such actions are costly, time consuming, and demoralising for all concerned. While they may lead to behavioural change, they do not necessarily lead to attitude change. Attitude is deemed to be a core requirement for being a professional.

What now follows is what I mean by values, attitudes, and behaviours.

Values

> *We do not act rightly because we have virtue or excellence, but we rather have those because we have acted rightly.*
>
> (Aristotle 384-322 B.C., Greek philosopher and scientist, student of Plato and teacher of Alexander the Great).

Values are the preferences we have for taking concerning appropriate courses of action or for seeking particular outcomes. They are guiding principles or standards which reflect our sense of right and wrong and help us to choose what is important, useful, desirable, constructive, and helpful (following Fromm, 1947). When we use a phrase such as *people ought to be treated with respect* or *people are treated equally in our SME*, we are making a statement reflecting the values that we hold. Our values have a propensity to influence our attitudes and behaviour.

For example, if you consider that people ought to be treated with respect but you work in an SME where some staff talk about others behind their back or rudely dismiss the opinions of others, then you may consider that your SME's reality does not match its rhetoric and develop an attitude that it is not a nice place to work. Accordingly, your productivity may decrease, you may be absent from work more often, or you may form an intention to leave the SME. By contrast, if such negative behaviours do not exist or are promptly addressed, it is more than likely that you will hold positive feelings towards your SME and act in accordance with the goals and objectives of the SME in mind. Thus, values help us explain what we do and why we choose that course of action. They are *the glue, which binds us together*.

Our values tend to be established at an early age and are influenced by parents, siblings, relatives, extended family, religious upbringing, teachers, and school colleagues. They tend to align with what is considered to be our national culture and thus we share that set of values in common with others. Australian culture is predicated on values of fairness, equality, justice, freedom, and respect. Sharing these values enables us to develop opportunities and certainties without which a culture would collapse. We would lose our sense of identity and self-worth.

Attitudes

Attitudes are affective, behavioural, and cognitive structures by which we make sense of, and form judgements about, our world. They are affective because they are formed emotionally, behavioural because they create a tendency for action, and cognitive because they help us evaluate and form an understanding or belief of the item or object in question. That is, they form the basis for the favourable or unfavourable approaches we take to thinking, feeling, or responding to some object, concept, or situation within our environment. Attitudes are important to us because they help us acquire knowledge through reasoning, intuition, or perception, thus enabling us to understand the events affecting our lives.

Generally speaking, attitudes are the helpful or unhelpful thoughts and feelings we hold about a person, place, object, or episode occurring in our lives. We may be conflicted in our attitudes because we may simultaneously possess both constructive and unconstructive attitudes towards a person, place, object, or episode occurring in our lives. They can create a paradox for us that may be difficult to explain, either to the self or others. For example, we may work in an SME which prides itself on the quality of its work while being aware that the way the work is undertaken could present a health and safety risk to the people performing that work.

Because they are individually formed and shaped, it is difficult to assess whether or not they are formed by nature, nurture, or a combination of both. That is, we are unsure if attitudes are innate or learned. Such uncertainty means they are also difficult to define. If they are difficult to define, then they also are difficult to measure, monitor, and change. Attitudes may remain permanent or they may be impervious to change. Equally, given that they may be influenced by a person's life experiences, they may be susceptible to change.

Behaviour

Behaviour is the action or actions a person takes in relation to their internal and external environment. One of the most often cited social psychologists, Kurt Lewin, stated in his 1936 book, *Principles of Topological Psychology*, that behaviour is a function of the person and their environment. He developed the equation $B = f(P, E)$. Thus, behaviour is how a person responds to the various stimuli or inputs within their internal and external environments.

Medical science informs us that behaviour is controlled primarily by the endocrine system and the nervous system. Our most common understanding is that complexity in the behaviour of a person is related to the intricacy of their nervous system. Even though the endocrine system and the nervous system are separate systems, they often work together to help the body function properly.

Given that human beings have a complex nervous system when compared to other organisms, then it may be argued that humans have a greater capacity to learn new responses and change their behaviour. Those responses may be internal or external, mindful or intuitive, obvious or hidden, and intentional or unintentional. Behaviours may be innate or learned, and they may be unlearned.

The action taken will change a person's relationship with their environment because actions have consequences. Those consequences may be planned or unplanned; acceptable or unacceptable, and are dependent on the actions of the endocrine and nervous systems.

What I am arguing here is that behaviour is a subjective experience, often influenced by actions and events beyond our control and outside our understanding. Our behaviour may relate to, or be influenced by, the actions and behaviours of others and/or to the responses generated by our endocrine and nervous systems. In attempting to understand, therefore, what helps our employees to be productive, we need to account for their experiences and the attribution of meaning employees give to those experiences.

Summary

Professionalism may be summarised as the way in which each individual's attitudes towards his or her role, work colleagues, customers, and the working environment are displayed. If they demonstrate a level of competency and performance, or a willingness to improve their competency and performance, including ongoing professional development, in the completion of a set of common roles and functions, then it may be argued that they are displaying the attributes of professionalism. Employees who belong to a profession recognised by the state also will be required to abide by a code of practice or a set of ethical expectations.

In the next chapter, I am going to argue that while values, attitudes, knowledge, and skills are vital in any job, the way in which they are used is equally important. I am going to suggest that SME professionalism requires the development of a set of qualities appropriate to your business so as to guide the actions and behaviours of staff to ensure appropriate application. This set of qualities is not meant to be prescriptive or descriptive. They are offered as a guide for you, bearing in mind that your set may vary, depending on your type of business and your values and vision, mission, and strategies.

Chapter 6

Qualities for Professionalism in SMEs

Introduction

Qualities are the guiding principles or potentialities seen to be necessary for SMEs to become more professional. In this chapter, a set of qualities are suggested and discussed. The set includes commitment to excellence, honesty, integrity, respect for others, compassion, transparency, fairness, professional responsibility, social responsibility, and altruism. Within each quality are listed some of the behaviours that could be instilled within your SME so that you may bring these qualities to fruition. The chapter concludes with a set of requirements for being a professional and a summary.

A set of qualities for professionalism in SMEs

While values, attitudes, knowledge and skills are vital in any job, *the way in which they are used is equally important*. SME professionalism requires that a set of qualities appropriate to your business and stakeholders be developed to guide the actions and behaviours of staff to ensure appropriate application. A set will vary depending on your values and vision, mission and strategies. To help you develop such a set, a list of generic qualities for professionalism is proposed, including the attributes of commitment to excellence, honesty, integrity, respect for others, compassion, transparency, fairness, professional responsibility, social responsibility, and altruism. These qualities apply to all aspects of professional life including interactions with any person in your supply chain, your staff, and indeed your personal relationships. While the list is not exhaustive, it may serve as a set of indicators to guide you in the development of a set of behaviours unique for your SME.

Commitment to excellence

Excellence is a somewhat nebulous word often used in organisations to promote quality and distinctiveness. When applied to performance, it can be used as a benchmark for performance and as a tool by which performance is assessed. Those benchmarks, usually framed in terms of quality and service, may be unrealistic rather than pragmatic. It is sometimes used to praise noteworthy performers on the achievement of a task. It can also be used as a tool for punishment if excellent performance is not achieved. It is a subjective term that can cause anxiety and result in performance being measured out of context. At best, it ought to be used as a guide to which an employee might strive to improve performance rather than as a weapon for destruction. Some examples of expected behaviours include the following:

- Do the best job that you can while striving to exceed expectations at all times; go the extra mile and seek to simplify systems and reduce bureaucracy.
- Use your initiative and encourage others to do the same.
- Be passionate about what you do and how you do it.
- Commit to lifelong learning by taking responsibility for your own learning, critically reflecting on your competencies, and the further knowledge and skill development required. Address personal barriers to accomplishing learning and growth.
- Take responsibility for learning by attending, being prepared and engaging with the learning; be prepared to extend your boundaries.
- Listen to the opinions of others, engage in debate, challenge, and be prepared for, and accept challenge, and be prepared to see things differently learn from others.
- Reflect with colleagues on the success of group work.

Honesty

Honesty means being sincere and truthful in what you do. It means being open, straightforward, and forthright in your communication with others. It means being candid and upfront with others. It also means being respectful of the rights and obligations of others and giving and receiving feedback in non-threatening and non-defensive ways. As well as a personal dimension, being honest also means how you use and relate to the assets of the SME and how you relate to others in the supply chain. Some behavioural examples include the following:

- Using SME assets for their intended purpose and not for personal convenience or gain.
- Refusing personal gain from others in the supply chain.
- Communicating appropriately in an honest and timely manner; saying what you think respectfully and with consideration for the feelings of others.
- Saying when you are unclear about expectations or when you do not understand or follow something and ask for help.
- Accurately representing actions and events; avoiding misrepresentation of the truth.
- Reflecting on your personal reaction to encounter with others and accepting responsibility for your actions and their consequences; admitting and accepting mistakes and endeavouring not to make the same mistake twice.
- Recognising, appropriately disclosing, and managing conflicts of interest.
- Be forthcoming with information; not withholding and/or using information for power.

Integrity

Like honesty, integrity relates to truthfulness and candour. You need to be aware of your value system and the value system of others with whom you come in contact. It requires that you lead by example, be consistent, firm, and fair in what you say and do, not favouring anyone above anyone else. That is, do not let personal relationships or likes and dislikes impede your treatment of each individual. Act without bias or discrimination. You are seen to be dependable, trustworthy, and steadfast in all that you do. You are dedicated, resolute, determined, and persistent. You treat others as you would like to be treated. Some behavioural examples include the following:

- Understand and communicate your values, morals, principles and ethics, and stand by them.
- Abide by rules or challenge them constructively.
- Keep your promises/word.
- Take care in what you do and accept the consequences of your actions.
- Do what is right rather than what is easy.
- Have the courage to say what you think but do so respectfully.
- Treat others in the way you like to be treated.

Respect for others

Most people want to be respected for what they do. We value the admiration and opinions of others if we are in open and honest relationships. Self-respect contributes to our self-esteem and feelings of self-worth.

On 10 December 1948, the General Assembly of the United Nations adopted and proclaimed the Universal Declaration of Human Rights. In summary, the declaration was a statement of intent as to how nation states ought to behave towards each other and how people throughout the world ought to be treated by their nation states, across borders, and within their workplaces. The intention was to ensure freedom, justice, and a peaceful world in which people could live lawfully, free from fear and oppression, and able to achieve their aspirations. Fundamental to the declaration was the notion of human rights and the dignity and worth of each individual.

Article 1 of the declaration states that, 'all human beings are born free and equal in dignity and rights. They are endowed with reason and conscience and should act towards one another in a spirit of brotherhood' (The Universal Declaration of Human Rights, 1948). Some examples of how respect may be applied in behavioural terms are

- remember that other people have rights and act accordingly; treat people as equals;
- recognise and respect personal and sexual boundaries;
- avoid bias (e.g., gender, race, age, sexual orientation) in interactions with others;
- articulate and embrace the many positive aspects of difference among people and demonstrate awareness of how such differences affect personal interactions;
- demonstrate a commitment to resolving conflicts in a collegial manner;
- persuade people to new ideas as opposed to bullying them;
- be approachable and listen to others;
- respect people's time and be punctual;
- show sensitivity and respect for the needs, feelings, ideas, and wishes of others in your daily activity;
- demonstrate humility in interactions with others;
- recognise that appropriate dress and appearance demonstrate respect for yourself, others, and for the work environment.

Compassion

Compassion is often thought of in the helping professions, particularly in the medical and social-work fields. But it equally applies to SMEs where empathy, care and concern for the well-being of staff and customers ought to be paramount. Kindness and consideration are not attributes simply for those dealing with the sick. People become distressed at work through the actions of their colleagues, customers, or suppliers or from the pressures of work. They may become anxious and apprehensive if they realise that the SME is facing financial difficulty or if change is being proposed. Behaviours consistent with compassion are

- recognise and respond to the aspirations dreams, hopes, anxieties, and fears of staff and stakeholders; and
- assist colleagues in dealing with the challenges of their work.

Transparency

The global financial crisis of the late 2000s happened for a number of reasons. One of those reasons was the lack of transparency in some organisations. That lack of transparency relates to ambiguity in strategy and planning, an inability to be clear about what is required, and why certain goals need to be achieved, and comprehensible, yet clear and simple instructions. Transparency means that you need to operate your SME with no hidden agendas. You need to create an environment where people are clear about your intentions and expectations and where they are able to articulate clearly, and without fear, their views. Such an environment requires open and unambiguous communication that wherever possible, it is conducted face to face rather than by email, text message, or social networking sites. Behaviours relating to transparency are

- be open about your intentions and expectations and state them clearly, firmly, and non-defensively. Reveal your agenda.
- relay facts and observations rather than rumour and innuendo.
- develop your goals, objectives, and tasks in consultation with your staff. Articulate your goals clearly.
- keep your communication clear, unambiguous and simple, avoiding jargon or the latest 'management speak'.

- create an environment where staff feel confident that they can state their suggestions, ideas, and opinions freely and without fear of retribution.
- be available to staff at all times but where possible do so in a face-to-face situation rather than electronically.
- keep your staff informed and tell it like it is, whether good or bad news. If original goals and expectations need to change to meet current and future business objectives, let people know early what needs to happen and clearly explain why.
- speak directly to people and avoid talking about them behind their back.
- involve staff in the decision-making process, particularly when those decisions are likely to affect them.

Fairness

Most people like to be treated fairly. When staff perceive that they are being treated equally, fairly and consistently, their attitude towards you and their work will be enhanced. There may be some fundamental differences in your workplace because of factors such as tradition, more experience, and thus superior knowledge and skills, religion, beliefs, and cultural values. These factors may affect people's attitude. More importantly, your attitude to, and management of these factors, will have a vital bearing on the work environment. Moreover, some are more ambitious, or indeed mischievous, than others and may seek to impress you. You need to be aware that this is happening and reiterate your approach to fairness. Fairness may be indicated if you

- treat everyone equally and provide equal opportunity for all.
- promote according to merit and ability rather than on length of service or personality.
- consider the needs of all staff.
- value and consider the suggestions, ideas and opinions of all staff and explain why you prefer some of those factors above others.
- ensure an equal distribution of work based on knowledge, skills, and abilities while recognising the need to provide challenge and opportunity.
- do your fair share.
- are consistent with the application of your values, policies, procedures and rules.

- ensure staff are equipped to do the job by providing the necessary resources and development opportunities.
- hold staff responsible and accountable for what they do and ensure you apply the same rule to yourself.
- recognise and reward good work; identify and correct unsatisfactory work.
- encourage staff to learn from honest mistakes but do not accept malicious intent.

Professional responsibility

Some people working in SMEs work in occupations that have professional standing and an accompanying set of responsibilities and standards. They are required to act in accordance with codes of conduct or professional body rules. Such occupations include accountants, engineers, lawyers and solicitors, and medical practitioners. However, not all people owning or managing an SME will have professional responsibilities. While what is outlined in this category will mainly relate to the aforementioned types of occupations, they may also have relevance for others. Behaviours include:

- adheres to established professional codes of conduct;
- identifies ethical issues relating to their situation and acts in an ethical way;
- practices their profession according to accepted standards;
- identifies and appropriately deals with inappropriate behaviours of all, bringing inappropriate actions to the attention of appropriate bodies;
- develops strategies for coping with the challenges, conflicts, and ambiguities inherent in professional work;
- being present and punctual for scheduled activities.

Social responsibility

There is a recognised need for organisations to become more attuned to the environment in which they operate. This includes protection of the environment and relevant ecosystems, responsible behaviour within the community it serves, good governance, ethical practice, and social equity. The International Organization for Standardization (ISO, 2011) states that social responsibility enables organisations to contribute to sustainable development by way of socially responsible behaviour. The overall performance of an organisation may be assessed by its performance in relation to the society in which it operates and its environmental impact. Organisations, including SMEs, increasingly are subject to greater scrutiny by their various stakeholders, including owners, shareholders, customers, suppliers, sponsors, donors, and financiers.

An SMEs performance as a socially responsible entity may impact on its competitive advantage. It may also impact on its reputation and influence customers and suppliers in their relationships with you. It could affect your ability to attract and retain staff, and maintain their morale, commitment, and productivity. It could affect your relationship with your customers and suppliers, government, the media, and the community in which you operate.

Thus an SME ought to operate in accordance with accepted social principles. The way your SME may do so will need to accord with your business strategies and the community in which you operate. As with any project, if you want to be socially responsible, you could do the following:

- Identify a suitable project that aligns with your business.
- Identify goals, objectives, targets, and performance measures.
- Allocate resources and a budget; even voluntary work will need support.
- Take action.
- Evaluate and reassess.
- Publicise what you are doing so that people are aware and able to respond.

Altruism

Following on from social responsibility and extending the core concept, I here propose that altruism may be a worthy consideration. Altruism is selfless concern for the welfare of others. In many cultures and religions, it is a core aspect of how people ought to behave towards each other. It moves beyond concepts of duty and loyalty to focus on helping others without seeking reward or recognition for so doing. It can be a pleasurable experience.

In an Australian study, Madden et al. (2006) carried out research in fifty-two small—to medium-size enterprises (SMEs) across Australia. They were particularly interested in why SMEs engaged with their communities, how they did so, and impediments they perceived in giving. They conducted five focus groups and fifteen face-to-face in-depth structured interviews with SME owners and chief executive officers in five Australian states from September 2004 to March 2005. They invited small business clients of a number of law and accounting firms located in major cities around Australia to participate, taking particular care to ensure that participants came from both urban and rural locations, from different business sectors, and were from SMEs of varying sizes. They established that SMEs prefer to avoid giving cash, favoured supporting local causes, and would benefit from the development of best practice, giving guidelines and templates.

They also identified four key barriers to SME engagement with their community. They are as follows: the number of requests received; the lack of a formal process for handling requests; a strong sense that business priorities, particularly the need for survival, must take precedence; and concerns that the contribution might not be used prudently rather than wasted in administration costs or large remuneration packages for high-ranking staff of the recipient organisations.

Overall, however, they found strong motivation and desire on the part of SMEs to be involved in, and engaged with, their local communities. An altruistic approach was seen as a duty. Behaviours could include

- placing the interests of others above self-interest; and
- giving up some personal needs to meet needs of others.

A set of requirements for being a professional

There are six requirements that ought to be considered for a professional approach to working in an SME. The first requirement is that a professional has a basic set of interpersonal skills, including assertiveness, the ability to mediate and resolve conflict, a genuine and unconditional regard for others, and self-awareness. The second requirement is that a professional is able to develop further, and improve, that set of basic skills, and has the motivation to do so. The third requirement is that a professional has the skills necessary to utilise their knowledge and understanding of theoretical constructs underpinning their role. The fourth requirement is that a professional is able to help SME employees take responsibility for actions, including their relationships with all SME stakeholders. The fifth requirement is that a professional has the necessary skills to address any ethical issues that may be encountered. The sixth and final requirement is that a professional is able to adopt different approaches in performing their role in the SME as circumstances dictate.

Summary

In this chapter, I have outlined a set of qualities that you may find interesting for your SME. Within each quality I have listed some of the behaviours that could be instilled within your SME so that you might observe and evaluate your progress and determine what action might be required if your aspirations remain unfulfilled. You and your staff may already have a well formed set of behaviours, but adopting the notion of lifelong learning and continuing development will help to enhance those behaviours. In the following chapters, I discuss a number of skills that I see as core to enabling the development of professionalism in SMEs. I start with self-awareness.

Chapter 7

Self-Awareness

Know thyself.

(Plato 427-347 BC,
ancient Greek philosopher, in the dialog 'Alcibiades')

Introduction

We ought not to be afraid of change. Along with death and taxes, it is one of the certainties in our lives. Being ready and willing to embrace change requires that we have an informed self-understanding and a willingness to adapt and change our skill set as required. That skill set may include the values we hold; our personal integrity and professionalism; and how we maintain our health and well-being in situations that we may find stressful. Change may require some personal adjustment on our part so that we can come to know ourselves, accept ourselves, and forget ourselves. That is, self-awareness is a vital component for becoming more professional.

In this chapter, becoming professional is the first notion explored. Then follows how we might go about recognising a lack of self-awareness, including a number of typologies that may be seen to help such recognition.

The next section covers becoming self-aware, and it includes a discussion on the *self* and the importance of self-awareness.

Two major theories have guided explanations of self-awareness. They are the Johari Window and Transactional Analysis. Each of these theories is thus explained, including ego states and contemporary transactional analysis theory. A brief summary and a pointer to the following chapter on mindfulness conclude this chapter.

Becoming professional

As an owner or manager of an SME, you will be well aware of a number of tasks you are required to complete on a daily basis. In your role, you have a planning and organising responsibility, you are required to solve problems and make decisions, and to communicate with your stakeholders. All these functions need to be carried out to ensure the smooth running of the business so that it not only survives but also thrives. Moreover, we often recognise the limitations of others when these functions are not completed satisfactorily. By contrast, we sometimes overlook or seek to hide from others the limitations we recognise in ourselves.

It is important that we perform our role to the best of our ability. Equally, it is important that we reflect on that performance in an endeavour to improve. We ought not to be content with doing just enough to get the job done. Rather, we ought to strive to remove errors and deficiencies and without necessarily waiting for others to point out such things to us.

As an organisational entity, it also is important that the SMEs do what is right, not only in terms of accepted community expectations but also in terms of employee expectations. This means that we must act in accordance with accepted society and workplace norms, including treating our employees well. No amount of so-called professional qualifications and degrees can facilitate such treatment. Essentially, how we do so relates to our values and attitudes.

Impression management has no place in the modern SME. Being a 'yes-man' [sic] by accepting orders and instructions from above without question, or by keeping the 'boss' informed of what some people are doing in order to self-promote at the expense of a colleague ought not to be tolerated.

Equally, those who indulge in workplace bullying or harassing are not being professional. The person who belittles others, tells untruths about their colleagues, criticises others without being aware of all the circumstances, or withholds information, is not acting professionally. Nor is the manager who listens to the impressionist, overlooks or indulges in inappropriate behaviours, fails to address such behaviours, or dismisses concerns without due consideration being a professional.

Such actions suggest a limited intrapersonal skills set. *Intrapersonal skills* may be defined as how we understand ourselves and how we relate to others. The skill set includes the values that we hold, our personal integrity and professionalism, and how we maintain our health and well-being in situations that we may find stressful. This may require some personal adjustment on our part so that we can come to know ourselves, accept ourselves, and forget ourselves. That is, self-awareness is a vital component of intrapersonal skills.

Recognising a lack of self-awareness

There are a number of ways by which we might recognise a lack of self-awareness in either ourselves or others. What might indicate bad manners or rudeness to some people, such as talking loudly on a mobile phone or queue jumping, also may indicate a lack of self-awareness. Other identifiers may be a person who is unable to remain for very long in a job, unable to sustain a friendship or relationship for more than a few weeks, continually interrupts when another person is talking or is easily influenced by others. They may also seek to blame others when things do not work out as well as they might like.

Equally, there are a number of reasons why people might lack self-awareness. They may lack the ability or willingness to reflect critically on their attitudes or behaviour. They may be deficient in their sense of values or moral purpose. They may be argumentative to the point that colleagues and significant others find it difficult to offer them meaningful feedback.

What now follows are nine suggested typologies of people we may recognise. You may even recognise yourself. That being the case, whether or not you decide to take action and seek ways to improve is up to you.

The 'know it all'

This person knows everything about everything. What is more, they are always right. They never let up enforcing their point of view. They are dogmatic and pedantic. Their opinion is the only one they are prepared to entertain. Their decisions are always right and beyond reproach or questioning. They believe in their infallibility and in truth and righteousness. If you disagree, they become more arrogant in tone and manner. Their non-verbal messages begin to reflect their feelings. They become louder in their tone of voice, begin to visibly rock back and forth, and start pointing their finger. The colour in their face changes to a redder shade. They go on ad nauseam until such time as you can take it no longer and just give in to them.

Similarly, there is the *know it all* who appears to compromise. They will appear to agree, after some debate, to a decision taken in a meeting. Deep down, however, other forces are at work. Once outside the meeting, they will begin to politic and attempt to undermine decisions. They will spread innuendo, rumour, and falsehoods about others and seek to re-establish their superiority.

People find it difficult to work with them because they tend not to be a team player.

The 'whinger'

To whinge is not seen as a particularly Australian characteristic. When we think of whingers, we tend to think of our past so-called colonial masters. Unfortunately, whinging appears to be a trait that has rubbed off on some in the workplace.

This person will whine and moan about anything and everything. They can see the fault in others but fail to recognise it in themselves. They do not like the colour of their uniform, their customers, their colleagues, the cricket results, or the outcome of last night's reality TV show. They deplore your taste in music.

Next time you are on your favourite social network site, think carefully about the comments you are reading. Look more closely at who says what and how often. You may suddenly recognise the family member or friend who constantly finds fault with their spouse, their children, their work colleagues, their boss, the neighbours, or the weather. Indeed, you may recognise that you are guilty of so doing. If these messages annoy you, it is time to offer some constructive feedback to that person, but privately and not through the social network. Failing that, you could close contact with that person.

I will stop now in case you think I am whingeing.

The 'egotist'

Our ego is a wonderful part of us. It shapes our personality and helps us to understand who we are and how we fit into our world. It gives us our sense of self-worth and self-esteem. It helps us to define ourselves and to distinguish ourselves from others. As well as our sense of self, Freud (1920, 1923)[5] considered our ego to be a set of psychic functions including judgment, tolerance, reality-testing, control, planning, defence, synthesis of

---

[5] These texts in their original form may now be difficult to locate. *Beyond the Pleasure Principle* is a particularly difficult read. For general information about Freud, his life, and his work, I suggest using the Internet.

information, intellectual functioning, and memory. It helps us determine what is real, organise our thoughts, and make sense of them and the world around us. As Skyhooks (1975)[6] once sang, 'Ego Is Not a Dirty Word.'

But there are exceptions.

A person who has an exaggerated sense of their own self-importance is called an egotist. The egotist tends to speak mostly about themselves and is seen to be conceited, self-absorbed, self-centred, and selfish. They regale you with the most amazing stories about themselves that can leave you bored to the point of exhaustion. They think nobody listens to them, that life is against them, and that they should be noticed. They tend to want to share their pain with the world, often over social networking sites, so that others will massage their egos with support and sympathy. These are not attractive qualities. They lack self-awareness.

The 'manipulator'

Some people present as genuinely charming and helpful. But the ones lacking self-awareness are a little different. Behind their charm offensive lies the 'cunning plan' to manipulate others or to create a situation in which other colleagues are seen to be incompetent or unprofessional. It is a defence mechanism on their part to ensure that others are being subject to closer scrutiny while they escape seemingly unscathed.

The most obvious examples may be seen on the so-called reality TV shows. I make this statement with a cautionary note. There may be a question as to whether contestants on these shows are behaving genuinely or merely acting out a perceived role. Nonetheless, the manipulator will show they are stubborn, untruthful, dishonest, and lacking in personal integrity. Once discovered, they are soon abandoned by friends and colleagues who no longer are able to tolerate their behaviours.

To identify whether or not you might fit this category, reflect critically on your own behaviours. Ask yourself if you are continually trying to besmirch the reputation of colleagues, talk about colleagues behind their back, or seek to damage others in some way.

---

[6] If you do not have a copy of the original album or the later CD version, you will find this song on YouTube.

The 'chopper'

The 1969 movie *Easy Rider* featured, among other things, two motorbikes cut to a size and style not previously encountered by the general public. They were termed choppers. While they served as a symbol of freedom and soul searching by their riders, the un-self-aware 'chopper' is the opposite.

This person will chop you off mid-sentence, or hurry you to provide the information or answer they want to their timescale. They do not allow you the time to think or to offer a considered response. They show disinterest in what you are saying and a complete disregard for your right to have a voice. They have no awareness of your freedoms.

Their actions illustrate a lack of listening skills. You are annoyed by this behaviour and your attempts to be assertive and to offer constructive feedback are rebutted. You feel that you are not valued and begin to question your own role and capabilities.

They more than likely lack an ability to do a little soul searching.

The 'criticiser'

Australians are known for their sense of humour. Tinged with sarcasm and a good deal of teasing and mockery, we use it to cope with all sorts of difficult situations. We also use it to bring down others we perceive to be more successful than us or to bring back to our level those we perceive to be getting beyond themselves—the tall poppy syndrome. We use humour, among other tools, to denigrate the achievements of prominent others.

Most people are able to use repartee to return in kind the humour we experience. However, when a work colleague appears to be critical of colleagues, customers, and suppliers, it sounds a warning that needs to be heeded. Constant criticism of others, judging their behaviours while ignoring their own limitations, is debilitating for all concerned. It is a characteristic of a person's behaviour that indicates a lack of self-awareness.

We are all entitled to be treated with respect and dignity in the workplace. If our performance is found wanting, then our actions ought to be addressed. Learning and development opportunities ought to be offered to help us address our shortcomings, not constant fault finding, unfathomable instructions, or unsupported assertions. Such actions from others in the workplace could border on workplace bullying and harassment.

The 'irrationalist'

This person is unable and unwilling to listen to reason. They appear to lack the ability to think clearly or to see any problem from other than their perspective. They seldom agree that they have made a mistake or have limitations. They hardly ever apologise. They consider that apologising is a sign of weakness, rather than of strength.

They consider that others are being unreasonable or unhelpful. If a mistake has happed or an error occurred, it is the fault of someone else.

They are frustrating and infuriating. They will annoy you and others and more than likely they will upset the positive dynamics in your SME.

The 'bullocky'

Australian bullock drivers or bullockies were famous for their swearing. Their reputation was enhanced if they had an extensive and imaginative range of abuse with which to get their bullocks moving. Swearing has not been contained to that occupation; rather, it is used in all walks of life. While swearing might be used when physical pain is felt or when telling an anecdote, using it simply in an attempt to shock others simply demonstrates that you have a limited vocabulary.

Some people in the workplace appear to consider that if they swear at others, their power is enhanced and people will bend to their will. I call this person the bullocky. If they think people will accede to their demands or comply with their instructions because they have been sworn at, then the bullocky needs to think again as nothing could be further from the truth. Most people consider that those who swear are uneducated or poorly educated and lacking in appropriate language skills or ill-informed, insensitive, disrespectful, tactless, and tedious. They are considered to lack self-awareness.

Swearing, when used as abuse, has no place in the Australian workplace.

The 'despot'

A despot thinks that they are born to rule. They consider that they have absolute power in an SME when that power may in fact be quite limited. They are attempting to create an illusion in order to shore up their position. They tend not to work collaboratively or co-operatively and if they treat their customers and suppliers in a similar way, they may begin to wonder why their business is suffering.

There is a lot to be said for consulting with your staff, keeping them informed, and involving them in the decision-making process. People who are empowered to make decisions are usually more effective and efficient. Productivity is enhanced.

The despot or autocrat is not viewed favourably in a nation that prides itself on democratic and egalitarian values.

For example, in the floods that engulfed 75% of the State of Queensland in December 2010 and January 2011, many heroic deeds were performed as people came to the aid of complete strangers or carried out deeds that more than likely saved lives. But two questionable acts stand out: The first is the action of looters seeking to take advantage of the misfortunes of others. The second is the act of a reasonably highly placed person in a government department who sent an email to staff who may or may not have been affected by the floods, either directly or indirectly, demanding that if staff were absent, that they should produce proof including photos of how they were affected. Many people lost all their worldly possessions, including any form of photographic recording equipment, in the floodwaters. These actions were soundly derided by the community generally and indicate that such behaviour is not well regarded. The acts also may be indicative of a lack of self-awareness.

One way to become professional is to become more self-aware.

Becoming self-aware

The self

There are a number of ways that owners, managers, and people working in SMEs might begin to become more self-aware. The first is to begin to think more positively about the *self* (Avolio and Luthans, 2006). Here I use *self* in relation to organisational, group, and individual identity. Like those writing in the field of positive psychology such as Luthans et al. (2007) and Gardner and Schermerhorn Jr. (2004), I argue that it is not management that provides an individual with the potential for improvement or instils in people the motivation to succeed. Nor do management provide the capability that people have for assuming responsibility or the inclination to focus their actions on the achievement of organisational goals. These characteristics are already inherent. Rather, it is a responsibility of management, and by extension leadership, to provide the opportunity and to facilitate and develop a workplace culture whereby people are able to recognise and extend these human characteristics for themselves (following Gardner and Schermerhorn Jr., 2004).

I suggest a return to more positive approaches about how managers and leaders regard and believe in their staff—a return to the messages of Dewey (1916) and McGregor (1957).

Dewey (1916) considered that human beings should be seen as having unlimited potential. Such potential could be developed and enhanced by increased opportunities within the social framework of the individual. Past experience and the wider environmental context could be utilised for achieving successful development outcomes. An SME owner, manager, or leader ought, therefore, to be a guide or facilitator, building on their employees' experiences in a process of individual self-growth. I am of the view that keeping a positive mindset about staff, and helping them towards positive and constructive change, is a way forward in establishing a professional approach within your SME.

Similarly, McGregor (1957) respected inherent human abilities. Unlike current fixations with the cult of celebrity and the trite obsession with supposed reality television shows and with performers whose purported talent is far surpassed by their egos, McGregor recognised innate talent. He understood that people have a willingness to accept responsibility, that they have the ability to be creative and innovative, and that they have the desire for personal growth. Certainly the better run contemporary organisations have been able to build upon McGregor's ideas by utilising the skills and talents of their staff and by trusting them to perform. Witness the growth of partnership arrangements, involvement, and participation schemes and self-directed work teams in some organisations (Murdoch et al., 2007).

The message for owners, managers, and leaders in SMEs, therefore, is that the establishment of their SME as a professional entity begins with them and their beliefs about, and attitude towards, themselves and their staff.

To do so requires self-awareness in terms of understanding how you act with others, the impact of those actions, and the interpretations of those acts on others. It means you need to understand how you behave in a group situation, that you are able to reflect critically, and that you are willing and able to learn as an outcome. Such outcomes appear to be consistent with the view that self-awareness is vital in identifying your strengths and weaknesses.

The importance of self-awareness

Being more self-aware enables you to focus and improve on your weaknesses, such as poor interpersonal communication or lack of assertiveness. Such awareness is a pre-requisite for helping others to cope with change and the demands placed upon them in SMEs attempting to survive and thrive in the contemporary environment. Being aware of your own processes and actions may help you become more aware of the processes and actions of others within your sphere of influence, including your staff, customers, and suppliers. You can serve as an ideal role model for the appropriate actions required, thereby assisting others with their learning.

Self-awareness is multi-faceted. It is enhanced by developing a positive self-concept in any learning environment and in applying that enhanced self-concept in your daily life. Most people develop their self-concept by *reflected appraisal*, a process of formulating how they see themselves based on how *significant others* such as staff, friends, and their family see them, or how they think those people see them. The development of self-understanding and self-awareness is an ongoing learning and internalisation life process. It forms part of your commitment to lifelong learning to become more professional.

Such learning will enable you to become more attuned to how your entrenched values, attitudes, and actions may impact upon other people. Self-awareness involves critically reflecting on your internal processes such as your thought processes, your emotional responses and attitudes, and your problem-solving choices in determining new courses of action. Critical reflection enables you to learn something about yourself from the experience and you are likely to experience personal change and a feeling that life is better as a result (following Sheehan, 2000).

You may become more attuned to your preferred communication style. That style may enhance your ability to listen actively to others and bring benefits from a revitalised appreciation of the importance that active listening contributes to your interpersonal relationships. You may find that you become more assertive, more prepared to resolve conflict, and less prone to anger in situations of conflict (following Sheehan, 2000). You may also become more proactive, a better time manager, more open to and tolerant of others and more willing to help other people.

Paradoxically, you may find you are more attuned to how people communicate and that new awareness may cause frustration when you observe inappropriate or inattentive action(s) in your relationships.

Arguably, one of the most often cited and used models for becoming more self-aware, and for better understanding individuals and their behaviours in groups, is the Johari Window (Luft, 1961, 1969)[7]. I suggest this is a useful model for better understanding of the self where the focus is on the development of the so-called soft skills, such as learning, leadership, team learning, and systems thinking in contrast to the development of the technical skills required in your SME. Soft-skill development requires an understanding of professionalism and associated qualities, values, attitudes, and behaviours, and intrapersonal and interpersonal understanding and development.

Johari window

The Johari Window model was developed by American psychologists Joseph Luft and Harry Ingham in the 1950s while they were conducting research on group dynamics. Luft and Ingham called their model 'Johari' after combining their first names, Joe and Harry. The Johari Window has been widely used for personal development training including self-understanding and self-awareness, where it is sometimes referred to as a 'disclosure/ feedback model' and an 'information processing tool'. It also has been used for helping to improve individual and intra—and inter-group communications, interpersonal relationships, group dynamics, and team development.

The Johari Window actually represents information about the knowledge, skills, emotions, attitudes, opinions, meanings, and motivation of a person in relation to their work colleagues from four perspectives, which are described below. The model can also be used to represent the same information for a group in relation to other groups. When the model refers to 'self', it means oneself; and when it refers to 'others', it means other people in the person's group or team.

The underlying principle is that as a work team matures and communications improve, so too the performance improves. Less energy is spent on internal issues relating to miscommunication, lack of co-operation, mistrust, and the need constantly to clarify meaning and understanding. More effort is devoted to achievement of the shared vision, the aims and objectives of the SME, and to productivity.

---

[7] While the original sources can be a little difficult to locate, there are any number of useful and accurate articles available on the Internet.

The Johari Window has four panes or perspectives that are called 'regions', 'areas', or 'quadrants'. Each of these regions contains and represents information known about the person, in terms of whether the information is known or unknown by the person, and whether the information is known or unknown by others in the group.

The Johari window's four quadrants are as follows:

1. What is known by the person about him/herself and is also known by others—open area, open self, free area, free self, or 'the arena'
2. What is unknown by the person about him/herself but which others know—blind area, blind self, or 'blindspot'
3. What the person knows about him/herself that others do not know—hidden area, hidden self, avoided area, avoided self, or 'facade'
4. What is unknown by the person about him/herself and is also unknown by others—unknown area or unknown self

The primary representation of the Johari Window is shown below in Figure 7.1, with each quadrant depicted as the same size. The quadrants can be changed in size to reflect the extent of 'knowledge' of/about a particular person in a given group or team situation. In new groups or teams, the open free space for any team member is small because shared awareness is relatively small. As the team member becomes better established and known, so the size of the team member's open free area quadrant increases.

The aim in any SME should always be to develop the 'open area' for every person, because when we work in quadrant 1, with others we are at our most effective and productive, individually and as a group. Quadrant 1 is the area where good communications and co-operation occur, free from ambiguity, disruption, mistrust, uncertainty, disagreement, and misunderstanding. Communication is open, honest, and transparent. Information is imparted in a non-threatening manner and received non-defensively.

Figure 7.1: The Johari Window

1 Open/free area	2 Blind area
3 Hidden area	4 Unknown area

Johari quadrant 1—open/free area

An employee who has worked longer in an SME will tend to have a larger open area than a new staff member. A new employee will start with a relatively small open area because comparatively little knowledge about the employee is shared initially. The size of the open area can be extended horizontally into the blind space, by asking for, and actively listening to, feedback from other staff members. This process is known as 'feedback solicitation'. Similarly, other employees can help a staff member expand their open area by offering feedback. Such feedback ought to be offered sensitively, thoughtfully, and respectfully.

The size of the open area can also be expanded vertically downwards into the hidden or avoided space by the person's disclosure of information and feelings about themselves to other employees. Colleagues may assist in this process by asking the person about themselves, but in a non-intrusive way.

An SME owner/manager can play an important role in facilitating feedback and disclosure among employees, and in directly giving feedback to employees about their own blind areas. An owner/manager has a responsibility to promote an SME culture where open, honest, positive, helpful, constructive, and sensitive communication is valued. Encouraging positive development in quadrant 1 for everyone is a simple yet fundamental aspect of effective SME leadership.

Johari quadrant 2—blind area

Johari quadrant 2 relates to what is known about a person by other SME employees but is unknown by the person him/herself. The aim ought to be to reduce this area and thereby to increase the open area in order to increase self-awareness. This can be achieved by seeking, and actively listening to, feedback. Such feedback ought to be offered sensitively and constructively, and by encouraging disclosure. Information disclosed ought to be received non-judgementally and should not then lead to punishment or withdrawal of reward. Rather it ought to be seen as a learning opportunity.

The extent to which an employee seeks feedback and the matters on which feedback is sought must always be the employees' choice. Some employees are more resilient than others.

The blind area is not an effective or productive place for individuals or their colleagues because it is considered that in this area, people tend to be uninformed or deluded. It is sometimes said of this type of person that they are 'thick skinned'.

It is worth noting, however, that the blind area may include issues that are being deliberately withheld by a colleague or manager. We tend to find it difficult to work productively if we feel we are being excluded or that we are not being kept informed.

Johari quadrant 3—hidden area

There are things that an employee knows about him/herself but chooses to keep from their colleagues. This hidden or avoided self forms Johari quadrant 3, the hidden area, and represents information, understanding and emotions that an employee knows about the self but which is not exposed or is kept concealed from others. The hidden area could also include anything that a person knows but does not reveal, for whatever reason. They could be dreams, hopes, ambitions, desires, insecurities, fears, hidden agendas, manipulative intentions, and secrets. Undoubtedly, it is only natural that very personal and private information and feelings remain hidden. Indeed, it may be argued that certain information, feelings, and experiences have no place at work, and so can and ought to remain hidden. Typically, however, a lot of hidden information is not personal. Rather, it is work or performance-related and so is better situated in the open area.

The way to move such information and emotions into the open quadrant is by way of 'disclosure'. The aim of disclosure is to expose pertinent information and feelings about the self and therefore to increase our open area. By advising others how we feel and/or other information about ourselves, we reduce the hidden area and increase the open area. It turn, such disclosure enables better understanding, cooperation, trust, team-working effectiveness, and productivity. Reducing the size of our hidden quadrant also reduces the potential for misunderstanding, poor communication, ambiguity, and uncertainty, which all distract from and undermine workplace effectiveness.

The workplace culture and climate, which you, as an owner or manager, create, have a major influence on your employees' preparedness to disclose their hidden selves. Most employees have vulnerabilities, including the fear of judgement or retribution for their honesty, and if that is the case in your SME, they will hold back information and feelings. By contrast, if you have developed a positive and constructive workplace culture, an employee's ability and willingness to move more of the self into the open quadrant may enhance mutual understanding and awareness, thus facilitating enhanced individual and team performance.

As stated earlier in quadrant 2, the extent to which an employee discloses personal feelings and information and the issues which are disclosed, and to whom, must always be at their discretion. Some people are more able and willing than others to disclose. People should disclose at a pace, breadth, and depth with which they are comfortable. As with feedback, some people are more resilient than others and so care needs to be taken to avoid causing distress.

Johari quadrant 4—unknown area

Johari quadrant 4 contains underlying values, beliefs, behaviours, attitudes, information, feelings, capabilities, abilities, aptitudes, and experiences that are unknown to the employee and unknown to their colleagues. These unknown issues may be quite close to the surface, and can be positive and useful, or they can be deeper aspects of an employee's personality. Either way, they tend to influence behaviour in some way. Young employees tend to have large unknown areas as do employees who lack experience or self-belief.

Examples of unknown factors are as follows, with the first example particularly relevant and common to any organisation, including an SME:

- A skill, ability, or aptitude that is novel, underrated, or untested because of lack of opportunity, encouragement, confidence, or learning and development
- A natural skill or ability that an employee does not realise they hold
- A fear or aversion of which an employee is unaware
- An unknown illness
- Self-conscious or subconscious feelings
- Values, behaviours, and attitudes inherent from childhood

There are a variety of ways in which these unknown factors may be uncovered. They may be prompted through learning and development opportunities, through being given extra work responsibilities, by serendipity, by self-discovery, or through observation of and by others. In some circumstances, they may be revealed in deep or intensive group work or through counselling.

SME owners and managers can help uncover the unknown by creating an environment that encourages learning and self-discovery. They can assist by offering positive and constructive feedback when they observe a noteworthy action by an employee and by not counselling, chastising, or embarrassing their employee publicly, either directly or indirectly. They can encourage all employees to do likewise. Creating such an environment will help employees to fulfil more of their potential. In turn, the fulfilment of potential will enhance performance and productivity.

Whether new knowledge helps an employee to then move into quadrants 1, 2, or 3 depends on who discovers it, how it is disclosed, and what the employee chooses to do with the new knowledge. The process of self-discovery is a sensitive one. The extent, breadth, and depth to which an employee is able to explore or ascertain their unknown feelings must always be at their discretion. Some employees are more able than others to undertake such a journey.

One reason that such a journey needs to be handled carefully relates to why some information may be in the unknown quadrant. Memories and feelings may be repressed or held in the subconscious because they relate to trauma earlier in the life cycle. For some people, they may remain unknown forever. No attempt by an inexperienced or untrained medical expert should be taken to address such issues.

Johari window example—increasing open area through feedback solicitation and disclosure

This Johari Window model, shown in Figure 7.2, demonstrates how the open area may be enlarged by reducing the blind area. Such reduction may be achieved by asking for, and receiving, feedback. Another way to enlarge the open area is through the process of disclosure. Disclosure helps to reduce the hidden area. The unknown area may be reduced in ways mentioned in the previous section.

In an SME, where each employee has a strong mutual understanding of each other will be far more effective than an SME where the employees do not understand each other because there are a number of employees with large hidden, blind, and/or unknown areas. Owner/ managers and employees ought to strive to increase their open free areas and to reduce their blind, hidden, and unknown areas.

If an employee does not attempt to increase their open area, they are unlikely to perform to their best potential and may inhibit the performance and productivity of the SME. They are unlikely to be utilised to their full potential. They are likely to become dissatisfied at work and harbour intentions to leave.

Figure 7.2: Increasing the Open Area

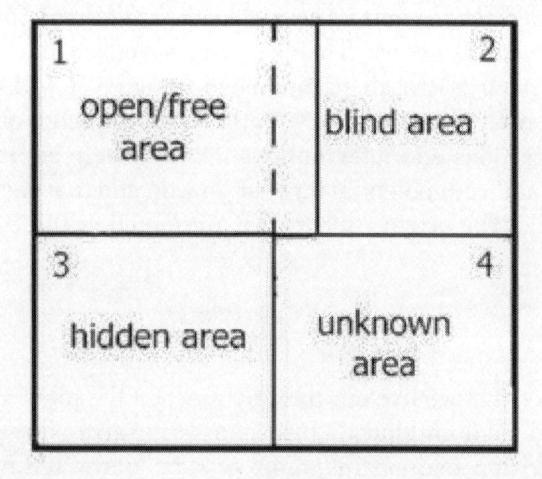

1 open/free area	2 blind area
3 hidden area	4 unknown area

Having discussed the Johari Window model as a tool helpful for understanding self-awareness, I now turn to two theories which I consider to be related and functional. The first theory is Transactional Analysis, and I think it is particularly practical for understanding deeper aspects of the 'unknown' area in quadrant 4 of the Johari Window. I think it also is useful for understanding employees, why they might act the way they do and, in turn, why we might react to them the way we do.

The second theory is emotional awareness. Given that emotion plays such a large part in working in an SME, I think that is important to have an understanding of this theory so that you may be able to understand the concepts of giving and receiving feedback and disclosure that form an important part of the Johari Window model.

Transactional analysis

Berne (1964) introduced his theory of Transactional Analysis (TA) in his book, *Games People Play*. The theory provides insight into how people communicate and suggests ways for how to improve communication. Premised on an understanding that we have rights, including the right to be accepted, and that we can change and grow our potential, the theory outlines how we have developed our human potential, how we treat ourselves, and how we relate and communicate with others. Berne postulated three ego states, parent, adult and child to explain his understanding.

TA is a contractual approach for conducting our interactions with others. Berne (1964) defines a contract as *an explicit bilateral commitment to a well-defined course of action*. That is, just as you conduct your business transactions in your SME, all parties need to agree. I will explore further the notion of contracting after I have outlined a little more of the theory. TA also offers suggestions and interventions that may help an understanding of self-awareness and your potential for your growth, and that of your employees, within your SME. The original model was presented as three circles, one for each ego state.

The script

Berne argues that we live our lives by way of a life plan or script that has been developed from childhood. Just as a script gives directions to actors in movies, television soap operas, radio or stage plays, telling them what to say, how to say it, when and where to move, so too do we act out our lives by reading the lines and deciding what will happen in each phase of our relationships with others and how those relationships will be conducted. Our script is developed from early childhood and subsequent life experiences. While we may not realise that we have devised a script, we can often find this to be the case by asking ourselves a few simple questions, such as the following

- What is my favourite childhood movie?
- What made it such a great movie?
- Who was my favourite character in the movie?
- Who do I identify with in that movie?
- Why do I still identify with that character?

Then consider the beginning, middle, and end of the movie and ask yourself:

- How is the story told in that movie reflected in my life today?

Another way of considering our script is to think about what your obituary might say. Consider the facts and events it might detail and how it might explain what you have done or contributed in your life. Think about what you would like to see in that obituary and what you could do now to influence the narrative. More than likely, it will contain details of your working life and something about your personal relationships.

Ego states

Berne formulated the concept of ego states to help explain how we conduct ourselves and how we relate to others. Ego states classify our cognitive, affective, and behavioural states. He termed these ego states Parent (P), Adult (A), and Child (C). Each ego state is given a capital letter to denote the difference between actual parents, adults, and children. It is important to understand that ego states do not of themselves exist. Rather, they are concepts developed and articulated in order to facilitate understanding.

Parent

The Parent ego state is our ingrained power base, developed from childhood and reinforced by learning, conditioning, and attitudes. Conditioning originates from parents, siblings, grandparents, teachers, aunts and uncles, other older people with whom we come into contact, friends we make in our lives, and people who might influence us in some way, albeit with little or no contact. Many people are inspired, for example, by Nelson Mandela, but have had no personal contact. Myths about others also develop this state, such as those about Santa Claus, the Easter Bunny, and the Tooth Fairy. Today we might add myths about our sporting heroes and music, movie, television, and so-called celebrity idols.

Our Parent ego encompasses a large number of subconscious yet evident understandings, usually personified by rules and directions conveyed to us as we were growing up so as to instil cultural, social, and moral obligations. Such instructions might include 'do it this way', 'if you do it that way, then you had better be sure you also . . . ', and 'never talk back to your elders', or similar. During maturity, our parent state is shaped further by external actions and demands, over which we may have little or no control. We can alter our parent state, but it requires a breadth and depth of self-awareness and self-understanding; and the commitment to change. Our parent state is our 'taught' understanding of life.

Adult

The Adult ego state forms in the latter stages of our first twelve months of life. In this state we form the ability to think and determine action for ourselves, based on our observations and interpretations. We respond to situations in ways that are open, honest, forthright, and respectful and are not unduly influenced by our past. We are spontaneous, aware of what is happening, and have the capacity for intimacy.

In this state, we see people as they are, rather than transferring or projecting some other self on to them, based on some past negative relationship or action. We seek information rather than stay fearful or make assumptions about the actions of others. We critically reflect on our experiences, revising how we relate to others, and use this new information and understanding to keep ourselves informed. Our adult state is our 'thought' understanding of life.

It is a state of what may be called a mature person who has their 'act' together.

It is the state that enables us to keep both our Parent and Child under control. If we want to change our Parent or Child ego states, we must do so through our Adult ego state.

Child

The Child ego state is an affective, cognitive, and behavioural state learned from childhood and which we use in our interactions with others. The Child ego state represents our emotional and senses 'being'. It is how we respond to, and understand, information formed from the use of our senses, particularly sight, sound, and hearing, and the emotional reactions that such data generates. Our actions may be positive and generate warm positive regard for others. Conversely, it is in this state that anger, antagonism, resentment, jealousy, or despondency tends to dominate reason. The Child takes control and reasoning disappears. Stress and depression may manifest. Like our Parent ego state, we can change it, but it takes willingness to do so. Our child state is our 'felt' understanding of life.

Contracting

As mentioned earlier, TA is a contractual approach for conducting our interactions with others. As a contract, all parties need to agree on why they want to do something, with whom, what they are going to do, by when, and any fees payment or exchanges that will take place. Such a contract forms a basis for performance management in your SME.

Just as with many business contracts you conduct, sometimes contracts are multifaceted and the partners have their own set of expectations. If you develop compatible expectations, then you more than likely will have an equal and fulfilling partnership based on trust and honesty in your dealings with each other. If not, then a discussion about everyone's expectations needs to occur to overcome any misunderstandings or misgivings. Such discussion, if carried out by all parties in the Adult ego state, may enhance understanding of each other and your particular expectations and requirements. A mutually satisfactory relationship will result.

On the other hand, if one party acts in the Parent or Child ego state, then the relationship will more than likely deteriorate. When that occurs, one or both parties may absent themselves from work and may form an intention to leave the SME. Productivity and performance will decline.

Contemporary transactional analysis theory

Many people in different fields have extended Berne's work. One of the more significant developments has been the expansion of the original PAC model into a nine-element model, as shown below in Figure 7.3, which initiates Controlling and Nurturing aspects of the Parent mode, each with positive and negative aspects, and the Adapted and Free aspects of the Child mode, also with positive and negative aspects, which essentially gives us the contemporary model. Modes are the term used by Temple (1999 updated 2002).

Parent

Parent is now usually represented as a circle with four quadrants:
Nurturing—Nurturing (positive) and Spoiling (negative).
Controlling—Structuring (positive) and Critical (negative).

Adult

Adult remains as a single entity, representing an 'accounting' function or mode, which can draw on the resources of both Parent and Child.

Child

Child is now usually represented as circle with four quadrants:
Adapted—Co-operative (positive) and Compliant/Resistant (negative).
Free—Spontaneous (positive) and Immature (negative).

Where Berne's early work suggested that successful communications were complementary (response echoing the path of the stimulus) and within a framework of adult to adult, the contemporary interpretation suggests that effective communications and relationships are based on matching transactions to and from positive quadrants, and within the adult to adult context. Stimuli and responses can come from any (or some) of these nine ego states to any or some of the respondent's nine ego states.

Figure 7.3 Ego States

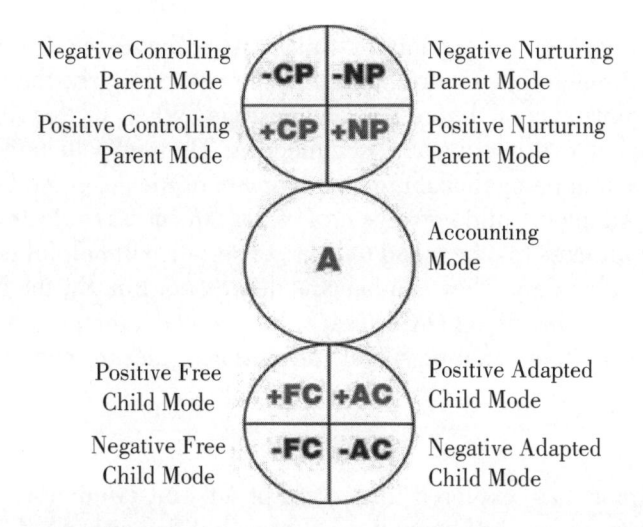

Negative Controlling Parent Mode	-CP | -NP	Negative Nurturing Parent Mode
Positive Controlling Parent Mode	+CP | +NP	Positive Nurturing Parent Mode
	A	Accounting Mode
Positive Free Child Mode	+FC | +AC	Positive Adapted Child Mode
Negative Free Child Mode	-FC | -AC	Negative Adapted Child Mode

Source: http://www.businessballs.com/transact.htm downloaded 24/01/10.

Effective modes

In the Positive Nurturing Parent mode, the sender sends the message *You're OK*. When in this mode the person is considerate and supportive. Similarly, in the Positive Controlling Parent mode, the message is *You're OK*. This is the mode that sets boundaries, offers constructive criticism, and is supportive but firm.

In the Positive Adapted Child mode, the message sent is *I'm OK*. From this mode, we learn societal rules and expectations. Similarly, the Positive Free Child sends the message *I'm OK*. This is the creative, playful, curious, and vivacious mode.

The Accounting mode sends *We're OK* messages. In this mode, the Adult is able to fully consider the present context. This mode enables us to choose which of the other effective modes to use, depending on the identified circumstances. It enables constructive problem solving and decision making to occur. In this mode, our responses are likely to be more appropriate and useful, such as the use of active listening and being non-defensive. It enables us to avoid outdated or past ways of acting, which experience and critical reflection tell us are likely to be inappropriate and unhelpful.

Ineffective modes

The Negative Controlling Parent transmits a *You're not OK* message and operates through fear, control, and punishment. Similarly, the Negative Nurturing Parent relays a *You're not OK* message. When in this mode, the sender is arrogant, overbearing, and domineering. They are reluctant to let go of control for fear of being thought to be inefficient or incompetent. Likewise, the Negative Adapted Child conveys an *I'm not OK* message. In this mode, the person capitulates to others and tends to experience unhelpful emotions, such as fear and anxiety. They can become depressed. Finally, the Negative Free Child sends a *You're not OK* message. In this mode, the person tends to be crude and primitive, ignoring social conventions, rules, or boundaries.

Summary

This chapter has explored the concept of self-awareness, arguing that to become more professional also required an enhanced level of self-awareness.

Self-awareness is a useful concept, although these have been arguments made that because it is a state of self-directed attention, it often becomes part of the subconscious and difficult to alter. It also tends to take a judgemental form, in that being social and evaluative in its motivation, we judge the appropriateness of our thoughts, feelings, behaviours, and actions. A judgemental approach can be limiting.

If that argument holds sway, then an alternative argument needs to be offered. That argument is presented in the next chapter on mindfulness. Mindfulness is a metaprocess whereby we are consciously aware of the internal focus on the self, including our thoughts, feelings and memories and we are able to acknowledge their existence. By metaprocess I mean the ability to reflect upon our actions and their outcomes and to discuss those reflections meaningfully so that higher order learning occurs.

Chapter 8

Mindfulness

Introduction

In our everyday lives, we participate actively, and to different degrees, with our *external* environment. We are influenced by events occurring in that environment. It is our *internal* experience or perception of those events, however, that shape our affective, attitudinal, behavioural, and cognitive responses and our ensuing actions. External and internal influences tend to be powerful and continuously impact how we perceive and interpret stimuli from these environments (following Carless and Roberts-Thompson, 2001).

Our internal focus may be influenced by our state of mind at the time. We may be focussed on the recall of previous events and feelings; on our hopes, fears, worries, dreams, and fantasies or on planning. At those times, we tend to behave automatically or mindlessly, without necessarily being aware of our actions and their impact on others. Our mind and body appear to be in separate places (Didonna, 2009).

Recall, for example, occasions when you have driven to work but later have been unable to recall much about the trip. You have driven that journey many times before and many of the actions taken in the driving of your car have been seemingly automatic. You have been on *autopilot* whereby your actions have been shaped by your known reality.

In this chapter the concept of mindfulness is explored using the following eight steps. First, mindfulness is outlined. Second, the development and use of the concept within a Western framework is sketched. Third, becoming mindful suggests what needs to be done. Fourth, inhibitors of mindfulness are suggested. Fifth, how mindfulness is different from self-awareness is addressed. Sixth, typologies for recognising mindfulness are provided.

Seventh, what being mindful will do is suggested. Eighth, using mindfulness in the SME workplace is proffered. The chapter concludes with a summary and an indication that adult learning is explored in the next chapter.

Mindfulness

Mikulas (2011) states that it is the 'contents of the mind', that is, our perceptions, memories, thoughts, and feelings, that ultimately shape our reality. Those 'contents' are what make us a unique human being, however flawed we may be seen to be or consider ourselves in actuality. What inhibits or distorts our actuality are the processes or 'behaviours of the mind'.

There are three fundamental processes of the mind. They are as follows:

1. *Clinging* to contents of the mind
2. *Concentration* or focus of the mind
3. *Awareness* or the extent and clarity of conscious experience

Mindfulness is the conscious awareness of our immediate experiences. It involves being aware of the inherent process of the mind (following Brown and Ryan, 2003; Kabat-Zinn, 1990). When we are aware of these processes, we are able to extend, limit, or reduce their power in defining how we react affectively, behaviourally, and cognitively. Awareness of, and attention to, our thoughts and feelings and the judgements that we make as a result of that awareness may be useful for monitoring and maintaining the effectiveness of our behaviours, actions, and reactions (Mace, 2008). We are able to respond thoughtfully, rather than irrationally (Didonna, 2009). Thus, the goal of mindfulness is to enable us to live fully in each moment in a non-judgemental way (Dekeyser et al., 2008; Didonna, 2009; Rapgay and Bystrisky, 2009).

Development and use of the concept within a Western framework

Since the early 1980s, the research, teaching, and practice of mindfulness as a psychological construct and as a form of clinical intervention has risen to some prominence. In a review of the three major areas of empirical literature on the effects of mindfulness on psychological health, Keng et al. (2011) pointed to the development of the concept from Buddhist tradition and its integration into Western medicine and psychology. The three areas of empirical research reviewed were the associations between mindfulness and various indicators of psychological health, the effects of mindfulness-oriented interventions on psychological health, and laboratory-based experimental research on the immediate effects of mindfulness inductions on emotional and behavioural functioning. They concluded that the positive psychological effects of mindfulness were improved subjective well-being, reduced psychological symptoms and emotional reactivity, and enhanced behavioural regulation.

Baer et al. (2004), Goldstein (2002) and Kabat-Zinn (2000) offered similar arguments. With a particular emphasis on the practice of meditation as part of Eastern spiritual tradition, they noted that regular practice of mindfulness meditation reduces suffering and develops positive qualities, such as awareness, understanding, insight, contemplation, compassion, and composure. With a view to the need for informed practice, Moore (2008) developed and reported on a mindfulness course that was designed to enable the development of mindfulness skills for clinical psychologists in training. A further intention was to provide an experience for the course participants that could be then used to enhance their future individual and specialised uses of mindfulness.

Mindfulness also has been found to help people cope with stress and to enhance self-worth. A study conducted by Palmer and Roger (2009) with a cohort of Canadian University students found that there were significant positive relationships between rational coping and mindfulness for those students. Thompson and Waltz (2008) explored the relationship between mindfulness, self-esteem, and unconditional self-acceptance. They found that mindfulness offered a means to accept oneself unconditionally and to achieve higher understanding of self-worth.

Another use for mindfulness has been found in therapeutic and counselling situations. Proulx (2008) studied patients suffering an eating disorder, bulimia nervosa. In this study, a reflective process was used to enable young women participants to recall past experiences, bring those experiences into their awareness, and to then take action to address their eating disorder. The six women involved in the study participated in an eight-week mindfulness-based treatment group. The aim of the treatment was not to cure the eating disorder but to provide the participants with coping skills, enhance their self-awareness, and help them address judgemental thoughts and self-harming behaviour. The outcome was considered to be successful.

Rosenzweig et al. (2010) explored mindfulness as a tool for helping chronic pain sufferers cope. They used a sample size of 133 participants with chronic pain conditions. Chronic pain was defined as lasting for six months or longer. The conditions included neck/back pain ($n = 51$), headaches/migraine ($n = 34$), arthritis ($n = 32$), and fibromyalgia ($n = 27$). Some patients had two or more conditions. Over a period of eight weeks, the participants were involved in a number of mindfulness techniques including awareness of emotions, breathing awareness, and mindful eating, listening, walking, and yoga. The results showed that some subgroups of patients dealing with the more physical aspects of pain, such as arthritis and back and neck pain, demonstrated a significant change in pain intensity and functional limitations due to pain following the treatments. The same outcome was not achieved to the same degree of significance for those suffering from psychological distress caused by headache and migraine, suggesting that mindfulness treatments are more effective at treating those with physical symptoms.

Becoming mindful

To be mindful requires that we do three things. The first is that we develop an awareness of both external and internal experiences as they exist in the present. The second requires that we focus on the present experience. The third entails that we approach those experiences by accepting all thoughts and feelings in a non-judgemental and open manner (Germer et al., 2005). To do so requires that we develop the ability to shift flexibly between our internal experiences encompassing our thoughts, feelings, memories, emotions and physiological sensations, and our external experiences. These latter experiences may include images, sounds, smells, touch, verbal and non-verbal cues, and our perceptions (Didonna, 2009; Hayes et al., 2004).

Thus being mindful requires that we have a degree of self-awareness but not to the extent whereby we are hindered in our actions by self-consciousness or a concern with how others might perceive us. Such a focus can be debilitating as we tend to be preoccupied with excessive self-monitoring or concern about the *self*, to the extent that we become anxious and stressed (Brown and Ryan, 2003). In such a state, we are unlikely to achieve mindfulness.

It seems apparent, therefore, that mindfulness may be conceptualised and practiced as sets of skills that can be learned independently of their spiritual origins and without meditation (Baer et al., 2004; Hayes and Shenk, 2006). The skills have been utilised in a number of therapeutic settings and while the interventions vary across those settings, there appears to be a common set of general instructions for mindfulness exercises. These instructions seem useful for the development of a skill set for an SME owner/manager attempting to guide their staff on a learning journey.

Prior to establishing the task(s) to be undertaken, some guidelines or parameters are established. Such guidelines usually encourage participants to approach the task with an attitude of responsive curiosity, attentiveness, and acceptance of observed phenomena while simultaneously abstaining from evaluation, self-deprecation, or attempts to disregard or alter the phenomena they observe (following Baer et al., 2004; Segal et al., 2002).

The most prominent general instruction is an activity focussing on any ordinary day-to-day activity that they experience. Such an activity might be walking, breathing, eating, or drinking. They may be given a small item of food such as a sultana or a sweet and asked only to consider it as an object with which they are unfamiliar. Participants are invited to focus their attention on that activity or object and to observe it carefully. They are asked to notice that their attention may wander into unrelated thoughts, recollections, or imaginations (following Baer et al., 2004). When such wandering occurs, they are asked to heed that they have wandered and then to recommence attending to the target they originally were asked to observe.

Participants are also asked to observe carefully any sensations or feelings that arise as a result of the task requirements. They are asked to make no attempt to evaluate thoughts as rational, to modify thoughts considered to be irrational, or to diminish unpleasant emotions. Rather, thoughts and feelings are simply noted and observed in passing (following Baer et al., 2004). Observational attention may be paid to the internal experiences, such as shifts in body posture, or intentions to do so, and the feelings that arise. Some encouragement of attention to objects in the external environment may also be suggested. Such objects may include other people in the room and the sights and sounds inside or outside the room.

Learning and using mindfulness may help develop what sometimes is called metacognitive insight (Teasdale, 1999) or decentring (Segal et al., 2002). Simply put, these terms mean that a person is able to develop a new perspective on their internal experience and that such development can lead to deeper self-understanding and personal growth. This perspective suggests that thoughts are *just thoughts*, are many and varied, are fleeting and short-lived, and do not impose an obligation to act.

A person using mindfulness practice may note an improvement in their self-observation skills. Such an improvement may enhance appreciation of sensations, understandings, and emotional states. Enhancement could lead to an improved ability to respond skilfully to these phenomena as they arise. A more skilful response may help them to cope with the ambiguities and uncertainties facing SMEs on a daily basis such as customer demands and expectations, the angry customer, the unhelpful supplier, and the disinterested staff member.

Inhibitors of mindfulness

What may inhibit achieving a state of mindfulness is public self-consciousness. Such consciousness may detract from present awareness because we focus on the expressed thoughts and interpreted and expressed feelings of others, rather than on the *self* (Brown and Ryan, 2003; Evans et al., 2009). If we are distracted constantly by what other people may be doing or saying, then we detract from our own present moment experience.

It may also be argued that giving consideration to others could be mindful in itself because one of the primary goals of mindfulness is to be aware of all that is happening in the internal and external environments. Other people serve as external stimuli. Careful consideration needs to be given to not becoming fixated on those stimuli to the extent that our own mindfulness is hindered (following Beitel et al., 2005). The key to mindfulness is to focus on your moment-to-moment experience.

Different from self-awareness

While self-awareness and mindfulness are both similar in that they are a state of being whereby you can focus on the *self*, they also differ in a particular way. Self-awareness is a state of self-directed attention (Fenigstein et al., 1975) and often becomes part of the subconscious. It also tends to take a judgemental form, in that being social and evaluative in its motivation, we judge the appropriateness of our thoughts, feelings, behaviours, and actions (following Silvia and Duval, 2001).

By contrast, mindfulness is a metaprocess whereby we are consciously aware of the internal focus on the self, including our thoughts, feelings, and memories (Bishop et al., 2004; Hick, 2008). We are able to acknowledge their existence. We also are able to recognise and attend to our cognitions utilising a non-judgemental and non-reactive awareness such that our thoughts and feelings do not define our response or our reality (following Langer, 1989; Phelan, 2010). We are able to regulate our physical, social, affective, and behavioural functioning while increasing understanding of the *self* and others (Kristeller and Wolever, 2011). Such recognition, regulation, and understanding can help SME staff to interact more appropriately with each other, their customers and suppliers, and significant others.

Recognising mindfulness

In Chapter 5, on self-awareness, nine typologies were offered for ways by which we might recognise a lack of self-awareness in the self or in others. There is a need then to identify a similar number of typologies to help recognise those people who may exhibit the characteristics of someone who is mindful.

What might indicate good manners or politeness to some people, such as keeping their voice down in public places or treating people respectfully, may indicate mindfulness. Other identifiers may be a person who offers more to their job than the requirements set out in their duty statement or position description, who is able to sustain friendships or relationships for more than a few weeks, who is able to develop and maintain deeper friendships than those that are sometimes considered to be friendships through social networking sites, who shares conversational time and space with others, and who is able to develop and sustain opinions and insight by careful consideration of facts and evidence. They may also accept responsibility when things do not work out as well as they might like, be prepared to be held accountable for their actions, and be prepared to learn from their mistakes.

While people who may be seen to exhibit the following qualities may not have undertaken mindfulness or mindfulness by meditation skill development, they nonetheless tend to demonstrate by their actions the types of attitudes and behaviours that may be identified with someone who is mindful. For example, they may demonstrate the ability or willingness to reflect critically on their attitudes or behaviour. They also may exhibit a strong sense of values or moral purpose. Moreover, they may be assertive in their views but respectful of the views and opinions of others and willing to seek compromise where necessary. Additionally, they may be open to receiving feedback and to reflecting on that feedback in constructive ways.

What now follows are nine suggested typologies of people we may recognise. You may even recognise yourself. That being the case, you may decide that you do not need to take any further action or you may seek out further ways to develop and grow.

The 'self-assured'

This person is authoritative, co-operative, and collaborative. They have knowledge, and they use it for developmental reasons rather than to laud it over others. Knowledge and insight is shared in a forthright manner, and they are prepared to listen actively to the views of others. Flexibility and an easy-going manner are strengths. Their opinion is important, and they seek to influence and persuade others to their views but in a context of shared understanding and mutual rights and obligations. Decisions are made with the best of intentions, and they accept that their decisions are not always right. They do not consider themselves to be beyond reproach or questioning. Indeed, they welcome constructive criticism in the interest of self-growth and continuous learning.

On those occasions, when they do make mistakes or errors of judgement, they are prepared to apologise. They are able to manage their emotions for positive benefit for themselves and others. Their non-verbal messages reflect positive feelings towards the self and others.

The self-assured person is a good team player and accepts the decisions that are made by the group even if they disagree with those decisions, as long as those decisions are made ethically, in a spirit of co-operation, and in an open and transparent manner. Once decisions have been made, they will work to implement agreements made, although they may seek further evidence to support their approach. While so doing, they do not attempt to belittle, criticise, or chastise others. They seek constructively to put an end to innuendo, rumour, and falsehoods about others in a spirit of respect and dignity for all.

People find it satisfying to work with them and often seek out their friendship and counsel.

The 'acceptor'

The acceptor realises that their thoughts and feelings are just that—thoughts and feelings. No greater significance is attached. Thoughts and feelings are recognised as transient moments in a more holistic existence.

It is highly unlikely you will ever hear this person complain. They accept themselves and others for who they are—a unique being with strengths and limitations.

Enhanced appreciation of, and sensitivity towards their own and others, sensations, understandings, and emotions are demonstrated. They are able to accept and respond skilfully, non-defensively, non-threateningly, and non-judgementally to customers', suppliers', and colleagues' demands, disinterest, unhelpfulness, and expectations as they arise. They are ideal employees for SMEs struggling to cope with increasing expectations, ambiguity, uncertainty, and complexity.

The 'individualist'

Mindfulness, or a strong sense of *self*, has helped to shape this person's personality. A strong level of self-understanding, self-worth, and self-esteem, and an understanding of how they fit into their environment, is evident. They recognise their strengths and frailties and are able to differentiate themselves from others. In Freudian terms, they are likely to have the sound psychic functions of judgement, tolerance, reality-testing, control, planning, defence, synthesis of information, intellectual functioning, and memory. They are able to determine what is real, organise their thoughts, make sense of them, and let them pass.

Such an understanding does not mean that they have an exaggerated sense of their own self-importance or that they are egotistical. Rather, the individualist knows the *self* and concurrently is concerned for others. They are likely to be caring, tolerant, sensitive to the needs of others, empathic and concerned. They do not self-promote and do not have a need to be noticed or the centre of attention.

The 'inspirationalist'

The inspirationalist is genuinely interested in their work, their colleagues, and others in their external environment. Because they have a sound awareness of their external environment, they tend also to have a solid understanding of their internal self. They are helpful and supportive towards others and appreciative of the help and guidance they receive. This person has no interest in playing organisational politics, indulging in impression management, or attempting to manipulate others to their way of thinking and acting. Openness to scruitinisation of, and feedback about, their performance, acceptance of responsibility for their performance, and the seeking of ways to improve are displayed. They set an example for others through actions rather than words. Others look up to them and attempt emulation.

Some people at the top in many sporting endeavours may be seen as examples, although I suggest such people with a degree of hesitation. On some occasions, some sports stars have served as an inspiration for many, only to fall from grace through a misdemeanour or two. Nonetheless, the inspirationalist will show they are tenacious, open and honest, respectful of their teammates and support staff, and of their opponents and have a high level of personal integrity. They are good team players.

To identify whether or not you might fit this category, reflect critically on your own behaviours. Ask yourself if you are supportive of, and helpful to, your staff, work colleagues, customers, and suppliers. Give consideration to how you praise others for their efforts and support them in times of crises.

The 'valuer'

A valuer is a person who has deep personal insight, moral fortitude, and inner courage or intestinal fortitude. They are at ease with themselves and as such, they tend to be at ease with others. An interest in acquiring knowledge through formal and informal learning opportunities, and in seeking to acquire wisdom from others, is apparent.

They are patient with people they encounter and are non-judgemental. In conversation, they allow you the time to gather your thoughts and gently inquire about your thinking in an endeavour to be helpful and considerate. Because they value you, they are interested in your views and opinions and strive to ensure that you have a voice. The protection of your rights and responsibilities is uppermost in their thinking.

The 'supporter'

While Australians are generally considered to be individualists, they are also recognised for their collective efforts. Such recognition quickly becomes apparent in times of crisis, such as flood, fire, cyclone, or drought. Australians quickly band together to help in any way they can, whether it be with physical, emotional, or financial support.

In these situations, we would rarely consider attempting to denigrate the misfortunes or achievements of others. We are even supportive of politicians we perceive as demonstrating leadership on such occasions, although there is a honeymoon period.

The supporter has strong awareness of both their internal and external environment. They may use gentle humour to diffuse a situation but never in a way that would offend. Sarcasm, mockery, and teasing have been eliminated from their repertoire.

This person is in tune with their thoughts and feelings and recognise them for what they are—thoughts and feelings. Thus, they are not offended by the inappropriate comments of others and quickly are able to diffuse such situations.

If a work colleague appears to be critical of colleagues, customers, or suppliers, they will confront the perpetrator and offer constructive feedback in a non-threatening and non-judgemental way.

They understand that we all are entitled to be treated with respect and dignity in the workplace, and they endeavour to ensure that such entitlements are achieved.

The 'rationalist'

The rationalist is articulate, lucid, and logical in a world where chaos seemingly rules. They are considerate of the views of others and are able to state their own views that are supported by facts and evidence. Those facts and evidence are considered carefully, with the evidence weighed up so that they make informed decisions using the best available data at the time. This person understands that new information may become available, and when that is the case, they are prepared to make alternative decisions, if deemed necessary. A willingness and ability to listen to reason and a well-reasoned argument, and to consider alternative conclusions that may be drawn from the same set of data, is demonstrated.

They do not blame others for their mistakes. Rather, they willingly admit mistakes and are not afraid to apologise. By so doing, they consider that they are continually learning about themselves and others. Such learning is seen as beneficial.

The 'humanitarian'

The humanitarian expresses themselves assertively and courteously. They do not entertain bitterness or ill will towards others and thus are able to express themselves in ways that do not harm or upset others. This person is polite, gracious, well-mannered, and tactful. You are unlikely to hear them swear, even in the most difficult of circumstances. Their reputation is enhanced because of the respect and dignity they display towards others in all their interactions.

An extensive vocabulary and a strong command of language are exhibited, but they do not use this strength to dominate or intimidate others. Their power is enhanced by their respectfulness towards their colleagues and significant others. They are well-informed, discreet, diplomatic, and sensitive towards others, and they are able to keep confidences.

The 'democrat'

Unlike the despot, the democrat realises and understands that all colleagues at work ought to be given a voice and have an equal say in decisions that may affect their lives. Having a voice means being involved in the discussion of ideas for creative and innovative solutions to problems facing the SME, including the need for, and demands of, change. They understand that by operating in an open and transparent manner, people are likely to become more engaged in their work and be prepared to give of themselves to their organisation, its customers and suppliers, and significant others.

This person has the capacity for self-renewal, for self-growth, and for achieving freedom within organisational constraints and boundaries which often inhibit the free flow of ideas, concepts, and philosophies. An aspiration to engage and participate on an equal basis is demonstrated. They are intimately connected to organisational systems and understand that being a democrat helps them to fulfil their potential and facilitate the potential of others.

Equality and freedom, and rights and responsibilities, in the workplace and in society, more generally, are important goals. They follow due process, help resolve grievances, raise issues that they see as important to address, mediate tensions and conflict before they escalate, and encourage a civil workplace. Power is shared. This person works collaboratively and co-operatively with colleagues and is helpful and responsive to customers and suppliers alike.

What being mindful will do

Mindfulness enables you to develop the ability to use your awareness and sensitivity to discern your feelings and to resist the temptation to respond impulsively and thoughtlessly. It will help you to influence without manipulation or abuse of authority those with whom you come in contact on a daily basis in the SME.

Being mindful may empower you to act receptively, authentically, and honestly and become emotionally intelligent (following Ryback, 2012). It will allow you to perceive situations differently than you have in the past, facilitate deeper learning, and assist you in the development of more meaningful relationships. It will enable you to move away from your traditional reliance on logic, linear thinking, intellect or technical analysis alone so that you become more innovative and creative in your problem solving and decision-making. You will be able to prioritise and act in ways that are more positive and constructive. You will move beyond the thoughts and feelings that typically have constrained and misguided you in the past.

The good news is that you are never too old to learn, develop, and improve. Forget the 'you can't teach an old dog new tricks' excuse that you may use to avoid learning something new, particularly when you think that there may not be any personal benefit from the new skill. You have heard yourself say 'That sounds interesting, but what's in it for me?' or 'I don't like broccoli' when you have never even tried it.

You have, however, learnt to use your computer, mobile phone, iPod, iPad, and social networking sites. You can Facebook and Tweet with the best. These are great technical skills to acquire and use. Now try to learn something about yourself that may help you on your personal journey of self-discovery. As you further develop the various characteristics of your mindfulness, you will find that you enhance your professionalism in your SME because you will further develop the following in you:

- Intuition
- Ability to trust and be trusted
- Sense of integrity and authenticity
- Appreciation of constructive dissent
- Creativity
- Problem-solving and decision-making abilities
- Leadership abilities
- Intrapersonal skills
- Interpersonal skills

Mindfulness takes practice. It requires an open mind and a willingness to learn, to take risks, and to accept consequences. If nurtured in a supportive environment, it will enable you to develop specific skills and abilities that underpin your self-understanding. The outcomes will be as follows:

1. The ability to recognise, assess, and articulate your thoughts and emotions accurately
2. The ability to access, recognise, and understand your thoughts and feelings as they are aroused and to recognise the contribution they make to self-understanding and the understanding of significant others
3. An ability to reflect upon, and make sense of, resultant knowledge that is identified
4. The ability to understand your thoughts and feelings for what they are and to use that understanding to promote emotional and intellectual growth

Using mindfulness in the workplace

Mindfulness may be helpful in a number of situations in your SME. If you are mindful, you may find that it assists you in the following:

- Appraising staff performance
- Counselling below-standard performance
- Resolving conflict
- Enabling people to work through an arduous issue with a co-worker
- Responding to defensive behaviours
- Offering and accepting constructive criticism
- Stating your opinions clearly and openly
- Challenging peoples' assumptions about yourself or your work
- Giving and accepting constructive criticism

The reason that mindfulness is helpful in the abovementioned situations is because it enables people to express and legitimise thoughts, sensations, emotions, hunches, and intuitive feelings that people often experience in work situations or when they are reflecting on a particular experience. It helps with the formulation of responses that may be expressed in non-threatening and non-defensive ways that enable a collaborative approach to problem solving.

Summary

It has been argued that professionals may be defined by their actions and by their values, attitudes, and behaviours. Furthermore, an SME owner and/or manager's attitude towards their employees, and their ability to manage those employees constructively, also is partly what defines them as a professional.

By contrast, inadequate people skills or soft skills may contribute to an unhealthy workplace in which productivity will be limited, job satisfaction will be low, and absenteeism and turnover is likely to be above average within similar occupations or industries. When such problems occur, a comprehensive approach is required to address the problem, particularly if SME owner/managers want to conduct their business in as professional a way as possible. A number of soft skill development tools, including the development of mindfulness in SME owner/managers were suggested as part of a solution for addressing the problem.

Self-awareness may be enhanced by way of learning and development. Similarly, an understanding of transactional analysis, the Johari Window and mindfulness may be gained through appropriate learning and development programmes. They are tools that may be added to a repertoire of skills necessary for enhanced professionalism within your SME. They facilitate the personal mastery seen by Senge (1992) as necessary for individual and organisational learning. As they are tools that can be learned, developed, and improved, in the next chapter, I will discuss adult learning.

Chapter 9

Adult Learning

Not since the dawn of the Industrial Revolution have managers had more to learn (and unlearn) about the art of business leadership.

(Toffler and Toffler, 1998: viii)

Introduction

If in my more than thirty or so years as a training officer, staff development officer, internal and external consultant, adult educator, tutor, lecturer, and learning facilitator I had invested $100 for every time I have heard someone say *you can't teach an old dog new tricks* or *here we go with the same old same old*, or *forget the bulldust* (or a very similar word) *just tell us how to do* it, I may just be retired and living somewhere near the beach by now. I am yet to understand why people are afraid of education. There probably are any number of explanations.

Perhaps they recall unhappy school days. Maybe they are afraid of what others might think of them if they appear to be unable to grasp a new concept. More than likely they are afraid of extending their boundaries and seeing learning as a useful developmental tool.

Another explanation might be that learning is not placed within a context suitable for understanding by those being asked to embrace change. This chapter sets out to address that explanation by first exploring learning within a context for learning and continuous improvement. The next section focuses on the importance of considering change as a learning process.

Having contextualised the chapter, attention then turns to a definition of learning, followed by some of the prominent theories relating to adult learning. These theories are grouped under the scientific approach to learning in organisations and progressive-humanist approaches to learning in organisations.

It is then argued that people learn differently, at different times, and on different occasions. Such learning is enhanced by a reflective process to learning so a definition of reflection and critical reflection is provided. The chapter concludes with an explanation of the importance of critical reflection as a tool for understanding, a summary, and a lead in to the next chapter on leadership.

Learning

Context for learning and continuous improvement

A number of continuous improvement learning initiatives may be identified as important for employees in SMEs. Building on Senge et al.'s (1994) notion that organisations are shaped by the ways in which people in them think and interact, the premise of my argument is that if you want to develop and change your SME for the better, you must give yourself, your employees, and even other stakeholders the opportunity to change the ways they think, feel, and interact. Such change requires that you develop and participate in real activities that will change the way people conduct themselves at work. You may do so by encouraging new ideas, innovations in the way you communicate, new management methods, an enhanced leadership style, and the integration of tools that will enable people to develop their potential and enhance their ability to cope with change. In return, you may expect to receive a greater range and intensity of dedication, engagement, involvement, participation, loyalty, improvement, and aptitude towards the completion of tasks and willingness to help you to succeed.

Let me be clear, however, that I am of the view that no one person, no matter how charismatic, charming, autocratic, or dictatorial they might be, can direct someone else to alter their attitudes, beliefs, skills, capabilities, perceptions, or level of commitment for the long term. You may do so by overt manipulation or through the use of threat, implied or otherwise, but coercive and manipulative practices always, yes always, fail in the long term.

Indeed, the Australian psyche is one of not tolerating or bending to petty officialdom, the abuses of authority, or to those who would see themselves as self-important. The outcome of standing up for one's rights can lead to political and personal benefits such as the right to be heard in organisational life and the right to engage in meaningful dialogue about problems and issues.

The right to freedom of speech and to political equality ought to be no less in our organisations than it is in our wider democratic, political, and economic systems. I understand this proposition as a generalisation but consider that such a suggestion is inherently important for understanding the tenet of what follows (Sheehan, 2006).

Engagement in meaningful dialogue and discussing issues and concerns openly and honestly, and without fear of retribution, can enable the fulfilment of initiatives such as enhanced systems thinking, goal and task completion, improved patterns of decision making, openness between employees, and enhanced intrapersonal and interpersonal development such as active listening, giving and receiving constructive feedback, and conflict resolution. By contrast, defensiveness will hinder the process of change, reduce productivity, and lead to workplace health and safety problems, absenteeism, and increased levels of turnover.

Improved patterns of problem solving, customer responsiveness, autonomy, and responsibility are measureable outcomes fundamental to continuous improvement processes. Such outcomes may be achieved through knowledge development that is constantly evaluated, and altered if necessary, to ensure the best utilisation of new knowledge and through ongoing management support to ensure individual and organisational improvement.

All such initiatives may be developed through learning. Learning ought to encompass formal and informal learning processes for individuals and the SME. It ought to be both discrete and continuous, and it may be formal, informal, and experiential and dialogic and creative. Employees taking part in learning programs ought to be required to use a range of abilities during their learning process (Sheehan, 1996), including reading this book.

Attention to the impact of change within SMEs from the perspective of the individual is important. It has been established that organisational change is often unsuccessful because management lacks understanding of how individuals are affected by the change process (following Robbins et al., 2011). Partly the lack of success stems from a limited understanding of the process of learning.

Such a process may best be described as the process by which we attain knowledge, incorporate this knowledge within what it is that we know already, make appropriate interpretations, and then apply new knowledge within the context of our everyday lives, including passing on that new knowledge to others (Higgins and Aspinall, 2011). Such transmission may happen in the SME by way of policies, procedures, rules, and daily routines. Thus knowledge acquisition is seen to be either a technical or social process (following Easterby-Smith and Araujo, 1999). Understanding knowledge acquisition, transformation, and application in this way means that many conventional learning theories have been founded on the basis that learning is an individual process, with a beginning and an end, and which somehow is separated from the rest of our activities and understanding. As such, learning follows from being 'taught' and by being assessed by pre—and post-test measures.

Learning is a much more dynamic process. Learning also takes place through practice and social interaction (following Chisholme, 2009). In this approach, learners are considered to be 'social actors' within an environment in which actions, reactions, and interactions comprise a rich fabric of knowledge, attitude, and skill acquisition. In turn, those 'social actors' participate in, and influence the development of, the socio-cultural practices of their SME and its community. In this understanding of learning, the learners not only acquire knowledge but also develop their identity and ongoing practice (Higgins and Aspinall, 2011).

What may be drawn from this perspective is that people working in SMEs need to be encouraged to make sense of, and give meaning to, their experiences. They need to be encouraged to reflect critically on their learning and how their new knowledge may be expressed through the development of new procedures and routines. It is a personal process, requiring collegiate and managerial support as some may find it difficult to contextualise and explain clearly to others.

An understanding of individual learning is paramount for an understanding of learning within your SME. I frame that learning within the subcontext of professionalism.

The Importance of considering change as a learning process

Expanding on the aforementioned arguments, it is clear that the concept of learning encompasses more than the acquisition of facts and knowledge. Learning is also a dynamic social process occurring within a social context that varies in meaning and understanding for each SME employee. Such variation suggests that learning be envisioned beyond the narrow confines of knowledge enhancement into a broader realm of social and emotional awareness. In this chapter, therefore, learning is contextualised within processes of change occurring because of a desire to become more professional in the SME.

Within such a context, individual learning will allow the SME to learn and change through the critical insight of those involved in the change process. The ability to learn depends on thinking processes, technical skills, security, role models, self-awareness, interpersonal skills, life pressures, intrapersonal understanding, and organisational memory. To learn in this way requires an ability and willingness to consider becoming more professional, to raise learning issues, and to be able to ask critical questions about the reasons for change. These concepts form the basis for contemporary notions of the SME as a learning organisation and one that is seeking continuously to improve.

By continuous improvement, I mean *an ongoing process of individual learning engagements directed to enhancing personal learning and growth that contributes to individual and SME effectiveness.* For such change to happen in an SME, employees will need to develop their learning to help them cope with paradigm shifts and to respond to a rapidly changing marketplace.

Within that rapidly changing marketplace, meeting customer requirements for quality and quantity at a reasonable price is paramount. They also require responsive and helpful customer service, the knowledge that a product is supported by warranty, and/or that refunds or exchanges are available and hassle-free.

The shift to professionalism may require some change in how you conceptualise your SME and what it is you are trying to achieve. It may be that you need to rethink your leadership approach and to consider ways in which you might share leadership as opposed to using it to control staff. You could consider partnerships with other SMEs to replace traditional relationships. It might be that you are seeking to expand internationally and thus need to be aware of the advantages and pitfalls of so doing. Professionalism requires a move to more co-operative rather than confrontational workplaces with a multiskilled and diverse workforce, rather than a narrow skill based and homogeneous workforce. You may need to create an environment where information is shared rather than controlled, and where there are systems that seek continual improvement, rather than systems and thinking that are constrained by rigidity.

Professionalism may also require a redistribution of power, with critical questioning by employees encouraged, as opposed to empowerment without consideration of the outcomes. Conflict needs to be identified as a part of organisational life, with systems developed to ensure that conflict is resolved, rather than leading to the creation of new tensions, conflicts, and differences, resulting in a lack of trust. Employees need to be given the opportunity to self-actualise, to feel personally secure, to have flexible work arrangements, to be able to develop their skills, and to have suitable reward systems, without being fearful of being punished for being creative and innovative. You also could consider developing systems that support learning and change to replace those that inhibit and block learning.

How those notions inform adult learning in the transition to a professional SME

The aforementioned changes suggest that owners, managers, and employees should make a number of systemic and individual changes within their SME. From the need for these changes, an extrapolation may be made of the need for adults to be involved in a process of continual learning as they come to understand the impact of a shift to professionalism for them as individuals. Some of the issues to be considered include the following:

- Change from individually based jobs to those that require more teamwork and integration.
- Break down barriers to change
- Re-envisage jobs and career paths as learning opportunities rather than the competence to complete set tasks
- Ensure flexibility in organisational structure
- Develop ways of integrating work and learning
- Encourage employees to recognise environmental uncertainty
- Do away with the supervisory position and introduce self-managing teams

What may be inferred from these suggestions is that employees need to be offered opportunities to learn to do things differently, and that part of the learning process requires them to reflect on, and learn from, their experience. You may need to rethink how you provide learning and development opportunities. Indeed, you may need to rethink your own motivation for learning and development and consider learning and development for the opportunities and possibilities it offers rather than as something that gets in the way of 'making money'. Some of the ways you might consider learning and development are as follows:

- Realise that training delivers content while learning occurs continuously
- Envisage learning as existing in all situations, rather than as only in those programmes specifically designed for the purpose of training employees in some new skill or technology
- Offer opportunities for the development of problem-solving skills as well as task skills
- Provide learning time

- Ensure learning programmes are designed to cater for individual learning styles and that learners are actively involved in the learning process rather than passive and uninvolved. Such programs could utilise mentors, learning contracts, learning resources, and learning-based system design
- Assure management and colleague support for new learning

Employees also have a role to play. They need to take responsibility for their own learning. They need to be open to new ideas, to be able to tolerate ambiguity and uncertainty, and to be able to question critically what is occurring in their workplace. Concurrently, they need to be supportive of others and to improve their communication processes.

Approaches to learning in organisations

To understand how employees may become more professional, some knowledge of approaches to learning in organisations is necessary, particularly from the perspective of adult learning. Adult learning theories will help explain how employees may come to understand their own affective, behavioural, and cognitive responses to the individual change required of them to become more professional. As a starting point, this section of the chapter defines adult learning.

An understanding of how adults learn is important so that those experiences might be contextualised. Two predominant schools of thought informed the concept of adult learning throughout the twentieth century. Knowles (1990) classified these schools of thought 'Scientific' and 'Artistic'. In this book they are termed 'scientific' and 'progressive-humanist'. The insights gleaned from the debates between proponents of each of these schools provide understanding of how learning might best be conceptualised. These insights are discussed following my definition of learning for the context of the arguments herein presented.

Definition of learning

Many definitions of learning rely on a behaviourist approach to understanding learning. Typically, those definitions tend to describe learning as a relatively permanent change in behaviour resulting from a person's experience (Sigelman and Shaffer, 1995), suggesting that learning is permanent and can be measured. Such change is not a result of either genetic disposition or maturation (Domjan and Burkhard, 1993). Given that much behaviourist research has been conducted with animals, it may be argued that behavioural definitions may be applied to any organism. But, as Kolb (1984) pointed out, humans are not only able to adapt to their physical and social worlds, as most organisms do, but they are also able actively to shape and create those worlds through a self-conscious process involving a reflexive awareness of our own beliefs and actions.

Thus, learning is partly a process whereby new concepts are developed, and continuously adjusted, through experience. Such learning uses all the human processes available, such as thinking, feeling, perceiving, reflecting and acting, and is not limited to cognition or perception alone. Brookfield (1990a) developed this argument. He suggests that learning is an activity of such significance, and of such a challenge to the learner's ego state, that account also needs to be given to the emotional experience of learning. Learning is defined as *a transformation in the learner's affective, behavioural, or cognitive states, whereby the learner is able to make sense of, and give meaning to, their learning experience. Further, the learner is able to recognise that experience as a learning experience, and is able to undertake endeavours to make appropriate changes to achieve a desired new state* (Sheehan, 2000: 31).

The scientific approach to learning in organisations

There is a long history of scientific approaches to adult learning, but a discussion of this history is beyond the scope of this book. Rather, what is intended at this stage is a brief mention of some of the major theorists and concepts within the behaviourist, cognitive, and social learning paradigms in an endeavour to inform you about these theories and concepts. The discussion will then move to an exploration of the artistic or progressive-humanist approach to understanding adult learning. It is the latter approach which underpins some of the core tenets expressed in this book.

1. Behaviourist theories

Behaviourists attempt to explain human behaviour in terms of cause and effect, by using the notion of external stimuli to arouse a behavioural response. Behaviourist theory is also termed stimulus-response or S-R theory. Arguably, the three most well-known proponents of behaviourist theory are Pavlov (1902), Watson (1930), and Skinner (1971). Some behaviourist theories attempt to frame learning within a statistical or mathematical dimension by way of stimulus sampling (Estes, 1950, 1970) or mathematical modelling (Norman, 1970).

Theories that fall within the behaviourist category may be summarised as relying on positivistic concepts of hypothesis testing and objective measurement to study learning behaviour (Burns, 1995). That is to say, they rely on an approach to science that suggests that it is possible for an observer to formulate a problem, develop a set of measurement criteria, examine phenomena, remain detached from the phenomena, and exclude value judgements from the whole process. Behaviourists, therefore, do not explain how a new behaviour is actually learned, remembered, and recalled (Thompson and McHugh, 1995), nor do they account for the affective state of the learner (Kolb, 1984).

Thus, account needs to be taken of people's subjective experience of learning and implementing that learning in the workplace. Account also needs to be taken of participant's attribution of meaning to those experiences. This is why your support as a manager, and the support of the employees' colleagues, is vital to the success of any workplace learning undertaken.

2. Cognitive theories

Cognitive theories encompass a broad range of approaches. They all have in common a focus on external behavioural indicators to the investigation of mental processes. Thus, they tend to focus on the following:

- Memory processes
- Semantic memory of words or symbols
- Mental processes, intelligence, and intellectual skills
- Aptitude
- Cognitive dissonance
- Lateral thinking
- Rules
- Structure

Memory, however, is episodic. That is, it relates directly to personal experience and thus depends on a person's personal script. As such, adult learners ought to be given the opportunity to build on prior life and work experiences. Moreover, learning occurs within a context of socio-cultural and environmental change and may be impacted by unforeseen events during a learning process. Social interaction is also an important construct in the learning process (following Chisholme, 2009; Sheehan, 2000).

Moreover, the learning setting needs to be conducive to a positive learning experience if the required learning is to occur. Learning environments are not sterile places where human beings may put aside their feelings and concentrate only on developing memory processes. Emotion also needs to be accounted for in the learning process (Chisholme, 2009; Kolb, 1984).

Such considerations recognise the dynamic nature of change and account for the role of previous experience, the way people give meaning to, and make sense of, their experiences and the application of insight. Their learning is more holistic than is suggested by the narrow confines of the stimulus-response approach of behaviourists.

While cognitive theories generally address some of the limitations of behaviourist theories, they nonetheless still encompass limitations that require mention. They are as follows:

1. Most are centred on acquiring, arranging, and remembering abstract symbols (Kolb, 1984).
2. Most tend to be based on a logical, linear, and mathematical approach to learning
3. Many ignore multiple intelligence (Gardner, 1993) and emotional intelligence (Goleman, 1996; Salovey and Mayer, 1990)
4. Many do not consider the environment within which learning occurs
5. Little attention is paid to reflection as part of the learning process

Thus, when considering the learning needs of employees as they work towards becoming more professional, the employees' wider social milieu in which the learning and implementation occur needs to be addressed. All learning occurs within a socio-cultural and socio-historical context that is authentic for each employee. Account also needs to be taken of the role of emotion, and how employees reflect on, and understand, their learning and implementation experience.

3. Social learning theory

Social learning theory tends to bridge the gap between behaviourist and cognitive approaches. It stresses the importance of learning new behaviours by observing and adopting the behaviours, attitudes, and emotional reactions of others (Bandura, 1969, 1977). The observation of the behaviours of others as part of a learning process implies that perception is also a crucial component of an employee's ability to learn.

Informal processes often occur in SMEs to help employees cope with organisational demands. In the past, 'sitting by Nellie' was a recognised form of learning new skills. This type of skill development is now termed 'mentoring'. Both approaches are a form of 'socialisation' as reflected in social learning theory.

The application of new learning from a formal programme of learning to the workplace is an important component of social learning. The application of learning is vital for successful learning outcomes. Application of learning occurs when new learning or activities experienced in a learning situation are utilised in another situation. Learners must be able to see the relevance of the new learning, and they need to have developed strategies for coping with new tasks and situations. The application of learning is enabled when adults have input to the design and organisation of learning programmes and when they have the support of the manager and colleagues for the implementation of that new learning in the workplace. Thus, self-responsibility and self-direction are key pre-conditions for adult learning, as is managerial and collegiate support. The latter is an important component of the social context in which learning occurs. The social context includes the following:

- Modelling and mentoring
- Positive and constructive support of managers, supervisors, and work colleagues
- An encouraging work climate
- Being given work roles or tasks relevant to the new learning
- The opportunity to apply new learning as quickly as possible in the workplace
- Positive and genuine feedback about their efforts

Progressive-humanist approaches to learning in organisations

Behaviourist, cognitive, and social learning theory approaches to conceptualising adult learning informed this chapter to the limited extent noted above, but the approach most pertinent to the arguments presented throughout is that advocated by those identified by Knowles (1990) as being in the 'artistic' school of thought. Such theories are termed 'progressive-humanist' in recognition of their dominant informing sentiments. Progressive-humanist constructs suggest that adult learners are capable of making decisions about their own learning needs.

Important foundational work in this approach has been done by Dewey (1916, 1933, 1938), Rogers (1969), Freire (1970), and Knowles (1980a, 1990). These four advocates are clustered together and mentioned briefly to help demonstrate the historical development of the approach. Their work is seen as informing later developments, particularly those of Mezirow (1978, 1981, 1985, 1991, 1994, 1996a, b), Brookfield (1987, 1988, 1990a,b, 1995), and Revans (1980, 1982a,b, 1991). Other significant theorists who may be identified within the progressive-humanist approach and whose work is included here are Kolb (1976, 1984, 1985), and Honey and Mumford (1982, 1986, 1989, 1990, 1992).

These last three mentioned have been instrumental in developing notions of the need to consider the different learning styles of adult learners. All of the aforementioned theorists moved beyond the limitations of behaviourist, cognitive, and social learning approaches by recognising education as part of a wider socio-political, socio-economic, and socio-cultural context. They recognise learning as an intentional, value-laden, and culturally dependent engagement, inseparable from its cultural context. Adults could therefore use education and learning in self-development and liberation. All these latter aspects are seen as important as an underpinning for the qualities of professionalism previously outlined in Chapter 4.

1. John Dewey, Carl Rogers, Paulo Freire, and Malcolm Knowles

Ideas underpinning humanistic constructs in adult learning are derived from pragmatism, existential philosophy, phenomenology and humanism. One of the earliest 20th century proponents was John Dewey. Dewey (1916) considered that human beings should be seen as having unlimited potential. Such potential could be developed and enhanced by education within the social framework of the learner. Past experience and the wider environmental context could be utilised for achieving successful learning outcomes. A teacher ought, therefore, to be a guide or facilitator, building on peoples' experiences in a process of learner self-growth.

Dewey was a strident critic of the scientific, or traditional, approach to learning. One of the criticisms related to the assumption made in the scientific approach that learners were *empty vessels* into which was poured all knowledge and wisdom from the teacher. Dewey envisioned a more holistic approach to learning. He argued that the free expression of individuality by the learner was more important than the imposition of knowledge and discipline from teachers. He also argued that learning through experience was more important than learning from tests and teachers, and he valued the importance of the learner's needs, as opposed to the teacher's needs. An active, rather than passive, approach to learning was also important.

Grounded in his work as a psychotherapist, Carl Rogers (1969, 1983) formulated a theory of experiential learning. Within the educational context, Rogers focused on the relationship between teacher and learner (Burns, 1995). Reflecting his work as a therapist, Rogers considered that the role of education was to create a better functioning person. In that way, the learner would be able to reach a state of self-actualisation. In identifying two types of learning, namely cognitive and experiential, Rogers proposed that cognitive, or meaningless, learning did not address the needs of the adult learner. On the other hand, experiential learning was seen to account for the needs of the learner because it allowed the learner to build on previous experiences. The learner, then, was seen to be personally involved, able to contribute responsibly, and able to evaluate their own learning. Under these circumstances 'real' learning occurred. The role of the teacher was to 'facilitate' the learning process.

Based on work undertaken with the indigenous people of Brazil, Paulo Freire (1970) envisaged learning as a process for achieving freedom from oppression. Freire argued that colonialists, by their social construction of language, imposed a false sense of identity on indigenous people. To overcome that false consciousness, he utilised literacy programs to develop adults so that they could better understand themselves within their socio-cultural context. Thus he saw adult learning within the context of a social milieu.

Often considered as one of the leading thinkers in adult learning theory, Malcolm Knowles (1970, 1975) argued that pedagogical approaches to learning were more suited to children. He argued that adults learned under a different set of circumstances and made different assumptions about their world than did children. From that position he developed a theory specifically for adult learning, which he termed 'andragogy'. Building on the work of Rogers, Knowles also envisaged learners as essentially self-directed, able to utilise and build on past experiences, and responsible for their own actions. Adult-learning programmes were seen, therefore, as needing to encapsulate these fundamental elements. Moreover, adult-learning programmes ought to focus on process rather than content, with the teacher adopting the role of guide or facilitator to help learners explore and experiment with content and process issues.

In some of his later work, Knowles (1980a, b, 1984) modified his earlier stance by recognising that, under certain conditions, adults could also learn under a set of pedagogical assumptions, while 'andragogical' approaches would be more pertinent given a different set of circumstances. Knowles's work has had a profound effect on subsequent studies of adult learning (Mumford, 1993b). One such effect is a cautionary note offered by Bagnall (1994). In pointing out that Knowles (1970) presents two-dimensional poles of andragogy and pedagogy as separate concepts, Bagnall suggests that Knowles's perceptions are limited. The dimensions, rather than being distinct polar opposites are 'continuously variable' (p. 38).

2. Jack Mezirow

Jack Mezirow (1990, 1991) suggested that there are three levels to adult learning, termed 'instrumental', 'communicative', and 'emancipatory' and that these levels form the basis of transformative learning. He clearly bases these levels on the distinction of knowledge formulated by Habermas (1972) of instrumental, practical, and emancipatory knowledge. He believes that he has formulated a 'comprehensive, idealised, and universal' model of adult learning (Mezirow, 1994: 222).

Instrumental learning involves the learner in learning to control or manipulate his or her environment in order to establish a foundation for the 'truth' by objective measurement. Such an approach aligns with task-oriented problem solving. This approach also suggests that an indicator such as workplace productivity improvement may measure learning outcomes. Instrumental learning is most obvious in organisations when procedural training is undertaken in order to achieve desired goals.

Communicative learning involves understanding others. The learner attempts to understand others by trying to understand such things as their values, intentions, ideals, moral decisions, and feelings. Instead of trying to determine truth, the learner seeks to understand others through understanding their justification for their personal beliefs. Such understanding may only be achieved through 'rational discourse' (Mezirow, 1994). Programmes that focus on developing a person's interpersonal communication style are examples of this type of learning. Understanding others in these types of programmes, or through other methods for learning 'rational discourse' requires three conditions for learning. The first is that the learners have equal opportunity to participate. The second is that they are free from coercion. The third is that they are open to alternative opinions, that they value the expression of those opinions, and that they care about the way others think and feel (Mezirow, 1994).

By emancipatory learning, Mezirow means the way adult learners transform their 'frame of reference'. These are the deeply embedded values and beliefs that adults hold, and that shape and direct individuals' everyday attitudes and actions. They provide us with the predisposition to act and strongly influence what we do, or do not, perceive, comprehend, and remember (Mezirow, 1991, 1994, 1996a, b). The way that adults might alter their frames of reference is by a process of critical reflection. They scrutinise their basic beliefs and how they have come to that set of beliefs. They challenge themselves to understand what those beliefs are, how they have developed, and if they might be changed. It is an introspective process that lies at the heart of transformational learning.

The strength of Mezirow's (1990, 1991) transformative learning is its multidisciplinary approach. Mezirow draws from psychological, psychotherapeutic, sociological, and philosophical discourses. Moreover, in formulating a theory of transformative adult learning, Mezirow addresses the importance of the need to include how adult learners make sense of, and give meaning to, their learning experience. Additionally, he places such learning within a social context.

3. Stephen Brookfield

Stephen Brookfield (1995) has built on Mezirow's notion of frames of reference, particularly extrapolating Mezirow's concept into a hierarchy of three assumptions. They are paradigmatic assumptions, prescriptive assumptions, and causal assumptions that selectively order and delimit what we learn because they define the limits of our expectations and thus impact upon our ability to perceive, comprehend, and remember.

Paradigmatic assumptions are those that humans use to construct order within their unique world. They help humans to categorise their understanding and view of the world, including their values, beliefs, aesthetic appreciation, and judgement criteria. They are developed during childhood and often rigidly adhered to in later life. We tend not to see them as assumptions, considering them to be our objective reality, and resisting efforts to challenge or change that reality. For example, in some Western cultures, some individuals equate the colour white with good or happiness and the colour black with evil or sadness. Prescriptive assumptions provide direction for what ought to happen when confronted with a particular situation. Causal assumptions are usually predictive and help us to understand how our world operates, and how we might change within that world.

For the purpose of the arguments in this book, an understanding of paradigmatic assumptions is important for three reasons. First, how SME employees make sense of, or give meaning to, their experience of becoming more professional will be impacted by how they filter information during any learning programme and how they implement new learning back in the workplace. Individuals tend to filter information on the basis of what supports their known world, rejecting information that is seen to challenge that world view. Second, a well-developed, sophisticated, and complex defence mechanism tends to come into action when it is felt necessary to defend our assumptions. Such a mechanism tends to protect the ego state. Third, a range of emotional reactions may accompany a change in how we make sense of, or give meaning to, an experience. Such emotions may range from what might be termed negative emotions, such as frustration, anger, confusion, and doubt to what might be termed positive emotions, such as happiness, joy, and exhilaration.

Like Mezirow, Brookfield also recognised the importance of a critically reflective process to aid understanding and change. He saw that reflection could become critical if two conditions were realised. The first was to use reflection as a tool to understand how power impacted upon relationships. The second was to question long-held assumptions that were perceived as useful in our lives, but that in fact, hindered our development. He labelled these as 'hegemonic assumptions'. Building on the work of Gramsci (1978), Brookfield pointed out that hegemonic assumptions were based on the notion that prominent societal ideas, structures, or actions were seen as natural and good. We do not realise that they have been formulated by a powerful minority whose interests were maintained by their further propagation. He therefore argued that there was a need to challenge accepted conventional wisdom, by way of critical reflection, in order to protect our own health and well-being.

4. Reg Revans

Reg Revans is credited with introducing the concept of 'action learning' as a way for adults to learn in organisations. Action learning incorporates the concepts of self-directed and reflective learning, with the learner able to build on previous knowledge and experience by using questioning to develop new learning. Revans formulated the equation $P + Q = L$, where P equals programmed knowledge, Q equals questioning insight, and L equals learning.

Action learning is a cyclical process involving planning, acting, observing, and reflecting, as is shown in Figure 9.1 (Revans, 1980, 1982a,b, 1991). It provides a mechanism for organisational members to work together to bring about organisational change by way of new competencies, group learning, the transference of learning to the workplace, and self-reflective inquiry.

Figure 9.1: The Action Learning Cycle

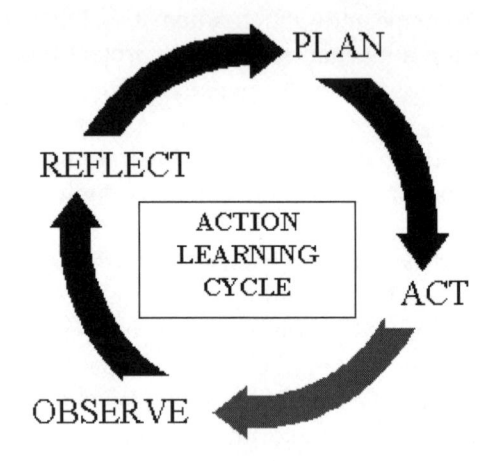

Source: Kemmis and McTaggart (1988).

As a process, it is closely related to the 'plan, do, check, act' cycle of the quality improvement model shown in Figure 9.2, and Kolb's (1984) learning cycle model, depicted in Figure 9.3. Understanding and using these models may assist individual and group learning by catering for different learning styles.

Figure 9.2: The Quality Improvement Model

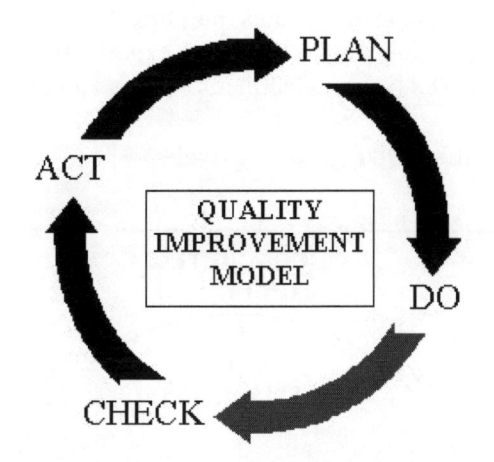

```
         PLAN
    ↗         ↘
ACT  ┌─────────┐  
  ↑  │ QUALITY │  ↓
     │IMPROVEMENT│
     │  MODEL  │ DO
     └─────────┘
    ↖         ↙
        CHECK
```

Source: Crosling and Munzberg (1993).

Some words of caution. Action learning has been criticised for its paucity of detail and for its narrow approach to the use of projects for problem solving. While employees are given the opportunity to learn within the context of the workplace, paradoxically the real demands and pressures of the workplace could impact negatively on their decision-making processes. Furthermore, action learning does not tell us about the learning experiences of action learners and does not provide a model of learning. The action learning equation of Revans may also be seen as attempting to objectify what is a subjective process since it is predicated on quasi-scientific notions of measurement and control.

5. David Kolb

David Kolb (1984) has argued that individual learning is a transactional process between personal knowledge and the external environment. Learning is seen as a social process whereby experiential learning opportunities occur within a cultural and social framework. Experiential learning maximises developmental opportunities within this framework. He appears to have developed his theory from a number of conceptual frameworks.

These frameworks include behaviourist theories stressing the need for active participation, cognitive theories that include the importance of past experience, and humanist constructs pointing to the need to draw on a learner's past experience. As such, Kolb's experiential learning model, as illustrated in Figure 9.3, is an eclectic approach to adult learning.

Figure 9.3: Kolb's (1984) Learning Cycle

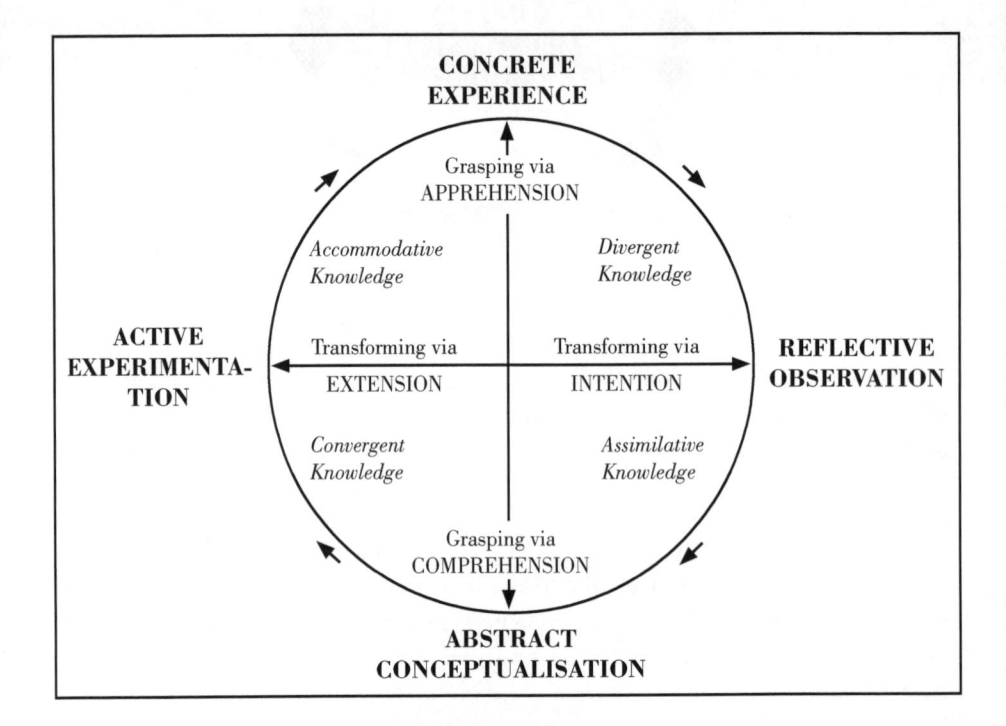

```
                    CONCRETE
                   EXPERIENCE
                        ↑
                 Grasping via
                 APPREHENSION

         Accommodative        Divergent
           Knowledge          Knowledge

ACTIVE    Transforming via   Transforming via   REFLECTIVE
EXPERIMENTA- ←─────────────────────────────→  OBSERVATION
 TION       EXTENSION          INTENTION

          Convergent          Assimilative
           Knowledge           Knowledge

                 Grasping via
                COMPREHENSION
                        ↓
                   ABSTRACT
              CONCEPTUALISATION
```

Experiential learning theory is portrayed in Kolb's learning model as a cycle. According to Kolb (1984), the learning process draws on orientations that are polar opposites: active and reflective, concrete and abstract. Dimensions relate to the apprehending or grasping of information and then the transforming or processing of that information. The model shows these dimensions in opposite quadrants of a learning cycle, with concrete experience

(CE) opposite abstract conceptualisation (AC) and reflective observation (RO) opposite active experimentation (AE). Observations are assimilated into a 'theory' from which new implications for action may be deduced and new experiences created. Participants are seen as moving through a linear regime of concrete experience, reflective observation, abstract conceptualisation, and active experimentation.

To help learners categorise their learning styles, Kolb (1976) devised a learning style inventory (KLSI) that used a self-description questionnaire as a measurement of learning styles. Kolb's Learning Style Inventory has been criticised for its psychometric weaknesses such as poor construct and face validity, poor reliability (Allinson and Hayes, 1988), abnormal distribution, and its general psychometric limitations (Bostrom, et al., 1993). Such criticism has carried on to the derivative Learning Style Questionnaire (LSQ), which is seen as quasi-experimental and unnecessarily complex (Caple and Martin, 1994).

6. Peter Honey and Alan Mumford

Peter Honey and Alan Mumford have further developed Kolb's theory (Honey and Mumford, 1989, 1992; Mumford, 1987, 1988, 1991, 1992, 1993a, 1994). Using a similar cyclical model, as shown in Figure 9.4, Honey and Mumford term their learning style categories, 'activists', 'reflectors', 'theorists', and 'pragmatists'. The model shows these categories in opposite poles of a learning cycle, with activist opposite theorist, and reflector opposite pragmatist. Participants are seen as moving through a linear regime of activist, reflector, theorist and pragmatist. Activists tend to be task oriented, and learn best when involved in activity. Reflectors prefer to plan, to observe and to listen, learning best when given time to analyse and consider new information. Theorists are unable to tolerate ambiguity and uncertainty, learning best from ideas and concepts they find interesting. Pragmatists need to see the relevance of new material to reality, learning best from models that they can imitate.

Figure 9.4: Honey and Mumford's (1992) Learning Cycle

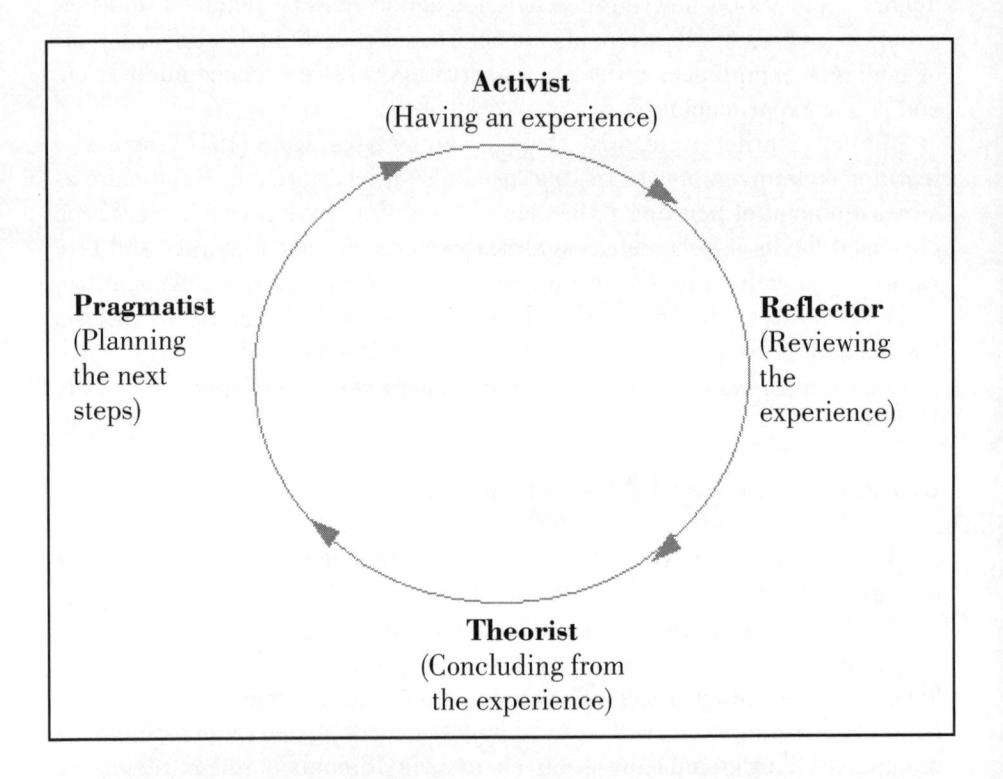

Activist
(Having an experience)

Pragmatist
(Planning the next steps)

Reflector
(Reviewing the experience)

Theorist
(Concluding from the experience)

Like Kolb, Honey and Mumford used a number of instruments to develop and test their model. Instruments included the Learning Style Questionnaire (LSQ) (Honey and Mumford, 1982; Mumford and Honey, 1992) and the Learning Diagnostic Questionnaire (LDQ) (Honey and Mumford, 1990, 1992). By extrapolation, criticism similar to that applied to Kolb may be advanced against the Honey and Mumford model and measurement instruments.

Notwithstanding any criticisms, the progressive-humanist approaches to learning suggest a number of issues to be considered when moving towards a more professional SME. They are as follows:

1. People ought to be treated with respect and with an acknowledgement that they are responsible and able to make their own choices
2. The wider social milieu within which adults conduct their daily lives is an integral part of a learning program

3. Notions of measurement and control ought to be avoided because adult learners are encouraged to evaluate their own learning outcomes
4. Reflection and critical reflection form part of, and are necessary for, emancipatory learning to occur
5. People learn differently, at different times, and on different occasions

Definition of reflection and critical reflection

As mentioned in point 4, above reflection and critical reflection are valuable components of the learning process. Drawing on the aforementioned theories, these terms are now extrapolated from the definitions in Sheehan (2000: 45-46).

Reflection is defined as *a process by which employees learning new skills are able to draw on their observations and interpretations of events that occurred during the completion of tasks in a learning programme to integrate an understanding of those events. Such understanding ought to be used in an endeavour to make the changes deemed necessary to move to the desired new state of a more professional SME.*

Critical reflection is defined as *a process by which employees learning new skills are able to examine and challenge their own beliefs and the assumptions on which those beliefs are founded. They endeavour to understand how their beliefs are developed, to recognise the debilitating effects of those beliefs, and to make decisions about how to change their beliefs in order to move to the desired new state of a more professional SME.*

The Importance of critical reflection as a tool for understanding

Critical reflection may serve as a tool for your understanding of your ability to consider events that occur during your learning and implementation processes. It may help you to understand, and give new meaning to, those experiences. New meaning aids understanding and appreciation of the need to alter past habits and assumptions and to take action to form new understanding and perspectives.

In a study by Sheehan (2000), most of the participants used critical reflection as a tool to assist their learning, to understand their experience, to challenge long held beliefs, and to make appropriate changes to achieve a desired new state. Participants found that critical reflection aided their learning outcomes, helped them make sense of their experience, helped them to make sense of previous learning experiences, and helped them determine personal strategies for future action. They offered comments like the following:

> *Until you sit down and reflect on what you've done, you really don't get any idea of just what you have learned* (p. 210).

> *I continually evaluate myself on the experiences that I've had* (p. 210).

> *Reflection is a tool that I bounce off in making a decision. I'm only going to be a better person for it* (p. 210).

Generally, there was no one indication of learning. Many events, and critical reflection on events, combined to help participants create a more complete understanding of their learning. One participant admitted, however, that he could have taken more opportunities during the learning programme to reflect on his learning, noting that, *I probably didn't do [enough] reflecting* (p. 210).

In this chapter it has been argued that learning and understanding how adults learn was considered to be important for understanding how people working in SMEs might cope with a change process. Contextual understanding was deemed to be important as was some understanding of different approaches to understanding how adults learn. Critical reflection was viewed as a key to successful learning and change outcomes.

But if such learning and change is to occur, another ingredient is important, and that ingredient is leadership. Thus, the next chapter explores leadership.

Chapter 10

Leadership

All of the great leaders have had one thing in common: it was the willingness to confront unequivocally the major anxiety of their people in their time. This, and not much else, is the essence of leadership.

(J. K. Galbraith, 1908-2006, American liberal economist)

Introduction

The central tenet of this chapter is that an SME leader's primary role is to create, maintain, and sustain an organisational culture in which their staffs' inherent abilities are valued, admired, and respected. Changing from a less-than professional to a more-professional SME requires discipline, commitment, risk, and critical self-reflection. But the benefits include enhanced individual and organisational performance (following Gardner and Schermerhorn Jr., 2004), improved supplier relationships, and increased customer satisfaction.

If you are an owner/manager of a one-person SME or if you work in a quite small SME, say less than three to ten staff, you may wonder whether or not you need to know much about leadership. After all, if you are a one-person operation, then you could argue that you have no one to lead. But leadership is often defined as a process whereby one party influences another to achieve a particular goal. Or, as seen in the definition at the start of this chapter, it also may be about managing anxiety. Customers and suppliers may sometimes need to be influenced or they may be anxious, so the above definition could provide some insight into why it might be worthwhile understanding a little more about leadership.

Perhaps more importantly, in the context of the arguments presented in this book, leadership is seen to be a core process for the achievement of sustainability (Epstein and Buhovac, 2010).

A leader is sometimes defined as someone who achieves goals through the work of others. Such definitions suggest at least three things need to be understood:

1. Leadership is a process; that is, it is a dynamic phenomenon.
2. Leadership involves other people.
3. Leadership is concerned with an outcome in terms of goal achievement.

I suggest, therefore, that understanding leadership is important for you, no matter what the size of your SME. In your day-to-day activities, whether you are working with staff, customers, suppliers, financiers, or people in your network, you will be demonstrating your qualities of leadership.

This chapter, therefore, seeks to identify what are the characteristics of leaders that might be most appropriate for the development of professionalism within an SME. This is not to suggest that the characteristics herein identified mean that leaders who do not possess such characteristics are therefore incapable of owning or managing an SME. Rather, it may identify that skill development is required.

An overview of a general understanding of leadership is provided first. Second, an overview of major leadership theories is proffered. These theories, in turn, are trait theories, contingency or situational theories, transactional leadership theories, transformational leadership theories, and authentic leadership theories. While it is important to have at least a basic understanding of these theories, it also is considered necessary to understand how leaders might be developed. Thus, the next sections are entitled developing leaders and leadership, and what I mean by leadership development.

General understanding of leadership

It has long been recognised that healthy relationships at work are paramount for organisational productivity and success. It is sometimes argued that it is a leader's responsibility to help create and nurture such relationships. Thus, leaders need to develop a climate of trust, meaning and dialogue (Gobillot, 2006). Leaders also need to understand that we live within an era of constant change, and they must understand the nature of change as it applies within their SME.

From an industrial and organisational perspective interest in, and attention to, leadership and theories of leadership emerged in the early twentieth century. That interest continues in contemporary organisations, particularly in times of crisis such as those currently being experienced because of the global financial crisis in many industrialised nations. Despite the plethora of studies devoted to understanding its features, leadership remains a somewhat nebulous concept and underexplored in terms of SMEs.

Theories of leadership abound. Leadership is seen to be a multifaceted social process that engages everyone in the organisation. Generally speaking, a leader is that person who is able to collaboratively develop and communicate the shared purpose and goals of their organisational unit. The leader is one who involves others in the planning process, ensuring that each team member is clear about their roles and responsibilities and is able to provide support and development to help those team members achieve their objectives. Such support includes encouragement, recognition, and reward. A leader is one who takes corrective action if and when required. A leader is able to engender support because they are seen to be trustworthy, open, honest, supportive, fair, and consistent. They are able to resolve conflict if necessary.

It may be argued that there is an inherent ambiguity when trying to identify those characteristics of leadership that contribute to, or prevent, appropriate practices in SMEs.

Overview of major leadership theories

Early leadership theories tended to focus on the qualities that distinguished those seen to be leaders in contrast to those of their followers. The theories that have then followed have tended to be an eclectic mix exploring a range of variables such as 'great man' (following Weber, 1947), traits (McCall Jr. and Lombardo, 1983; Stogdill, 1974), behaviours (Blake and Mouton, 1964; McGregor, 1957; Pavlov, 1927; Thorndike, 1913; Watson, 1930), situations (Fiedler, 1967; Hersey and Blanchard, 1969; House, 1971), transactions (Bass, 1985; Weber, 1947), and relationships (Burns, 1978). For the purposes of this chapter, four major theoretical categories have been selected to help achieve the intention of the chapter. They are trait, contingency or situational, transactional, and transformational theories.

Trait theories

Trait theories emerged in the 1920s and were based on an assumption that people inherit certain qualities and traits that characterise them as a leader. Trait theories often identified particular personality or behavioural characteristics shared by leaders. Stogdill (1974) identified traits such as assertiveness, being alert to the social environment, being ambitious and achievement-orientated, and being cooperative and dependable as critical to leaders. Furthermore, he identified a skill set encompassing conceptual ability, creativity, diplomacy, tactfulness, persuasiveness, and enhanced social skills.

McCall Jr. and Lombardo (1983) identified four primary traits by which leaders could succeed or fail. They were as follows:

1. *Emotional stability and composure* by which was meant that leaders were calm, confident, and predictable, especially when under pressure
2. *Admitting error*, that is admitting mistakes rather than concealing those mistakes
3. *Good interpersonal skills* in that leaders were able to communicate and influence others without using manipulative, negative or coercive methods
4. *Intellectual breadth* in that leaders had the ability to comprehend a wide range of issues as opposed to having a constricted area of expertise exacerbated by insularity.

More recently, the concept of emotional intelligence may be added to the trait list. Covey (1996) asserts that emotional intelligence embraces traits such as interpersonal relations, kinaesthetic ability, conceptual and creative thinking, perspective, proportion, and correlation. Cooper and Sawaf (1997) see emotional intelligence as the capability to comprehend, appreciate, and apply the influence and insight of emotions as a source of human energy, information, association, and influence.

Goleman (1998) suggests that emotional intelligence has two parts: personal competence and social competence. Personal competence refers to how we self-manage and includes traits such as self-awareness, self-management, and motivation. Social competence refers to how we manage relationships and includes empathy and the social skills necessary for responding appropriately to others.

Contingency or situational theories

Researchers next began to consider the circumstances or situations that influence what leadership behaviours will be effective, resulting in the development of contingency or situational theories. It was seen that leaders can scrutinise their situation and alter their behaviour to improve their leadership effectiveness. Major variables were leadership style, the characteristics and qualities of followers and the tasks they were set, characteristics of the work environment, and the external environment.

According to contingency theory, no leadership style suits all situations. Thus, leaders need to choose the course of action most appropriate for their circumstances. It was seen that the problems encountered in their individual circumstances would require decision-making appropriate to that situation and thus necessitate a different leadership style to match. Arguably, better known theories here include Fiedler's (1967) leadership contingency theory, Hersey and Blanchard's (1969) situational leadership model, and House's (1971) path-goal theory of leadership.

While these theories have had intuitive appeal for some leaders, there appears to be little consistent research support (French et al., 2008). It could be argued that, given the uncertainty with which many SMEs are faced, a leader constantly changing his or her style to adapt to follower maturity or to the situation could leave followers bewildered and uncertain. It then follows that leaders themselves may become anxious, confused, and apprehensive. In turn, such feelings may result in inappropriate workplace behaviours such as bullying, hostility, duplicity, and poor communication and problem solving.

Transactional leadership theories

Transactional leadership or management theories first mooted by Weber (1947) and later developed more fully by Bass, (1985) focus on the role of supervision, organisation, and group performance. These theories base leadership on the notion that followers are motivated by a system of rewards and punishment set to help achieve agreed goals. When employees are seen to be successful, they are rewarded; when they are seen to fail or make a mistake, they are reprimanded or punished. Leadership becomes a series of transactions between the leader and followers.

Ulrich et al. (2008) go a step further. They suggest that good leaders ought to follow five essential rules or a code of leadership so as to become a better leader. Those rules are as follows: shape the future, make things happen, engage today's talent, build the next generation, and invest in yourself.

Leaders thus need to be in close contact with their followers so that they can observe their successes or failures, suggesting a preoccupation by those leaders with authority, close oversighting of employee performance, control, power, status, and strict performance management. A lack of trust also is evident. Transactional leaders tend to focus on short-term, bottom line performance, tactical decisions, and the use of targets and measurements to justify their position (following Kotter, 1990). In such transactions, leadership may be perceived as destructive (following Illies and Reiter-Palmon, 2008).

If, however, the goals are not mutually agreed, or if support systems are not consistently in place to help staff achieve the goals, then staff may determine that they are being treated inappropriately. Similarly, if discussion is stifled and the questioning of the leader's ideas and suggestions is deemed to be detrimental to the achievement of goals, then unmet expectations become mired in ambiguity, complexity, policies and procedures, and rules. Unmet expectations could lead staff to conclude that they are being bullied with consequent feelings of anxiety and impaired performance tending to manifest, leading to distress and ill-health (following Keashly and Neuman, 2010; Neuman and Baron, 2011).

Transformational leadership theories

By contrast to transactional theories, transformational leadership or relationship theories focus on the associations, rather than transactions, between leaders and followers. Transformational leaders motivate and inspire people by helping employees engage with, and share in, the vision and mission of higher order tasks. The requirement is to work for a common good rather than narrow self-interest, but in ways that individual potential may still be achieved.

Since the late 1970s, many ideas of leadership have focused on how leaders and followers interact and influence one another. Burns (1978) viewed leadership as a relationship whereby all actors in the system were able to transcend higher order goals. That is, followers could become leaders, and leaders could become 'moral agents'. Thus, transformational leaders were seen to have high ethical and moral standards or potential to develop such standards (following Kanungo and Mendonca, 1996). The strength of the association lies in the interpersonal relationship between the primary actors.

The implementation of the association requires leaders to be inspirational and able to overcome environmental and organisational barriers for the achievement of the SME's vision and mission. By building meaning, purpose and values, the leader enables staff to release their potential for the achievement of long-term objectives. Internal structures and systems are realigned when necessary and jobs are redesigned to ensure they are significant and challenging (following Covey, 1996) for the performance of task requirements. Transformational leaders build relationships through motivation and empowerment, open and honest communication, team leadership, and an understanding and embracing, of diversity.

In contrast to a transactional leader, a transformational leader encourages 'eustress', the arousal state where people are engaged and working to optimal levels (following Selye, 1987) as opposed to 'distress' where anxiety and impaired performance result in ill-health or burnout. The transformational leader does so by providing a secure base, nurturing creativity, and inspiring people to reach peak performance (Bass and Avolio, 1994; Goleman, 2006). Such leaders have often been described as charismatic.

A limitation of transformational theory, therefore, lies in the notion of charisma. Charismatic leaders are seen to have charm, highly developed intrapersonal and interpersonal skills, a warm personality, magnetism and allure (following Northouse, 2004). People appear to be drawn to their company and want to work with leaders with those attributes. Partly this may be because followers project, from a Freudian perspective, an idealised notion of leadership on to that person (following Kets de Vries, 1993). Similarly, and also from a Freudian perspective, followers may transfer their feelings for significant others in their past on to their organisational leader (following Fincham and Rhodes, 2005). Many leaders of financial institutions that have experienced difficulties in the global financial crisis have been described as charismatic.

Another limitation is that it is often argued that to be a transformational leader, a person needs to have their leadership skills developed. Such skills are said to include managing your own performance, learning how to create a productive environment, learning how to self-assess the impact of those skills, and learning how to calculate the business benefits of being a transformational leader. What still remains unclear, however, is how best these skills might be learned (following Fincham and Rhodes, 2005; French et al., 2008; Leitch Review of Skills Report, 2006) and implemented.

Authentic leadership theory

More recently, authentic leadership has been seen as a conduit for change.

Authentic leadership is seen to be

> a *process that draws from both positive psychological capacities and a highly developed organizational context, which results in both greater self-awareness and self-regulated positive behaviours on the part of leaders and associates, fostering positive self-development.* (Luthans and Avolio, 2003: 243)

An authentic leader must be self-aware and self-accepting (Gardner et al., 2005) and display confidence, hope, optimism, and resilience (Gardner and Schermerhorn Jr., 2004). Gardner and Schermerhorn Jr. (2004) and May et al. (2003) suggest that displaying positive psychological capabilities assists leaders to frame moral dilemmas, respond transparently, and act as ethical role models. All of these attributes are considered to be part of a professional approach to leadership in an SME.

Furthermore, leaders must be authentic in their actions and relationships. Such relationships are characterised by transparency, openness, and trust; guidance towards worthy objectives; and with an emphasis on self-development (May et al., 2003) and follower development (Gardner et al., 2005). By so doing, authentic leaders help to build a positive and productive organisational climate in which their followers' motivational tendencies are enhanced (Avolio and Luthans, 2006). While these arguments have been drawn from research in large organisations, they equally may be applied to a leader in an SME.

Developing leaders and leadership

The aforementioned theories provide a number of ideas about the nature of leadership. What they do not reveal is how leaders might be developed, nor do they address what leadership development might mean within the context of an SME.

SMEs appeared to have been abandoned by government and universities when it comes to skills development. Individuals are left to their own motivation for the development of their skills, particularly in relation to leadership. But such development ought to be a shared responsibility between government, the tertiary education sector, and SMEs. The focus ought to be on the development of the skills appropriate for enabling individuals to ensure professionalism within their SME. That is, there needs to be a move beyond the development of technical skills to the development of skills that are seen to be economically valuable to the individual, the SME, and society.

Such skills are often termed *soft skills*. Leadership skills are a good example for such movement.

Moreover, the development of leadership skills as an underpinning to the development of professionalism within SMEs seems to be an imperative for improving national competitiveness during times of economic uncertainty. SME employers need to take responsibility for leadership development, and the government ought to ensure that learning opportunities appropriate to their needs are supported and incentivised.

There is a range of ways such incentivisation could occur. A national award could be offered similar to that of the Australian Quality Awards. Such an award would help raise the profile of SMEs who demonstrate a drive towards professionalism. Best practice ought to be identified and encouraged. Access opportunities for individuals need to be improved, particularly within the tertiary education sector. A new economy needs to be developed between higher education and SMEs.

What I mean by leadership development

Leadership development emphasises social capital through building networked relationships, enhancing cooperation, and creating organisational values, such as commitment, trust, and respect. Such development also aligns with the suggested qualities outlined in Chapter 6. Leadership development considers not only the leadership process but also the role of followers.

The primary focus of leadership development ought to be on strategies to build your interpersonal competence. Such competence includes self-awareness as outlined in Chapter 7 and mindfulness as outlined in Chapter 8. The intention is to build your leadership capability by broadening your range of knowledge, skills, and abilities. Such development ought to include recognition and integration of appropriate adult learning, including transformative learning theories, as discussed in Chapter 9.

Transformative learning theories focus on the need to include early life experiences where the role of the parent is fundamental to developing concern for others and society, the promotion of maturity, self-efficacy and worth, and the development of appropriate values and principles within their children. Such theories align with the suggested qualities required for professionalism in SMEs as explored in Chapter 6 and accord with the theory of transactional analysis as outlined in Chapter 7.

It is well recognised that a competent leader adds value to an organisation whether that organisation is large and complex or an SME. Not all leaders are born. Most need some level of development. Thus, leadership development also ought to be part of an SME's strategic thinking in terms of the skills required for surviving and thriving.

Your development as a leader in your SME ought to be based on the premise that SMEs operate in volatile and uncertain environments. Thus, your development ought to be about dealing with complexity, ambiguity, and uncertainty as opposed to preparing you for a world that is stable and predictable—one where you are in full control of information and where your decisions are precise and binding. Your development therefore ought to be evolutionary, transformational, and continual. It also ought to provide you with skills that are portable, transferable, and able to meet future market needs.

Complexity is a common theme in current international management literature. Although mostly focussing on large organisations, and in particular, public services, the premise also holds for SMEs. A 2006 study by Prosser and his colleagues in Wales suggested that complexity was a major challenge for organisations undergoing transformational change. In Northern Ireland, Birrell (2008) explored public sector reform, noting a continuing agenda public sector reform since the restoration of devolution in 1999. He examined the range of reforms, structural changes, and the principles used to underpin the reform process. The number of issues confronted suggested a highly complex operating environment for the public sector.

It may be that many models of organisational development, including leadership development, set as they often are in large organisations may seem outside the scope of organisational life within an SME. The reality is, however, that whatever the type and size of the organisation, my narrative concerns the development of people. Put to one side, therefore, notions of gender, nationality, organisational size, hierarchy, bureaucracy, the plethora of research developed in North American and European contexts, and stay focused on the notion of leadership development being an essential prerequisite for the professionalism of your SME.

Rather, be aware that tensions will exist between a recognised need for development and the pull of the workplace to ensure your availability at all times. It will be a fine balancing act but one that nonetheless ought to be undertaken. Equally, be aware that if you do engage in leadership development, that attempts to implement your new skills may not always meet with immediate success. You will need to be patient, self-confident, and persistent.

Leadership development is usually effective. Such effectiveness will be influenced by the learning environment, the quality of development to which you are exposed, the context of the development, your willingness to engage openly with new learning, and your willingness to implement your new learning in the workplace. Equally there may be other factors such as the organisational environment in which you attempt to apply your new skills (following Sheehan, 2000), gender, age, and diversity.

My argument in this section is based on an assumption that you will be a willing participant in your development. You are interested in ways that you might improve your performance. If you seek to enhance your development needs because you have been required to as part of new government regulations, as an outcome of performance management, or because you have been told to undertake a particular learning programme for which you can see no immediate benefit, then it is unlikely that you will engage to the extent required.

The notion of professionalism for SMEs is a complex one. Such complexity recognises the need for development of task-based competencies. Equally, leadership development requires a level of affective commitment that may occur through coaching, mentoring, and/or action learning approaches to leadership development. Your individual development is a fundamental part of enabling you to cope with change and to facilitate change within your SME.

Any reluctance on your part to do so may be viewed by an owner/manager or by your staff as suggesting a lack of confidence and an unwillingness to engage in self-development. Such a view may have negative connotations for your role within the SME.

Summary

It has been argued that leadership is paramount to the effective operation of an SME. In this chapter some of the major theories of leadership have been covered and an argument has been advanced for how leaders might be developed.

Leadership obviously does not occur in a vacuum. Rather, a leader is part of a team and that team also bears responsibility for ensuring SME effectiveness. In the next chapter, therefore, the notion of team learning is addressed.

Chapter 11

Team Learning

The team that plays together stays together (with acknowledgement to the hundreds of people who have said so).

Introduction

In Chapter 9, I explored some of the theories of adult learning. While I have a particular understanding of these theories and a lean towards those I favour, I do not mean to suggest that any one theory or type of learning is necessarily better than any other. Rather, my argument is that there ought to be a general awareness and understanding in SMEs of the various theories. Such awareness will enable an informed decision to be made about the type of theory, or theories, most applicable for helping you, and your SME colleagues, to learn to become more professional. Your choice may depend on your role and the type of work you do, the tasks performed, your maturity level, and that of your staff, and the environment within which you operate (following Love et al., 2004).

This chapter commences with an explanation of what team learning entails. It is argued that team learning enables the team to come to a deeper understanding of each other so that they work more closely and harmoniously together to achieve the SME's goals. One way to do so is by ensuring there are meaningful conversations. Thus, the next two sections cover meaningful conversations and how to hold a meaningful conversation.

Then follows two sections on the roles required to ensure team learning occurs. The first section is entitled roles for team learning, and the second is entitled roles for SME team learning. The penultimate section in this chapter suggests ways for identifying that team learning is occurring. A summary concludes the chapter.

What team learning entails

As the name implies, team learning is about people in an SME learning together, rather than as individuals. Such learning may be particularly relevant to SMEs because it is often asserted by owners and managers of SMEs that it is difficult for them or individual staff to attend any type of formal training programme. They argue that it is difficult to release staff or difficult to find the time or that the learning programme offered is not relevant to their needs.

Team learning may, therefore, be more suitable to your needs.

Team learning enables the team to come to a deeper understanding of each other so that they work more closely and harmoniously together to achieve the SME's goals. Rather than operate as individuals, they work on behalf of each other. The synergy thus created ensures that the whole is greater than the sum of the parts. Value is added. Individuals align as a unit that becomes self-sustaining and self-perpetuating.

By self-sustaining, I mean they continue their efforts, rarely faltering in their ability to work together for the common good of the SME.

By self-perpetuating, I mean that they imbue the spirit of the way they work into all that they do. Employees new to the SME connect to the feeling evident within the workplace. They pick up on the *vibe*. They adapt easily to how things are done and quickly comply with expectations.

Such SMEs have meaningful conversations. A meaningful conversation ought to mean that there are no *undiscussables*. Undiscussables are issues which most people working in the SME know exist but which they individually and/or collectively decide not to discuss. Such disinclination may impact inappropriately on the effectiveness of the SME. I am here arguing that if undiscussables can be raised and discussed in a climate of openness and honesty and without fear of retribution for the expression of constructive opinions, then the issues may be surfaced and resolved. In a professional SME, there would be very few, if any, undiscussables worthy of note.

A word of caution also needs to be offered. Such a desire may be an ideal aspiration, but the reality may be somewhat different. It is unlikely that people will reveal all or everything about themselves. Indeed, it may be psychologically dangerous for them to do so. Honesty and openness are desired states, but they may also be perilous ones. Nonetheless, agreeing a process by which such conversations may be held could be a useful starting point[8].

Meaningful conversations

Large organisations love meetings. They think that gathering a group of people together in one room for a two—or three-hour meeting will enable greater discussions and debate about issues which will then lead to better decision making. What they forget, however, is that some of those people are lost in their own self-importance, intent on playing politics, or focussed on impressing their manager. They facilitate the process of discussion and outcome by way of lengthy agendas and minutes.

Agendas and minutes are a great way to kill meaningful conversations during the meeting.

The agenda often is set by the chair of the meeting. While the chair may circulate a message prior to the meeting, asking for items for the agenda, they then choose what items actually make it to the agenda; or they place your item so far down the list that time does not allow your item to be discussed. Your item is 'held over' to the next meeting. By then, of course, the time to deal with the issue has passed.

Similarly, minutes are supposed to reflect what is discussed at the meeting. They also are used to provide action points and an outcome in terms of a person responsible for completing the action and a completion date for that action. In the often 'too busy to read lengthy documents' climate in many large organisations, minutes are often presented in abbreviated form of actions to be taken. A person who has attended the meeting will be left wondering if those minutes bear any resemblance to what they recall being discussed. Moreover, the minutes are often distributed sometime after the completion of the meeting, perhaps even just prior to the next meeting. Unless people attending the meeting have kept careful and detailed notes, they may be left vulnerable to criticism for a failure to complete an agreed action.

Then there is the meeting and its aftermath. At the meeting, the chair will frequently dominate proceedings. Unless they are a skilled facilitator, they will overlook or choose to ignore input from others. Often, they do so

---

[8] For a very useful process for discussing the undiscussables, see Dick, B. (1997). Discussing the undiscussable: A workbook for improving group effectiveness and openness [on line]. Available at: http://www.scu.edu.au/schools/gcm/ar/arp/dtuwb.html.

because they fear being challenged. Thus, they do not encourage debate or discussion; they merely seek rubber-stamp approval for their ideas.

Many of these types of meetings are soon seen as pointless and irrelevant. People attending, or required to attend, such meetings inevitably overtly or covertly resist involvement. They absent themselves from the meeting in body and/or in spirit. Such meetings tend to drain time and energy from participants. People begin to wish they were elsewhere, withdraw, daydream, become anxious, and only involve themselves in a cursory manner.

Chisholme (2009) provides some insight into such meetings in large organisations using a case-study approach with three diverse organisations. Case study one involved a medical device company (MDC). Formed in 1979 in the US, to respond to the needs of the medical community for innovative products, MDC expanded rapidly. By 2002, it employed approximately 13,500 people, with about 4,000 employed in Europe. Arguably, it was considered to be one of the leading medical device companies in the world, with a focus on producing products for minimally invasive therapies for the treatment of cardiovascular disease, vascular disease, and non-vascular disease.

The management group met monthly, with each meeting lasting five to six hours. Formally, the group lacked a shared sense of purpose and belonging. Individuals struggled with their role and authority, and lacked clarity about their role and function. Informally, there was a shared sense of each individual's purpose in the group that largely stemmed from reflections of interpersonal behaviour on inter-group dynamics. Lack of purpose and understanding manifested in individual anxiety and social defence behaviours. Group members exhibited signs of covert and unhelpful practice within the organisation, which was seen as destabilising. Staff resistance to their power and identity resulted because of poor leadership from the senior management group.

In turn, feelings of anxiety permeated the senior management team. Social defence mechanisms worsened. Hidden agendas flourished. There was a lack of affinity for others and a contrasting concern for self. Complex issues were suppressed or avoided by individuals as trust deteriorated. The blame game was played. Managers blamed the environment, the system, the organisational structure, processes used, their staff, and each other. They displaced their anxiety rather than dealing with it through a meaningful conversation.

Case study two related to a software company, TSC. TSC, founded in 2001 with a merger of five companies, specialised in life and materials science modelling and simulations, informatics, nanotechnology, and scientific operating platform technology in the biopharmaceutical industry.

It delivered software and service solutions to pharmaceutical, biotechnology, and industrial chemical research organisations and to materials-based industries, including automotive, aerospace, electronics, and energy. It also serviced major pharmaceutical corporations and academic and government laboratories. It employed 550 staff worldwide, with 60% of its employees being PhD-qualified scientists.

Top management had high employee turnover, with one vice president, having seventeen managers in ten years. The market was static and facing a reduction in value, rather than opportunity. There were concerns about return on investment, resulting in pressure on staff to sell more products and to deliver new product innovation quicker.

TSC faced high market expectations for new products, expectations that the research and development arm was unable to meet. There were concerns about current and future profitability of the European business. Only one person in the senior management group had experience of management outside the company.

The senior management group, comprising six heads of department, met monthly and shared responsibility for the conduct of the meeting. Meetings appeared to be open but often the group had to rely on limited information. An understanding of the business performance at a European level was lacking because they only had access to global data. There was a realisation, however, that business performance was poor. The group tended to rely on the US parent company. Decisions made were of a regional tactical nature rather than strategic. There internal group struggles concerning leadership and the company culture appeared to be a nebulous concept. These struggles were acknowledged by the chief executive officer.

At one meeting, there were a number of items on the agenda for discussion. They included, developing a positive culture and a cohesive unit, work to enhance peoples' understanding of what other departments do, the general business plan, and adding value to the workplace by introducing group activities and social events. There also was a realisation that some managers were unsure of their managerial control responsibilities, they did not know how to deal with difficult issues, there was limited trust and openness within the group, and they did not know how to deal with conflict. All these issues were resulting in anxiety at a group and individual level.

Participants in this case study admitted that they did not address the issues. They simply hoped to avoid them and that by so doing, the issues would dissipate. They too displaced their anxiety rather than dealing with it through a meaningful conversation.

Case study three involved a professional sound equipment company (PSEC) that was founded in 1973 by two entrepreneurs. The company is based in the UK and Switzerland. PSEC provided audio mixing consoles and related equipment to emerging music touring businesses and to recording studios and radio broadcast stations. They were very successful, with their equipment being associated with the creation of the *British Sound*. An innovative transportable mixing desk, a device used for the purposes of live performances, quickly became popular with bands and performers such as Pink Floyd, Texas, and Bryan Adams. The company has a network of eighty-eight distributors selling and supporting its products worldwide.

While a profitable organisation, they operated in a competitive market place. The management group was facing a number of challenges including an aging workforce, an eroding analogue technology, significant opportunities in digital technology, and skills shortages in new technology areas. There also was pressure from the parent company to be more innovative more quickly in order to meet customer demand in a growing and competitive professional sound market. The need for change was recognised.

At one stage, the managing director gave a presentation to the workforce. The presentation covered group performance, product development, facilities upgrade, and new product presentations. While the messages delivered were mostly of a positive nature, feedback from staff after the meeting indicated a mostly negative interpretation of what had been presented. Culturally, the workforce was bruised from recent redundancies and not receptive to positive news. A lack of trust and suspicion about motives appeared to permeate the workforce, conditions that often are indicative of the psychological withdrawal of employees.

Stacey (1996) asserted that in destabilising conditions, taken-for-granted assumptions ought to be discarded. In their place, the creation of an environment conducive to question ought to occur.

Redundancies often leave a bitter taste in the mouths of those remaining in the workforce. They are worried if they might be next and filled with anxiety. This is not the time for a manager to assume that they can shape an employee's feelings. This is a time for the restoration of the psychological safety net. People need to feel that they can be themselves without fear of penalty. They need to know that they can voice their opinion without fear of retribution or punishment. Managers have to be adept at dealing with the expression of a depth of feeling inherent at such times. They need a high level of emotional intelligence. They need to be able to hold meaningful conversations.

Meaningful conversations are first and foremost about cultural change (Chinowsky and Molenaar, 2007; Chinowsky et al., 2007). People need to be receptive to new ideas, and there needs to be support and encouragement for all to be involved. The first responsibility for so doing lies with the owner/manager of the SME. It is their role to ensure that such conversations occur and that good ideas are identified and explored in depth.

An SME in which meaningful conversations are held will reflect on their meetings and conversations. They will explore not only the task elements of their meeting, but they will also take the time to explore the processes used. In this way, they are able to identify areas for improvement. By so doing, they will learn to function more effectively.

Meaningful conversations enable deep, as opposed to surface, learning to occur.

Surface learning transpires when team members of the SME respond to problems or issues by detecting errors and correcting them but failing to address why those errors occurred in the first place. The focus is on solving the problem rather than exploring the actions that enabled the problem to occur. Failure to delve more deeply into why a problem occurred suggests an organisation where punishment of mistakes and fear of failure permeate organisational culture. Such a culture inhibits deeper learning. The status quo is maintained and errors continue to occur.

Deep learning, by contrast, means that the new meanings and understanding discovered by team members contributes to deeper self and team understanding by way of critical reflection. The perceived problem is not dealt with in isolation. Rather all avenues are explored. Those avenues might be a lack of awareness or training, exploration of group norms and leadership behaviour, and examination of the SME's policies and procedures or tactical or strategic intentions. Such understanding helps to avoid potential areas where problems may occur and ensures that those problems do not reoccur. Thus the propagation of new learning facilitates a change in knowledge and understanding, competencies and routines (following Holt et al., 2000), group norms, and organisational climate and culture. Organisational memory is enhanced (following Love et al., 2004).

Such learning is neither ideology or idealistic. Rather, it is realistic, practical, challenging, and doable. It will enhance team learning. It will improve productivity.

How to hold a meaningful conversation

An SME that adopts team learning will demonstrate a great deal of meaningful conversations. Meaningful conversations move beyond the realm of dialogue, in which ideas or information are exchanged between parties. Indeed, they move beyond the realm of debate and discussion typified by meetings in which a chair or vocal participant dominates proceedings.

Rather, meaningful conversations require participants to move beyond the surface exchange of data, into a deeper exploration of the assumptions underpinning ideas, into the meanings behind those ideas, and into making sense of, and understanding, at a deeper level, what a person is saying and why.

Such exploration requires a number of insights from SME employees. It requires that

- they accept that differing opinions and ideas will be advanced;
- those opinions and ideas are freely given and open to challenge;
- there will be no punishment or penalty to pay for ideas that are offered contrary to popular dogma;
- all ideas are offered in the spirit of team learning;
- ideas offered do not breach the fundamental rights of others;
- ideas are offered in accordance with legal requirements; that is, they are not sexist, racist, homophobic, ageist, or deliberately inflammatory;
- ideas advanced are explored in depth, taking into account the assumptions behind those ideas;
- all members of the SME, no matter what rank or profession, are able to, and encouraged to, express their ideas;
- ideas freely offered will be discussed on merit as opposed to the rank or influence of the person advancing the idea;
- there will be support and encouragement for the expression of ideas;
- people listen actively;
- people do not get defensive;
- inquisitiveness is encouraged;
- early adjudication of discussion is resisted;
- critical reflection occurs;
- there will be no attempt at one-upmanship (following Senge, 1992; Senge et al., 1994); and

- if need be, the services of a trained facilitator are used to help put a process in place for successful outcomes.

Roles for team learning

It is well known that in any team, people play a role or a number of roles. Indeed, the number of roles played vary from four (Parker, 1990; Senge, 1992) to fifteen (Davis et al., 1992). Clearly, roles played in an SME will depend on the size of the SME. This section, therefore, is predicated on an assumption that the SME will consist of three or more people.

It also needs to be understood that when talking about *role* in this section, I do not mean the role as specified by the job function, task or responsibility, position or profession. Rather, here I refer to role in terms of a particular intention or action carried out by an individual in their daily work activity and that may be seen to guide or contribute to the team's success. The roles may vary from time to time, based on a particular way of working or on what role a person feels comfortable adopting in a group. They are interchangeable and, in a small SME, a number of roles may be performed by one person. Alternatively, because of the number of people in an SME, there may be an absence of some roles.

Arguably, the most well-known exponent of the number of team roles is Belbin (1993). Originally suggesting that there were eight team roles, he later revised his thoughts to suggest that there were nine. Those nine were as follows:

1. **Plant**: the person is creative, imaginative, serious minded, knowledgeable, a problem solver, and unorthodox
2. **Resource investigator**: an extrovert who is enthusiastic, curious, open to exploring possibilities, develops contacts, and responds to challenge
3. **Coordinator**: a person who is mature, confident, calm, controlled, able to clarify goals, encourages decision making, delegates, and is a good chair
4. **Shaper**: challenges and thrives on pressure, overcomes obstacles, outgoing and dynamic
5. **Monitor evaluator**: strategic and discerning, restrained, cautious, sees all options, and judges accurately
6. **Teamworker**: co-operative, mild, perceptive, diplomatic, a good listener, builds on ideas, and is sensitive

7. **Implementer**: disciplined, reliable, hard-working, conservative, and efficient
8. **Completer/finisher**: conscientious, meticulous, seeks out errors and omissions, follows through, and delivers on time
9. **Specialist**: single-minded, dedicated, and is able to provide rare and specialised skills

Roles for SME team learning

I argue here that a professional SME will require at least four roles. They are as follows:

1. Instigator—the person who takes responsibility for initiating action for the benefit of team learning
2. Role model—the person to whom others look to provide wisdom and counsel and to guide them in meaningful conversations
3. Protector—the person who protects the interests of the less capable members of the team to ensure that they are not disenfranchised
4. Reflector—the person who leads critical reflection of processes utilised within the team learning environment

Such roles may not always be apparent or visible to team members. They may shift over time and as circumstances necessitate. They may emerge by osmosis or serendipity.

By osmosis, I mean that the roles performed will be gradual and often unconscious. The knowledge generated from the effective performance of the roles will be absorbed in an evolutionary way into team learning. It is the continual exposure of team members to the actions of the role adopters that will enable learning to occur gradually and thus become part of a synergistic whole as opposed to being imposed by some formal process.

By serendipity, I mean that the learning outcomes from team learning will become apparent over time and as a process of discovery. Such discovery will be seen as useful to team learning and performance.

The team learning that emerges in these ways will enhance functional performance and SME productivity.

Nonetheless, people will need to understand the roles being performed and the value of enabling the roles to be acted out in a way that is natural and tolerant of different motivations. Meaningful conversations may serve as an ideal process to more deeply understand the roles being enacted and how those roles contribute to team learning. Understanding also requires that people are flexible in their approach and realise that their transformation is both beneficial and continuous (following Raiden and Dainty, 2006). A tolerance of the diversity and individualism inherent in an SME therefore is important, as is the ability to understand, and the willingness to accept, that people learn in many different ways. Some of those ways have been discussed in Chapter 8.

Some SMEs have a daily routine directed by customer demand for that day. A small medical or dental practice may be busier on a given day because of the health needs of their patients on that day. By contrast, a small construction firm may be more projects driven.

A project may have been obtained through a competitive tendering process, an alliance with others, or through a network arrangement or joint venture (following Butcher, 2011). In managing a project, an SME employee may have to address different customer expectations, attend to supplier issues, or deal with subcontractor performance during the life of the project. They also may have to deal with changing environmental conditions.

Identifying that team learning is occurring

You may well ask how you will be able to identify that team learning is occurring. You may also be wondering how team learning is contributing to performance and productivity in your SME. There are reasonable musings. There are some things you can seek to identify:

The first thing to understand is that team learning ought to be part of your drive to the establishment of your SME as a professional organisation. Thus, team learning is part of your cultural change process.

There is neither a descriptive or prescriptive solution to how you might do so. There are some steps that you may like to take that will facilitate the process, and they are depicted elsewhere in this book.

SMEs face a variety of challenging and complex business situations. Many of those challenges are similar. Equally, many are unique. Different situations call for different solutions. Flexibility, the ability to adapt, and the ability to understand and tolerate ambiguity are key concepts that need to influence your cultural shift.

You may argue that your SME is not large enough to enable team learning, or meaningful conversations, to occur. Equally, you may suggest that your staff are not mature enough to engage with the process of change. The financial crisis may mean that you want to focus solely on *making money*. You may also think, *why fix it if it is not broken*? These may be relevant arguments. On the other hand, they may suggest a blinkered approach to your business and how that business might be improved. Your focus ought to be not only on task completion and the performance targets but also on continuous improvement.

Such arguments need to be considered. If you truly desire becoming more professional, then you need to be able to reconcile your arguments within a framework of change in an often uncertain and ambiguous business climate. Your learning, and that of your staff, needs to be embraced within a change process that recognises current business opportunities, the strategies in place to meet a desired future state, the organisational structure, and the culture permeating all that occurs in your SME.

Furthermore, you need to be open to understanding that team learning is not a destination, it is a journey. The destination is unknown although you have some ideas of where you would like to go. To facilitate travel on your journey, you will need to embrace new knowledge, import learning ideas from other fields, such as benchmarking against other SMEs, formal and informal learning opportunities, networking, and engaging with learning and development providers.

You will recognise that team learning is occurring when

- you notice that meaningful conversations are occurring;
- knowledge is shared openly;
- people begin to look for more challenging tasks;
- staff seek opportunities for more responsibility;
- absenteeism and turnover declines;
- conflict situations are reduced;
- customers express satisfaction and praise;
- suppliers comment on performance; and
- performance management becomes a conversation rather than an onerous task.

Summary

This chapter has covered the necessity for team learning to be an integral part of an SME as it moves towards being more professional. It was argued that one way for such learning to occur was to hold meaningful conversations. Roles for team learning also were addressed and ways in which team learning could be identified as occurring were suggested.

The next chapter focuses on systems thinking.

Chapter 12

Systems Thinking

Introduction

Like large organisations, SMEs do not operate in a vacuum. They operate within a socio-economic, political and technological environment which is open and in which chaos is the norm. The best they may hope to achieve is to comprehend that environment, realise that it is subject to constant change, and endeavour to bring some measure of understanding to that chaotic system so that all stakeholders are confident their requirements will be satisfied.

It would be rare to find an SME that operates as a closed system.

That being the case, this chapter discusses the notion of systems thinking. In Chapter 3, it was pointed out that Senge argues that one of the problems of management is that simple solutions are often applied to complex systems problems and that managers tend to think that cause and effect adjoin a temporal and spatial framework.

When such thinking drives action, the most immediate and apparent solutions are implemented, particularly in relation to short-term solutions. But short-term solutions often lead to significant long-term costs. Such thinking also suggests a limited understanding of organisations. Systems' thinking transcends such limitations and enables more appropriate managerial action.

This brief chapter commences with a section called systems thinking explained. In this section, it is argued that appreciation of an SME as a part of a system is important for a deeper understanding and appreciation of Senge's other four disciplines as discussed in earlier chapters and as applied to SMEs.

The next section identifies how you will know systems thinking is occurring. A summary concludes the chapter and briefly introduces the final chapter on change and its consequences.

Systems thinking explained

Understanding the system within which an SME operates requires a number of insights. An owner and/or manager must understand how each individual component of their external and internal environment interrelate and act. Externally, they need to be politically aware, economically astute, technologically confident, and aware of the broader environment within which they operate, such as community concerns, changing demographics that may affect their business, product and service demands, and ethical considerations. They need to be able to see, interpret, and anticipate the forces that may impact the business. They need to be able to connect with wider issues.

Such connection requires an understanding of, and empathy towards, other SMEs, your customers, the community within which you operate, and your supply chain. When financial concerns are paramount, as exacerbated for many by the recent global financial crisis and its aftermath, the temptation is to become contractually harsher with your supply chain or to give the customer a little less. These may be useful short-term strategies for survival, but they will have long-term ramifications. Your actions will have consequences.

You may find that, as recovery occurs, your suppliers no longer want to do business with you, or that their terms become less amenable. More than likely your supply chain is not large, so opportunities for finding new suppliers are limited.

Similarly, you probably do not have an extensive customer base. People have long memories. If they feel they have been mistreated, they will look elsewhere. In the long term, your business will suffer. The quick fix is not the answer.

Professionalism helps indemnify you during such times. Customers and suppliers, who are more than likely suffering themselves, will be receptive to your needs if you treat them in a professional manner. They will understand the need for short-term solutions and help you to achieve those solutions if you maintain a professional relationship.

Internally, connectivity also is important. An owner and/or manager must understand how all parts of their business interrelate, particularly as a business begins to grow or if it has more than one site. Equally, employees of the organisation also need to understand how all parts of the business operate and how the completion of their tasks impacts upon the ability of their colleagues to complete their tasks and to meet customer needs. Roles, responsibilities, accountabilities, and relationships all need to be understood clearly and appropriately administered.

The quick fix also is not the solution internally. Here the temptation is to reduce the number of working hours for employees or to reduce their learning and development opportunities. You may ask them to *do more with less* or to *work smarter, not harder*. Such glib phrases have little meaning and tend to break down trust. Job enlargement, job intensification, and/or deskilling are not useful solutions in professional SMEs. The consequences are changes in commitment and loyalty, loss of valued employees, job dissatisfaction and expressions of intention to leave, and lowered productivity. Employees understand predicaments if you are open and honest with them and work with them to help find more appropriate solutions.

There is no doubt that an owner and/or manager holds the responsibility for organisational performance. Endeavouring to become a more professional SME will mean that systems thinking will need to become an automatic outcome of daily activity. Personal mastery, team learning, mental models, and a shared vision are all embraced by systems thinking (Senge, 1992). It is the glue that binds together the other four disciplines to ensure those four disciplines work in harmony.

How you will know systems thinking is occurring

You may well ask how you will be able to identify systems thinking is occurring. You may also be wondering what such thinking contributes to performance and productivity in your SME. There are some things you can seek to identify.

An SME which understands and inculcates systems thinking will demonstrate the following:

- Early recognition of business opportunities
- Early anticipation of problems likely to occur and their impact
- Team learning
- Better preparedness to meet those problems
- Ability to anticipate the need for change and to adapt quickly to address changing forces
- Improved problem solving
- Better and more intelligent decision making

- Involvement of staff in the problem solving and decision-making processes
- Employees readily adapt to change and embrace new technology
- Employees demonstrate a willingness to learn as part of a continual learning process
- A more professional approach to doing business
- Improved supply chain relationships
- Enhanced customer satisfaction
- Enhanced job satisfaction
- Enhanced profitability

It is unlikely that your SME will become more professional overnight. It is unlikely that your SME will ever be perfect. Perfection is a goal towards which you may aspire. The way to get as near as possible to that goal is to avoid a repetition of mistakes, openly confront and deal with all the issues that may have resulted in those mistakes occurring, remove any semblance of a blame culture, avoid the *quick fix*, and encourage innovation, creativity, experimentation, and risk taking. You also need to share power and limit organisational politics.

Summary

Systems thinking requires the application of holistic approaches to problem solving. If there are policies and procedures in place that contradict each other, they need to be addressed. If operational outcomes do not align with strategies, then adjustments need to be made. If conflicting goals are evident, they need to be adjusted.

The aforementioned suggestions are indicators of the need for change. Change, therefore, needs to be understood, and in particular, the consequences of change need to be identified. The next, and final, chapter does so.

Chapter 13

SME Change and Its Consequences

Introduction

The basic argument offered throughout has been that SMEs need to change, to become more professional in their outlook and approach. In this way, they may be able to deal with the instability, complexity, ambiguity, and uncertainty of change and to cope with the ever-increasing pressures brought by change. Given the focus on change, it seems appropriate, therefore, to discuss some of the theories of organisational change and how such theories may be applied to SMEs.

In this chapter, therefore, some of the theories of organisational change and their application for SMEs are outlined. Many assumptions underpin organisational change so the next section discusses organisational change assumptions. One of the underlying arguments presented is that change ought to be seen to be part of a learning process so the next section discusses the importance of considering change as a learning process.

Change, and learning, does not occur in isolation. A conceptual understanding is important so that change may better be understood, made sense of, and given meaning. Thus, the next section is called the centrality of the conceptualisation of the learning experience.

For many, change also is a difficult and challenging process. New relationships with colleagues, customers, and significant others may need to be formed as an outcome from engaging in change and learning processes. The next section addresses the difficulty of reconstructing relationships. Such difficulty may relate to unfulfilled expectations, and this difficulty is explored in the experience of unfulfilled expectations.

Expectations need to be tempered by tolerance. The importance of a heightened tolerance of others is therefore explored. Understanding others may also mean that people gain a different understanding of themselves. This likelihood is explored in the penultimate section on a heightened understanding of self. A conclusion draws the chapter and the book to a close.

Theories of organisational change (and their application for SMEs)

Organisational change may be seen to be driven by a number of factors, including globalisation, technology, economics, complexity, and socio-political demands. It seems clear that organisations now exist within an *age of discontinuity* (following Drucker, 2008). That is, organisations have not been prepared for the social, economic, political, technological, and environmental demands experienced in recent years. As such, any preconceived formulas for dealing with organisational change are seen to be inadequate in the current environment. Even though Drucker's book was published originally in 1992, his argument still appears to be relevant today.

The focus of change may clearly be contextualised at an organisational level, with many models of change apparent in the organisational change literature. It has variously been suggested that change is incremental, planned, rational, a mixture of radical and incremental, and transformative. In attempting to delineate change processes, many theorists suggest a two—or three-phase approach.

The first phase is termed *first order change*, *single-loop learning*, *surface system learning*, or *adaptive learning*. First-phase change helps an organisation to cope with current problems by focusing on the correction of errors and the completion of tasks. The aim is survival, with little consideration given to what might be learned from addressing the problems at anything more than a superficial level. Broader aspects relating to, for example, addressing the assumptions and core processes underpinning the reasons for errors are not addressed. The same patterns of values, beliefs, and thinking continue in spite of efforts devoted to change, such as performance management, learning and development programmes, and counselling and disciplinary measures.

The second phase is termed *second order change*, *double-loop learning*, *deep system learning*, or *generative learning*. Second-phase change stresses creativity, experimentation, and feedback in a continuous learning process. In second-phase change, more fundamental issues, such as entrenched values, attitudes, and behaviours are addressed. Core processes such as the organisation's strategy, structure, and culture are examined with the intention of addressing the fundamental assumptions within those processes that may lead to error. Such change occurs in an environment where risk taking is encouraged and outcomes are rewarded, rather than punished. The aim is for ongoing systemic change and organisational effectiveness. Continuous improvement becomes an everyday activity and part of the culture.

Senge (1992) argues that organisations need to focus on both first—and second-phase approaches. However, learning aimed at improving how the organisation performs both phases, termed *deuterolearning*, is also seen as important (Cummings and Worley, 1997).

The focus in these models tends to be on organisational learning, with little or no account given to the individual in the learning process (following Sheehan, 2000). Equally, within an organisational change framework, change at the individual level needs to be considered as part of a learning process. Indeed, it may be argued that organisational change is often unsuccessful because management and leaders lack understanding of how individuals are affected by the change process (Sheehan, 2000).

Organisational change assumptions

A number of assumptions are left unexplored in the forgoing arguments. First, the concepts do not entirely account for rapidly changing socio-economic conditions, such as the previously mentioned global financial crisis, so that confusion exists as to whether organisations function within a stable environment or within an environment of uncertainty or discontinuous change. The argument is that SMEs need to be contextualised within a framework of environmental instability, discontinuity and complexity.

Second, there appears to be an assumption that managers are rational and logical human beings, in full control of information, and able to make incremental change (Dunphy and Stace, 1988). But such a notion is outdated and misplaced, as argued earlier.

Third, organisational change processes have marginalised many employees, particularly those in middle management positions (following Snape et al., 1994), and there is a view that managers are only interested in maintaining the status quo (Dunphy and Stace, 1988). It is suggested also that managers are not strategic in their approach to change, often instigating change in an unplanned and reactive manner. Clearly such an approach is flawed for any organisation, let alone an SME.

Fourth, some of the aforementioned arguments are also restricted in terms of second phase change. They fail to account for the experiences of people whose role it is to introduce new learning, knowledge, ideas, and techniques into the workplace. Little is known of the impact of change programs on such persons from their viewpoint, in terms of issues such as learning and implementing the new learning; their involvement in the change process; and the impact on them in terms of the learning. This argument was addressed in Sheehan (2000).

Fifth, debate also centres on the connection, if any, between learning and development and behavioural or attitudinal change in the workplace, the way adults learn, and the links between learning satisfaction and on-the-job performance. Within these debates relationships between variables are often unclear (Sheehan, 2000). In part, this failure relates to limitations associated with the methodologies used. Some methodologies fail to measure the impact of change as a result of exposure to a learning program from an individual standpoint. The individual's voice remains silent. Sheehan's (2000) study enabled some of those voices to be heard, thus enhancing our understanding of the problematic experiences faced by individuals learning, and implementing new learning. Such understanding is applicable to SMEs.

The importance of considering change as a learning process

The concept of learning encompasses more than the acquisition of facts and knowledge. Learning is a dynamic social process occurring within a social context that varies in meaning and understanding for each person. Such variation suggests that learning be envisioned beyond the narrow confines of knowledge enhancement into a broader realm of social and emotional awareness.

Building on the concept of second-phase learning, it may be argued that such learning will enable SME employees to learn and change through critical insight. The ability to learn depends on thinking processes, technical skills, security, role models, interpersonal skills, life pressures, and intrapersonal understanding. It also depends on organisational memory, support, and environment. To learn in this way requires the vision to rethink change in the context of organisational learning, to raise learning issues, and to be able to ask critical questions about the reasons for change. Thus, meaningful conversations, as covered in Chapter 11, are paramount to success.

The centrality of the conceptualisation of the learning experience

SME employees undergoing any type of change process, and particularly one where they are being asked to be more professional in their working relationships, ought to be able to conceptualise their experience. Conceptualisation encompasses employees' broadest understanding of how they give meaning to their individual subjective experience of learning and developing within and beyond the spatio-temporal borders of any learning programme they might attend. Moreover, conceptualisation is used here in the broadest meaning of the term *conceptual*. As such, conceptualisation is seen to vary in profundity, tempered by each employee's introspective ability to cognitively and affectively recall and implement new behaviours and actions.

It may be expected that employees will use their feelings, their perceptions of the feelings of others, their value systems, spatio-temporal perceptions, intuitions, previous experiences, professional standing, feedback, and observations to help them understand their experience and to become more professional. How they conceptualise their experience will impact on the judgements they make about what they could do differently.

Conceptualisation may give employees deeper self-insight and help them to challenge their belief systems so as to cope with individual change requirements. Conceptualisation may, therefore, be seen as part of a critically reflective and deeper self-awareness process.

An awareness of their own actions, and the actions of others, may be a vital insight for an SME employee.

It may enable them to assess their own performance, develop a new appreciation of other people, and enhance understanding of what they could do differently in implementing their learning. The SME will benefit from the transfer of learning.

Becoming more professional may serve as a catalyst for a changed approach to a reconsideration and reformulation of intentions at work. Employees may change how they approach their job, with the intention of improved performance, perhaps turning around a previous philosophy of looking more for what the SME might do for them, rather than what they might do for the organisation.

They are likely to have a desire to do things differently in the workplace.

They may contemplate what they want to achieve in the SME and made a deliberate and considered choice to take responsibility for being more committed members of the SME.

Commitment will lead to a sense of achievement and personal satisfaction.

The development of more fulfilling relationships may occur. Being able to reformulate the assumptions behind their actions and determine strategies to enhance their new understanding may help employees instigate new actions and improve their own performance and the performance of others in the SME.

But there also may be a flow-on effect outside the workplace. There could be change in interpersonal relationships. Such change may be important for a number of reasons. Employees will become more aware of the needs of other people with whom they maintain close relationships, such as their children, other family members, and friends. They may then be prepared to account for these needs in ways that include being assertive rather than aggressive in their interpersonal communication, being more intimate and open in relationships and being more attentive to others.

The changes may result in more secure relationships, improved, healthier relationships and enhanced understanding and valuing of others. Such changes are likely to be reciprocated, resulting in smoother, more positive interpersonal relationships and greater acceptance by others. Relationships that are reinvented and improved, by enhanced patterns of communication, changed power relationships, and new respect and affection for, and from, others, will have positive outcomes for them, their family and friends, and their colleagues, customers, and suppliers.

The difficulty of reconstructing relationships

A cautionary note needs to be sounded. The sense of a redistribution of power may create some difficulty. Perceptions that people hold of others, and the judgements that they made as a result of those perceptions, suggest that there may be some difficulty in reconstructing relationships, no matter how well intentioned the individuals might be towards such change. Emotional interplays may hinder successful outcomes and those interplays need to be well managed.

Some may recognise that their conflict resolution style is inappropriate and attempt to alter that style. For example, previously they may have perceived a loss of face when they withdrew from conflict and thus now have a desire to change to a more appropriate and collaborative mode of action in resolving conflict. While they may be willing to address the situation differently, they may encounter some emotional difficulty with pursuing such an outcome. The intention may be to confront and deal with the issue more appropriately. But some attempts to do so may result in a more aggressive approach to conflict resolution, to the detriment of all parties. Resulting frustration may leave them disillusioned, disappointed, and unwilling to further pursue matters to a more satisfactory conclusion.

Trust in relationships also may suffer. Development and maintenance of trust in interpersonal relationships is important but often difficult to attain. Meeting the challenge, however, is important for positive change outcomes to occur. Otherwise, there may be a likelihood of returning to a previous inappropriate and unsatisfactory mode of action.

Changed social structures as a result of attempts to become more professional may impact on the expectations of employees and the nature of interpersonal relationships within the SME. Unfulfilled expectations ought to be addressed.

The experience of unfulfilled expectations

Employees embracing new ways of working may have an expectation that others will do likewise. They may expect their colleagues to develop or improve through learning at the same rate as they do. If they judge others to be unmotivated or limited in their progress, then difficult situations may arise. Unfulfilled expectations may leave people disillusioned and dissatisfied. They may become frustrated.

It is useful to remember that individuals are the originators of meaning and explanation of their participation in events. An act of interpretation inevitably occurs in the expression of the explanation. Actions interpreted as social loafing, free riding, or inequity will hinder progress. The effort one expends may be impacted upon as a result of a perception of the effort(s) being expended by other SME members.

There may be, therefore, a need to modify expectations of other people. The judgements employees make of others could be turned into learning experiences for themselves. Clearer self-understanding may result along with a commitment to take responsibility for instigating change in the relationship.

Thus, unfulfilled expectations may serve as a catalyst for change in interpersonal relationships. In recalling and reflecting on incidents in which they were frustrated by other people, they may come to an understanding that the event was one of inner conflict. Partly that conflict may arise because they need to understand what is required of them by the other person. While they attempt to adapt their actions and their expectations of others, they may not always be successful because they may sometimes pre-empt their expectations of others. They may then realise they need to lessen or modify those expectations. Mindfulness, as explored in Chapter 8, may be a helpful tool for guiding them to deeper consideration of their thoughts and feelings on these occasions.

By modifying their expectations of others, SME employees may discover that they are able to reconstruct positive and successful relationships with those people. They may be able to see others from a new perspective that in turn enhances their self-understanding and heightens their tolerance of others.

The importance of a heightened tolerance of others

The personal-change process required for individuals in SMEs to become more professional can be an exciting and challenging time. A willingness to address change at a personal level, and support from management in so doing, may help employees become more tolerant of other people. That is to say, they will become more receptive to, and empathic with, the needs of some people—more liberal and open-minded in their thoughts and actions towards them, hold more respect for those people, and be more generous in their understanding of them. Such tolerance will help improve their work and family relationships.

Another importance of a heightened tolerance of other people will be that employees will be able to identify their own shortcomings in relationships, including how they communicate with people and the perceptions they frame of others. Such a realisation will help them to understand that they have a responsibility to improve their communication processes.

One outcome from such a realisation may be that employees will now be more prepared to manage the interactions between themselves and other people. Interaction management includes being more prepared to listen actively to others and to express themselves openly, rather than aggressively, to further improve interpersonal relationships.

They will have a deeper understanding of, and regard for, the views of other people because of their new way of looking at, and understanding, them. They are more likely to be willing to listen to others' opinions and to be less judgemental. They also are likely to appreciate that other people have as much right as they do to express an opinion.

Such understanding and appreciation will enable them to be more at ease with people and more confident about how they communicate with others.

A heightened tolerance and acceptance of others is paramount to positive working relationships within SMEs and within a broader multicultural community.

Moreover, in discussing the concept of situational sensitivity within a framework of 'continuing professional moral education,' Bagnall (1998: 326) highlights the importance of tolerance of others in a postmodern society. In order to work as professionals, SME employees need to demonstrate a tolerance of others. Such tolerance embraces recognition of the uniqueness of others, and respect for that uniqueness, even when such uniqueness may challenge, or conflict with, a person's preferences. In coming to such conclusions, employees will also demonstrate a heightened understanding of themselves.

A heightened understanding of self

As well as becoming more tolerant of others as they become more professional, employees will have the opportunity to develop a heightened understanding of themselves as a result of their experiences and understandings. A heightened understanding of *self* encompasses being open to the ideas, opinions, and feelings of other people and becoming less critical of others. Such understanding indicates that people are more confident about themselves, which will enable them to develop stronger relationships with other people. By critically reflecting on and appraising themselves, including their thoughts, feelings, and actions, employees will come to new understandings of what it means to work in their SME.

They will feel invigorated by their understanding of themselves and others and by the reconstructed relationships that develop. Such awareness may vary in scope and intensity for each employee. While some will be more attuned to the needs of others, and more reflective and understanding of themselves, others may continue to struggle.

Nonetheless, it is a struggle worth pursuing in the move to becoming more professional. A heightened self-understanding will manifest in enlightenment and confidence that, in turn, will result in a cycle of self-growth and improved relationships both at work and in peoples' wider social milieu.

There is another, perhaps unanticipated consequence for helping employees to develop in becoming more professional. Their new actions and reactions may, in turn, determine the actions of others in a cyclical process of action and reaction. This argument is consistent with the process of reciprocal determinism as defined by Bandura (1977), in which peoples' behaviours, cognition, and the environment constantly influence one another.

Conclusion

The thrust of this chapter has been that SMEs need to be aware of organisational change, its subtleties, and its consequences. It was suggested that a sound understanding of some of the theories of organisational change would assist with developing such awareness. A cautionary note was sounded that organisational and individual change can be fraught with difficulty. Dealing with those difficulties can result in more meaningful change.

The book has been underpinned by a similar argument.

SMEs operate in an era of uncertainty, ambiguity, and complexity. The ways that issues and problems have been dealt with in the past no longer suit SMEs facing the need for continuous change. Change is exacerbated by the socio-economic climate and by political and technological requirements. Equally, customer demand for better service ought to be a catalyst for change.

It has been argued throughout that such change may be facilitated by SMEs becoming more professional. A set of qualities necessary for professionalism were presented, and arguments were made throughout for tools and techniques suitable for becoming more professional.

References

ABS (2011). Counts of Australian Businesses, including Entries and Exits, June 2003 to June 2007, Catalogue number 8165.0, downloaded on 10 January 2011 from http://www.abs.gov.au.

ABS (2012). Counts of Australian Businesses, including Entries and Exits, June 2007 to June 2011, Catalogue number 8165.0, downloaded 11 July 2012 from http://www.abs.gov.au.

ACCI Small Business Survey (2012). Identifying National Trends and Conditions for the Small Business Sector, downloaded on 19 November 2012 from http://www.acci.asn.au.

AIM (2011). About AIM, downloaded on 14 February 2011 from http://www.aim.com.au.

APSC (2011). APS Code of Conduct, downloaded on 10 January 2011 from http://www.apsc.gov.au/conduct.

Allinson, C. W., and Hayes, J. (1988). The Learning Styles Questionnaire: an Alternative to Kolb's Inventory. *Journal of Management Studies*, 25(3), 269-88.

Australian Bureau of Statistics (2012). Consumer Price Index, Australia, September 2012, Catalogue Number 6401.0, downloaded on 25 October 2012 from http://www.abs.gov.au/ausstats/abs@.nsf/mf/6401.0?OpenDocument.

Avolio, B. J., and Luthans, F. (2006). *The High Impact Leader: Moments Matter for Accelerating Authentic Leadership Development*. New York: McGraw-Hill.

Baer, R. A., Smith, G. T., and Allen, K. B. (2004). Assessment of mindfulness by self-report: The Kentucky inventory of mindfulness skills, *Assessment*, 11(3), 191-206.

Bagnall, R. G. (1994). *Conceptualising Adult Education for Research and Development*. Queensland: Centre for Skill Formation Research and Development, Faculty of Education.

Bagnall, R. G. (1998). Moral education in a postmodern world: Continuing professional education, *Journal of Moral Education*, 27(3), 313-31.
Bandura, A. (1969). *Principles of Behavior Modification*. New York: Holt, Rinehart and Winston.
Bandura, A. (1977). *Social Learning Theory*. Englewood Cliffs, NJ: Prentice-Hall.
Bass, B. M. (1985). *Leadership and Performance Beyond Expectations*. New York: Free Press.
Bass, B. M., and Avolio, B. J. (1994). *Improving Organizational Effectiveness Through Transformational Leadership*. Thousand Oaks, CA: Sage.
Beer, M., Voelpel, S. C., Leibold, M., and Tekie, E. B. (2005). Strategic management as organizational learning: developing fit and alignment through a disciplined process, *Long Range Planning*, 38, 445-65.
Beitel, M., Ferrer, E., and Cecero, J. (2005). Psychological mindedness and awareness of self and others, *Journal of Clinical Psychology*, 61(6), 739-50.
Belbin, R. M. (1993). *Team Roles at Work*. Oxford: Butterworth-Heinemann.
Berne, E. (1964). *Games People Play: The Psychology of Human Relationships*. New York: Grove Press.
Birrell, D. (2008). The final outcomes of the review of public administration in Northern Ireland: Tensions and compatibility with devolution, parity and modernization, *Public Administration*, 86(3), 779-93.
Bishop, S. R., Lau, M., Shapiro, S., Carlson, L., Anderson, N. D., Carmody, J., Segal, Z. V., Abbey, S., Speca, M., Velting, D., and Devins, G. (2004). Mindfulness: A proposed operational definition, *Clinical Psychology: Science and Practice*, 11(3), 230-41.
Blake, R., and Mouton, J. (1964). *The Managerial Grid: The Key to Leadership Excellence*. Houston: Gulf Publishing.
Blewitt, J. (2010). Higher education for a sustainable world, *Education and Training*, 52(6/7), 477-88.
Bostrom, R. P., Olfman, L., and Sein, M. K. (1993). Learning Styles and End-User Training: a first step. *MIS Quarterly*, 17(1), 118-20.
Boulton, J., and Allen, P. (2007). Complexity perspective, in M. Jenkins, V. Ambrosini, and N. Collier (Eds.), *Advanced Strategic Management: A Multi-Perspective Approach*. Basingstoke: Palgrave Macmillan, pp. 215-34.
Bourne, G. (2005). A sustainable planet—a future for Australia, 2005 Annual Hawke Lecture, The Bob Hawke Prime Ministerial Centre, University of South Australia, 9 November.

Briggs, J., and Peat, F. (2000). *Seven Life Lessons of Chaos: Spiritual Wisdom from the Science of Change*. New York: Harper Perennial.
Brookfield, S. D. (1987). *Developing Critical Thinking*. San Francisco, CA: Jossey-Bass.
Brookfield, S. D. (1988). *Developing Critical Thinkers: Challenging Adults to Explore Alternative Ways of Thinking and Acting*. San Francisco, CA: Jossey-Bass.
Brookfield, S. D. (1990a). Using critical incidents to explore learners' assumptions, in J. Mezirow and Associates, *Fostering Critical Reflection in Adulthood*. San Francisco, CA: Jossey-Bass, 177-93.
Brookfield, S. D. (1990b). *The Skillful Teacher*. San Francisco, CA: Jossey-Bass.
Brookfield, S. D. (1995). *Becoming a Critically Reflective Teacher*. San Francisco, CA: Jossey-Bass.
Brown, K. W., and Ryan, R. M. (2003). The benefits of being present: Mindfulness and its role in psychological well-being, *Journal of Personality and Social Psychology*, 84(4), 822-48.
Bryde, D., and Meehan, J. (2011). Sustainable procurement practice, *Business Strategy and the Environment*, 20(2), 94-106.
Burns, J. M. (1978). *Leadership*. New York: Harper & Row.
Burns, R. (1995). *The Adult Learner at Work*. Sydney: Business and Professional Publishing.
Butcher, D. C. A. (2011). The 'learning organization' contractor in the UK construction industry, Unpublished doctoral thesis, University of Glamorgan, Pontypridd.
Caple, J., and Martin, P. (1994). Reflections of Two Pragmatists: a critique of Honey and Mumford's learning styles, *Industrial and Commercial Training*, 26(1), 16-20.
Carless, S. A., and Roberts-Thompson, G. P. (2001). Self-ratings in training programs: An examination of level of performance and the effects of feedback, *International Journal of Selection and Assessment*, 9(3), 217-25.
Chandler, A. D. (1962). *Strategy and Structure: Chapters in the History of the American Industrial Enterprise*. Cambridge, MA: MIT Press.
Chandler, A. D. (1977). *The Visible Hand: The Managerial Revolution in American Business*. Cambridge, MA: Harvard University Press.
Charmaz, K. (2006). *Constructing Grounded Theory: A Practical Guide Through Qualitative Analysis*. London: Sage.
Chinowsky, P. S., and Molenaar, K. R. (2007). Learning organizations in construction, *Journal of Management in Engineering*, 23(1), 27-34.

Chinowsky, P., Molenaar, K., and Bastias, A. (2007). Measuring achievement of learning organizations in construction, *Engineering, Construction and Architectural Management*, 14(3), 215-27.

Chisholme, H. (2009). An exploration into the nature and impact of anxiety in Senior Management Teams, Unpublished doctoral thesis, University of Glamorgan, Pontypridd.

Chowdhury, M. (2009). Sustainable kerbside recycling in the municipal garbage contract, *Waste Management and Research*, 27(10), 988-95.

CIPD (2011a). *Sustainable Organisation Performance What Really Makes the Difference?* London: Chartered Institute of Personnel and Development, downloaded on 17 February 2011 from http://www.cipd.co.uk/shapingthefuture.

CIPD (2011b). *Engagement for Sustainable Organisation Performance*. London: Chartered Institute of Personnel and Development, downloaded on 25 July 2011 from http://www.cipd.co.uk/shapingthefuture.

CIPD (2011c). *HR in Tough Times: Adapting to a Changing World*. London: Chartered Institute of Personnel and Development.

Cooper, R. K., and Sawaf, A. (1997). *Executive EQ: Emotional Intelligence in Leadership and Organizations*. New York: Gosset Putnam.

Corbin, J., and Strauss, A. (2008). *Basics of Qualitative Research: Techniques and Procedures for Developing Grounded Theory* (3rd ed.). London: Sage.

Covey, S. (1996). The competitive paradox, *Executive Excellence*, 13(3), 3-4.

Crosling, R., and Munzberg, B. (1993). *Total Quality Management* (2nd ed.). ACT: Department of Industry, Technology, and Commerce.

Cummings, T. G. and Worley, C. G. (1997). *Organization Development and Change* (6th ed.). Cincinnati, OH: South-Western College Publishing.

Daft, R. L., and Pirola-Merlo, A. (2009). *The Leadership Experience*. Asia Pacific Edition 1, South Melbourne: Cengage Learning Australia Pty Ltd.

Davis, W. K., Nairn, R., Paine, M. E., Anderson, R. M., and Oh, M. S. (1992). Effects of expert and non-expert facilitators on the small-group process and on student performance, *Academic Medicine*, 67(7), 470-74.

Dekeyser, M., Raes, F., Leijssen, M., Leysen, S., and Dewulf, D. (2008). Mindfulness skills and interpersonal behaviour, *Personality and Individual Differences*, 44, 1235-45.

Deming, W. E. (1986). *Out of the Crises*. Cambridge: Cambridge University Press.

Denzin, N. K. (1989). *Interpretive Interactionism*. Newbury Park: Sage.

Department of Environment, Water, Heritage, and the Arts (2010). *Sustainability Curriculum Framework: A Guide for Curriculum Developers and Policy Makers*. Barton, ACT: Commonwealth of Australia.

Dewey, J. (1916). *Education and Democracy*. New York: Macmillan.

Dewey, J. (1933), *How We Think*. Chicago: Henry Regnery and Co.

Dewey, J. (1938). *Experience and Education*. London: Macmillan.

De Wit, B., and Meyer, R. (2005). *Strategy Synthesis: Resolving Strategy Paradoxes to Create Competitive Advantage*. London: Thomson Learning.

Didonna, F. (2009). *Clinical Handbook of Mindfulness*. New York: Springer.

Domjan, M., and Burkhard, B. (1993). *The Principles of Learning and Behavior*. Pacific Grove, CA: Brooks/Cole Publishing Company.

Drucker, P. F. (2008). *The Age of Discontinuity: Guidelines to Our Changing Society*. Piscataway, NJ: Transaction Publishers.

Dunphy, D. C., and Stace, D. A. (1988). Transformational and coercive strategies for planned organizational change: Beyond the O.D. model, *Organization Studies*, 9(3), 317-34.

Easterby-Smith, M., and Araujo, L. (1999). Organizational learning: Current debates and opportunities, in M. Easterby-Smith, J. Burgoyne, and L. Araujo (Eds.), *Organizational Learning and the Learning Organization*. London: Sage, 1-21.

Ebie, S. (2011). An exploratory study on the adoption of managing equality and diversity (MED) by small to medium size enterprises (SME) in England and Wales, Unpublished doctoral thesis, University of Glamorgan, Pontypridd.

Ebie, S., and Djebarni, R. (2010). Equality and diversity management: An investigation into the business case for equality and diversity practise in SMEs, *International Journal of Diversity in Organisations and Nations*, 10(5), 145-68.

Economist Intelligence Unit (2011). Synchronised Slowdown, Thursday 16 June, downloaded on 21 June 2011 from http://www.eiu.com.

Epstein, M. J., and Buhovac, A. R. (2010), Solving the sustainability implementation challenge. *Organizational Dynamics*, 39(4), 306-15.

Estes, W. K. (1950). Toward a statistical theory of learning, *Psychological Review*, 57, 94-107.

Estes, W. K. (1970). *Learning Theory and Mental Development*. New York: Academic Press.

EU as Global Actor (2009). Education for sustainable development Merging with European Policy and Strategy, Lund, Sweden, downloaded on 13 April

2011 from http://unesdoc.unesco.org/images/0014/001486/148654e.pdf.

Evans, D. R., Baer, R. A., and Segerstrom, S. C. (2009). The effects of mindfulness and self-consciousness on persistence, *Journal of Personality and Individual Differences*, 47(4), 379-82.

Fenigstein, A., Scheier, M. F., and Buss, A. H. (1975). Public and private self-consciousness: Assessment and theory, *Journal of Consulting and Clinical Psychology*, 43(4), 522-27.

Fiedler, F. (1967). *A Theory of Leadership Effectiveness*. New York: McGraw-Hill.

Fien, J., and Wilson, D. (2005). Promoting sustainable development in TVET: The Bonn declaration, *Prospects*, 35(3), 273-88.

Fincham, R., and Rhodes, P. (2005). *Principles of Organizational Behaviour* (4th ed.). Oxford: Oxford University Press.

Fineman, S. (2003). *Understanding Emotion at Work*. London: Sage.

Freire, P. (1970). *The Pedagogy of the Oppressed*. New York: Herder and Herder.

French, R., Rayner, C., Rees, G., Rumbles, S., Schermerhorn Jr., J., Hunt, J., and Osborn, R. (2008). *Organizational Behaviour*. England: Wiley.

Freud, S. (1920). *Beyond the Pleasure Principle*. Translated by C. J. M. Hubback. London: International Psycho-Analytical.

Freud, S. (1923). *The Ego and the Id*. London: W. W. Norton.

Fromm, E. (1947). *Man for Himself: An Inquiry into the Psychology of Ethics*. New York: Henry Holt and Company.

Gallup Consulting (2010). Employee Engagement: What's Your Engagement Ratio? Downloaded on 25 July 2011 from http://www.gallup.com/consulting/52/Employee-Engagement.aspx.

Gardner, H. (1993). *Multiple Intelligences: The Theory in Practice*. New York: Basic Books.

Gardner, W. L., Avolio, B. J., Luthans, F., May, D. R., and Walumbwa, F. (2005). Can you see the real me? A self-based model of authentic leader and follower development, *The Leadership Quarterly*, 16(3), 343-72.

Gardner, W. L., and Schermerhorn, Jr., J. R. (2004). Performance gains through positive organizational behavior and authentic leadership, *Organizational Dynamics*, 33(3), 270-81.

George, C. (2007). Sustainable development and global governance, *The Journal of Environment and Development*, 16(1), 102-25.

Germer, C. K., Siegel, R. D., and Fulton, P. R. (2005). *Mindfulness and Psychotherapy*. New York: Guildford Press.

Glaser, B. G. (1998). *Doing Grounded Theory: Issues and Discussions.* Mill Valley, CA: Sociology Press.

Glaser, B. G., and Strauss, A. L. (1999). *The Discovery of Grounded Theory: Strategies for Qualitative Research.* New York: Aldine De Gruyter.

Gobillot, E. (2006). *The Connected Leader: Creating Agile Organisations for People, Performance and Profit.* London: Kogan Page.

Goffee, R., and Jones, G. (2005). Managing authenticity: The paradox of great leadership, *Harvard Business Review*, 83(12), 86-94.

Goldstein, J. (2002). *One Dharma: The Emerging Western Buddhism.* San Francisco, CA: HarperCollins.

Goleman, D. (1996). *Emotional Intelligence.* London: Bloomsbury Publishing.

Goleman, D. (1998). *Working with Emotional Intelligence.* New York: Bantam Books.

Goleman, D. (2006). *Social Intelligence: The New Science of Social Relationships.* New York: Bantam Books.

Gramsci, A. (1978). *Selections from the Prison Notebooks.* London: Lawrence and Wishart.

Gulf Oil and Gas (2012). *World Economy*—October 12, downloaded on 25 October 2012 from http://www.gulfoilandgas.com/webpro1/MAIN/Mainnews.asp?id=23543.

Habermas, J. (1972). *Knowledge and Human Interests.* London: Heinemann.

Handy, C. (1989). *The Age of Unreason.* Boston, MA: Harvard Business School Press.

Hanson, D., Dowling, P., Hitt, M. A., Ireland, R. D., and Hoskisson, R. E. (2002). *Strategic Management: Competitiveness and Globalisation.* Southbank, Vic.: Nelson Thomson Learning.

Hayes, S. C., Follette, V. M., and Linehan, M. M. (Eds.), (2004). *Mindfulness and Acceptance: Expanding the Cognitive-Behavioral Tradition.* New York: Guilford.

Hayes, S. C., and Shenk, C. (2006). Operationalizing mindfulness without unnecessary attachments, *Clinical Psychology: Science and Practice*, 11(3), 249-54.

Hersey, P., and Blanchard, K. H. (1969). Life cycle theory of leadership: Is there a best style of leadership? *Training and Development Journal*, 33(6), 26-34.

Hick, S. F. (2008). Cultivating therapeutic relationships: The role of mindfulness, in S. Hick and T. Bien (Eds.), *Mindfulness and the Therapeutic Relationship.* New York: Guildford Press, 3-19.

Higgins, D., and Aspinall, C. (2011). Learning to learn: A case for developing small firm owner/managers, *Journal of Small Business and Enterprise Development*, 18(1), 43-57.

Holt, G., Love, P., and Li, H. (2000). The Learning Organisation: Toward a Paradigm for Mutually Beneficial Strategic Construction Alliances. *International Journal of Project Management*, 18(6), 415-21.

Honey, P., and Mumford, A. (1982). *The Manual of Learning Styles*. Maidenhead: Berkshire.

Honey, P., and Mumford, A. (1986). *Using Your Learning Styles*. Maidenhead: Honey.

Honey, P., and Mumford, A. (1989). *The Manual of Learning Opportunities*. Maidenhead: Honey.

Honey, P., and Mumford, A. (1990). Learning diagnostic questionnaire, in P. Honey (Ed.), *Manual of Learning Opportunities*. Maidenhead: Honey.

Honey, P., and Mumford, A. (1992). *The Manual of Learning Styles* (3rd ed.), Maidenhead: Honey.

House, R. J. (1971). A path-goal theory of leader effectiveness, *Administrative Science Quarterly*, 16(3), 321-39.

Hulspas, L., and Maliepaard, F. (2011), Sustainability in Project Management: Analyzing two projects within Medisch Spectrum Twente. *PM World Today*, XIII(VIII), 1-25.

Illies, J. J., and Reiter-Palmon, R. (2008). Responding destructively in leadership situations: The role of personal values and problem construction, *Journal of Business Ethics*, 82(1), 251-72.

ISO (2011). ISO 26000—Social Responsibility, downloaded on 7 January 2011 from http://www.iso.org/sr.

Jämsä, P., Tähtinen, J., Ryan, A., Pallari, M. (2011). Sustainable SMEs network utilization: the case of food enterprises. *Journal of Small Business and Enterprise Development*, 18(1), 141-56.

Kabat-Zinn, J. (1990). *Full Catastrophe Living: Using the Wisdom of Your Body and Mind to Face Stress, Pain and Illness*. New York: Dell Publishing.

Kabat-Zinn, J. (2000). Indra's net at work: The mainstreaming of Dharma practice in society, in G. Watson and S. Batchelor (Eds.), *The Psychology of Awakening: Buddhism, Science, and Our Day-to-day Lives*. North Beach, ME: Weiser, pp. 225-49.

Kanter, R. M. (1983). *The Change Masters*. London: Unwin Paperbacks.

Kanungo, R. N., and Mendonca, M. (1996). *Ethical Dimensions of Leadership*. Thousand Oaks, CA: Sage Publications.

Kao, J. (1996). *Jamming*. London: HarperCollins Business.

Keashly, L., and Neuman, J. H. (2010). Faculty experiences with bullying in higher education, *Administrative Theory and Praxis*, 32(1), 48-70.

Kemmis, S., and McTaggart, R. (1988). *The Action Research Reader*. Waurn Ponds, Vic.: Deakin University Press.

Keng, S.-L., Smoski, M. J., and Robins, C. J. (2011). Effects of mindfulness on psychological health: A review of empirical studies, *Clinical Psychology Review*, 31(6), 1041-56.

Kets de Vries, M. F. R. (1993). *Leaders, Fools and Imposters: Essays on the Psychology of Leadership*. San Francisco, CA: Jossey-Bass.

Knowles, M. S. (1970). *The Modern Practice of Adult Education: Andragogy Versus Pedagogy*. Chicago, Association Press.

Knowles, M. S. (1975). *Self-Directed Learning: A Guide for Learners and Teachers*. New York: Association Press.

Knowles, M. S. (1980a). *The Modern Practice of Education: From Pedagogy to Andragogy* (2nd ed.). New York: Cambridge Books.

Knowles, M. S. (1980b). My farewell address ... Andragogy—no panacea, no ideology, *Training and Development Journal*, 34(8), 48-50.

Knowles, M. S. (1984). *Andragogy in Action*. San Francisco, CA: Jossey-Bass.

Knowles, M. S. (1990). *The Adult Learner: A Neglected Species* (4th ed.). Houston: Gulf Publishing Company.

Kolb, D. A. (1976). *Learning Style Inventory: Technical Manual*. Boston, MA: McBer.

Kolb, D. A. (1984). *Experiential Learning*. Englewood Cliffs, NJ: Prentice-Hall.

Kolb, D. A. (1985). *Learning Style Inventory, Technical Manual*. Boston, MA: McBer.

Kotter, J. P. (1990). *A Force for Change: How Leadership Differs from Management*. New York: Free Press.

Kristeller, J. L., and Wolever, R. Q. (2011). Mindfulness-based eating awareness training for treating binge eating disorder: The conceptual foundation, *Eating Disorders*, 19(1), 49-61.

Lagarde, C. (2012). Annual Meetings Speech: The Road Ahead—A Changing Global Economy, A Changing IMF, address to the 2012 Tokyo Annual Meetings International Monetary Fund World Bank Group, Tokyo, 12 October, downloaded on 25 October 2012 from http://www.imf.org/external/am/2012/speeches/pr03e.pdf.

Landsbury, R. D. (1978). *Professionals and Management: A Study of Behaviour in Organizations*. St Lucia, Queensland: University of Queensland Press.

Langer, E. J. (1989). *Mindfulness: Choice and Control in Everyday Life*. London: Harvill.
Leitch Review of Skills Report (2006). *Prosperity for All in the Global Economy—World Class Skills*. Norwich: HMSO.
Levy, M., and Powell, P. (2005). *Strategies for Growth in SMEs—The Role of Information and Information Systems*. Oxford: Elsevier/Butterworth-Heinemann.
Lewin, K. (1936). *Principles of Topological Psychology*. New York: McGraw-Hill.
Limerick, D., and Cunnington, B. (1993). *Managing the New Organisation: A Blueprint for Networks and Strategic Alliances*. New South Wales: Business and Professional Publishing.
Limerick, D., Cunnington, B., and Trevor-Roberts, B. (1984). *Frontiers of Excellence*. Queensland: Australian Institute of Management.
Love, P. E. D., Huang, J. C., Edwards, D.J., and Irani, Z. (2004). Nurturing a learning organization in construction: A focus on strategic shift, organizational transformation, customer orientation and quality-centered learning, *Construction Innovation*, 4(2), 113-26.
Lovelock, J. (2009). *The Vanishing Face of Gaia: A Final Warning*. London: Allen Lane.
Luft, J. (1961). The Johari Window, *Human Relations and Training News*, January, 6-7.
Luft, J. (1969). *Of Human Interaction*. Palo Alto, CA: National Press.
Luthans, F., and Avolio, B. J. (2003). Authentic leadership: A positive developmental approach, in K. S. Cameron, J. E. Dutton and R. E. Quinn, (Eds.), *Positive organizational scholarship*, San Francisco: Barrett-Koehler, 241-61.
Luthans, F., Youssef, C. M., and Avolio, B. J. (2007). *Psychological Capital: Developing the Human Competitive Edge*. Oxford: Oxford University Press.
Lysons, K., and Farrington, B. (2006). *Purchasing and Supply Chain Management* (7th ed.). London: Financial Times Press.
Mace, C. (2008). *Mindfulness and Mental Health: Therapy, Theory and Science*. New York: Routledge.
Madden, K., Scaife, W., and Crissman, K. (2006). How and why small to medium size enterprises (SMEs) engage with their communities: An Australian study, *International Journal of Nonprofit and Voluntary Sector Marketing*, 11(1), 49-60.

Mader, C. (2012). How to assess transformative performance towards sustainable development in higher education institutions, *Journal of Education for Sustainable Development*, 6(1), 79-89.
Maiden, S. (2011). Tax beater a turn off, *The Sunday Mail (Qld)*, February 27, downloaded on 13 April 2011 from http://www.couriermail.com.au/news/tax-beater-a-turn-off/story-e6freon6-1226012559734.
May, D. R., Chan, A. Y. L., Hodges, T. D., and Avolio, B. J. (2003). Developing the moral component of authentic leadership, *Organizational Dynamics*, 32(3), 247-60.
McCall Jr., M. W., and Lombardo, M. M. (1983). *Off the Track: Why and How Successful Executives Get Derailed*. Greensboro, NC: Centre for Creative Leadership.
McGregor, D. (1957). *The Human Side of Enterprise*. New York: McGraw-Hill.
Mezirow, J. (1978). Perspective transformation, *Adult Education*, 28, 100-10.
Mezirow, J. (1981). A critical theory of adult learning and education, *Adult Education*, 32, 3-24.
Mezirow, J. (1985). Concept and action in adult education, *Adult Education Quarterly*, 35(3), 3-27.
Mezirow, J. and Associates (1990). *Fostering Critical Reflection in Adulthood: A Guide to Transformative and Emancipatory Learning*. San Francisco, CA: Jossey-Bass.
Mezirow, J. (1991). *Transformative Dimensions of Adult Learning*. San Francisco, CA: Jossey-Bass.
Mezirow, J. (1994). Understanding transformational theory, *Adult Education Quarterly*, 44(4), 222-32.
Mezirow, J. (1996a). Transformational learning, *Training and Development in Australia*, 32(1), 9-12.
Mezirow, J. (1996b). Contemporary paradigms of learning, *Adult Learning Quarterly*, 46(3), 158-73.
Mikulas, W. L. (2011). Mindfulness: Significant common confusions, *Mindfulness*, 2(1), 1-7.
Miles, M. P., Darroch, J., and Munilla, L. S. (2009). Sustainable corporate entrepreneurship, *International Entrepreneurship and Management Journal*, 5(1), 65-76.
Mintzberg, H. (1973). *The Nature of Managerial Work*. New York: Harper and Row.
Mirvis, P., Googins, B., and Kinnicutt, S. (2010). Vision, mission, values: Guideposts to sustainability. *Organizational Dynamics*, 39(4), 316-24.

Moore, P. (2008). Introducing mindfulness to clinical psychologists in training: An experiential course of brief exercises, *Journal of Clinical Psychology Medical Settings*, 15, 331-37.
Mumford, A. (1987). Helping managers learn to learn: Using learning styles and learning biography, *Journal of Management Development*, 6(5), 49-60.
Mumford, A. (1988). *Developing Top Managers*. Aldershot: Gower.
Mumford, A. (1991). Individual and organisational learning: balance in the pursuit of change, *Studies in Continuing Education*, 13(2), 115-25.
Mumford, A. (1992). Individual and organisational learning: The pursuit of change, *Management Decision*, 30(5), 143-48.
Mumford, A. (1993a). Putting learning styles to work: An integrated approach, *Journal of European Industrial Training*, 17(10), 3-9.
Mumford, A. (1993b). *Management Development: Strategies for Action* (2nd ed.). London: IPM.
Mumford, A. (1994). Four approaches to learning from experience, *The Learning Organization*, 1(1), 4-10.
Mumford, A., and Honey, P. (1992). Questions and answers on learning styles questionnaire, *Industrial and Commercial Training*, 24(7), 10-13.
Murdoch, M., Mortimer, J., Colebourne, D., Daunton, L., Finniear, J., Hammett, L., Parker, G., and Sheehan, M. (2007). Employee involvement and participation in Wales, *Report for Acas Wales and the Partnership at Work Project*. Pontypridd: University of Glamorgan Business School, 14 August.
MYEFO (2012). Mid-Year Economic and Fiscal Outlook 2012-13, downloaded on 25 October 2012 from http://www.budget.gov.au/2012-13/content/myefo/html/index.htm.
MYOB (2012). MYOB March 2012 Business Monitor: The Voice of Australian Business Owners, March, downloaded on 25 October 2012 from http://www.myob.com.au.
Neuman, J. H., and Baron, R. A. (2011). Social antecedents of bullying: A social interactionist perspective, in S. Einarsen, H. Hoel, D. Zapf, and C. L. Cooper (Eds.), *Bullying and Harassment in the Workplace: Developments in Theory, Research, and Practice*. London: Taylor & Francis, 201-26.
Norman, D. (1970). *Models of Memory*. New York: Academic Press.
Northouse, P. G. (2004). *Leadership: Theory and Practice* (3rd ed.). London: Sage.
OANDA Currency Convertor, (2012). USD/AUD Exchange rate, downloaded on 19 November 2012 from http://www.oanda.com.

OGC (2009). Building the Procurement Profession in Government, downloaded on 7 January 2011 from http://www.ogc.gov.uk.
Palmer, A., and Roger, S. (2009). Mindfulness, stress and coping among university students, *Canadian Journal of Counselling*, 43, 198-212.
Paparone, C. R., Anderson, R. A., and McDaniel Jr., R. R. (2008). Where military professionalism meets complexity science, *Armed Forces and Society*, 34(3), 433-49.
Parker, G. M. (1990). *Team Players and Teamwork: The New Competitive Business Strategy*. Oxford: Jossey-Bass.
Pavlov, I. P. (1902). *The Work of the Digestive Glands*. Translated by W. H. Thompson. London: Charles Griffin.
Pavlov, I. P. (1927). *Conditioned Reflexes*. London: Oxford University Press.
Pereira, A. O., Soares, J. B., de Queiroz, R. P., and de Oliveira, R. G. (2007). Energy in Brazil: Toward sustainable development? *Energy Policy*, 36(1), 73-83.
Peters, T. J., and Waterman Jr., R. H. (1985). *In Search of Excellence*. Sydney: Harper & Row.
Phelan, J. P. (2010). Mindfulness as presence, *Mindfulness*, 1, 131-34.
Prosser, S., Connolly, M., Hough, R., and Potter, K. (2006). *Making It Happen in Public Services: Devolution in Wales as a Case Study*. Exeter: Imprint Academic.
Proulx, K. (2008). Experiences of women with bulimia nervosa in a mindfulness-based eating disorder treatment group, *Eating disorders*, 16, 52-72.
Putnam, L. L., and Mumby, D. K. (1993). Organizations, emotion and the myth of rationality, in S. Fineman (Ed), *Emotion in Organizations*. London: Sage, 36-57.
Raiden, A., and Dainty, A. (2006). Human resource development in construction organisations, an example of a 'chaordic' learning organisation? *The Learning Organization*, 13(1), 63-79.
Rapgay, L., and Bystrisky, A. (2009). Classical mindfulness, *Annals of the New York Academy of Sciences*, 1172, 148-62.
Ravi Kanth, D. (2009). Globalisation in retreat, *Business Standard*, Tuesday February 3 2009 downloaded on 19 November 2012 from http://www.business-standard.com/india/news/d-ravi-kanth-globalisation-in-retreat/14/10/347779/.
Revans, R. W. (1980). *Action Learning*. London: Blond and Briggs.
Revans, R. W. (1982a). What is action learning? *Journal of Management Development*, 1(3), 64-75.

Revans, R. W. (1982b). *The Origins and Growth of Action Learning*. Kent: Chartwell-Bratt.
Revans, R. W. (1991). Action learning: Its origins and nature, in M. Pedler (Ed.), *Action Learning in Practice* (2nd ed.). England: Gower, 3-15.
Robbins, S. P., Judge, T. A., Millett, B., and Boyle, M. (2011). *Organisational Behaviour* (6th ed.). Frenchs Forest, NSW: Pearson Australia.
Rogers, C. R. (1969). *Freedom to Learn*. Columbus, OH: Merrill.
Rogers, C. R. (1983). *Freedom to Learn for the 80s*. Columbus, OH: Merrill.
Rosenzweig, S., Green, J., Reibel, D., Greeson, J., Beasley, D., and Jasser, S. (2010). Mindfulness-based stress reduction for chronic pain conditions: variation in treatment outcomes and role of meditation practice, *Journal of Psychosomatic Research*, 68, 29-36.
Ryback, D. (2012). *Putting Emotional Intelligence to Work: Successful Leadership is More Than IQ*. New York: Routledge.
Salovey, P., and Mayer, J. D. (1990). Emotional Intelligence, *Imagination, Cognition, and Personality*, 9, 185-211.
Segal, Z. V., Williams, J. M. G., and Teasdale, J. D. (2002). *Mindfulness Based Cognitive Therapy for Depression: A New Approach to Preventing Relapse*. New York: Guilford.
Selye, H. (1987). *Stress without Distress (Pathway)*. Philadelphia, PA: Lippincott, Williams and Wilkins.
Senge, P. (1992). *The Fifth Discipline: The Art and Practice of the Learning Organization*. London: Random House.
Senge, P., Kleiner, A., Roberts, C., Ross, R., and Smith, B. (1994). *The Fifth Discipline Fieldbook: Strategies and Tools for Building a Learning Organization*. New York: Doubleday/Currency.
Sensis® Business Index (2011). Sensis® Business Index—Small and Medium Enterprises, June, downloaded on 15 July 2011 from http://www.about.sensis.com.au.
Sensis® Business Index (2012). Sensis® Business Index—Small and Medium Enterprises, September, downloaded on 24 October 2012 from http://www.about.sensis.com.au.
Sheehan, M. (1996). Learning and implementing facilitation skills: Setting directions, *Accountability and Performance*, 2(1), 73-93.
Sheehan, M. (2006). The Fight at Eureka Stockade: Down with the tyrant and bully, Inaugural professorial lecture, presented in the Glamorgan Business Centre, University of Glamorgan, 14 March 2006.
Sheehan, M. (2010). Globalisation: Conundrums and paradoxes for civil engineering, *Leadership and Management in Engineering*, 10(1), 10-15.

Sheehan, M. J. (2000). Learning and Implementing Group Process Facilitation: Individual Experiences, Australian Digital Thesis project at http://www.gu.edu.au/ins/lils/adt/.

Sheehan, M. J. (2011). The global financial crisis and natural disaster: Impact on the Queensland economy, *The Journal of Finance and Management in Public Services*, 10(1), 24-37.

Sigelman, C. K., and Shaffer, D. R. (1995). *Life-Span Human Development*. Pacific Grove: CA: Brooks/Cole Publishing.

Silvia, P. J., and Duval, T. S. (2001). Objective self-awareness theory: Recent progress and enduring problems, *Journal of Personality and Social Psychology Review*, 5(3), 230-41.

Skinner, B. (1971). *Beyond Freedom and Dignity*. New York: Knopf.

Skyhooks (1975). *Ego is Not a Dirty Word*. Melbourne: Mercury Records.

Smick, D. M. (2008), *The World is Curved: Hidden Dangers to the Global Economy*, USA: Penguin Portfolio.

Snape, E., Redman, T., and Bamber, G. J. (1994). *Managing Managers*. Oxford: Blackwell.

Spence, M., Biwole, V. O., and Gherib, J. B. B. (2009). Research on sustainable development in small and medium enterprises in Tunisia, *Journal of Small Business and Entrepreneurship*, 22(3), 355.

Stacey, R. D. (1996). *Complexity and Creativity in Organizations*. San Francisco, CA: Berrett-Koehler.

Stogdill, R. M. (1974). *Handbook of Leadership: A Survey of the Literature*. New York: Free Press.

Strauss, A. L., and Corbin, J. (1998). *Basics of Qualitative Research: Techniques and Procedures for Developing Grounded Theory* (2nd ed.). London: Sage.

Swan, W. The Honourable (2011). Budget Speech 2011-12, delivered on 10 May 2011 on the Second Reading of the Appropriation Bill (No. 1) 2011-12, downloaded on 29 October 2012 from http://www.budget.gov.au/2011-12/content/speech/html/speech.htm.

Teasdale, J. D. (1999). Metacognition, mindfulness, and the modification of mood disorders, *Clinical Psychology and Psychotherapy*, 6(2), 146-55.

Temple, S. (2002). Functional Fluency for Educational Transactional Analysts, downloaded on 29 October 2012 from http://www.functionalfluency.com/articles_resources/Functional_Fluency_for_Educational_Transactional_Analyst_1.pdf.

The American Express Global Customer Service Barometer (2012). Downloaded on 25 October 2012 from http://about.americanexpress.com/news/docs/2012x/axp_2012gcsb_us.pdf.

The Queensland Law Society Annual Report 2009/10 (2010). Downloaded on 14 February 2011 from http://www.qls.com.au.
The Universal Declaration of Human Rights (1948). Downloaded on 29 October 2012 from http://www.un.org/en/documents/udhr/index.shtml.
Thompson, B. L., and Waltz, J. A. (2008). Mindfulness, self-esteem and unconditional self-acceptance, *Journal of Rational-Emotive and Cognitive-Behavior Therapy*, 26(2), 119-26.
Thompson, P., and McHugh, D. (1995). *Work Organisations* (2nd ed.). Hampshire: Macmillan.
Thorndike, E. (1913). *Educational Psychology: The Psychology of Learning*. New York: Teachers College Press.
Toffler, A., and Toffler, H. (1998). In R. Gibson (Ed.), *Rethinking the Future: Rethinking Business, Principles, Competition, Control and Complexity, Leadership, Markets, and the World*. London: Nicholas Brealey Publishing, VIII.
Ulrich, D., Smallwood, N., and Sweetman, K. (2008). *The Leadership Code: Five Rules to Lead By*. Boston, MA: Harvard Business Press. von Bertalanffy, L. (1950). An outline for general system theory, *British Journal for the Philosophy of Science*, 1(2), downloaded on 19 July 2011 from http://www.absoluteastronomy.com/topics/Systems_theory.
Wals, A. E. J., and Schwarzin, L. (2012). Fostering organizational sustainability through dialogical interaction, *Learning Organization*, 19(1), 11-27.
Watkins, K. E., and Marsick, V. J. (1993). *Sculpting the Learning Organization: Lessons in the Art and Science of Systemic Change*. San Francisco, CA: Jossey-Bass.
Watson, J. B. (1930). *Behaviourism*. New York: Norton.
Weber, M. (1947). *The Theory of Social and Economic Organization*. Translated by A. M. Henderson and Talcott Parsons. New York: Free Press.
Weick, K. E. (1995). *Sense Making in Organisations*. Thousand Oaks, CA: Sage.

Further Reading

Australian Council for International Development, http://www.acfid.asn.au/code-of-conduct.
Australian Institute of Management (AIM), http://www.aim.com.au/about/conduct.html.
Berne, E. (1978). *What Do You Say After You Say Hello*. New York: Grove Press.
Crane, A., McWilliams, A., Matten, D., Moon, J., and Siegel, D. S. (Eds.) (2008). *The Oxford Handbook of Corporate Social Responsibility*. Oxford, England: Oxford University Press.
Dick, B. (1997). Discussing the undiscussable: A workbook for improving group effectiveness and openness [on line]. Available at http://www.scu.edu.au/schools/gcm/ar/arp/dtuwb.html.
Harris, T. A. (1967). *I'm OK—You're OK*. New York: HarperCollins.
Hay, J. (1996). *Transactional Analysis for Trainers* (2nd ed.). Watford: Sherwood Publishing.
Lapid, M., Moutier, C., Dunn, L., Hammond, K. G., and Roberts, L. W. (2009). Professionalism and ethics education on relationships and boundaries: Psychiatric residents' training preferences, *Academic Psychiatry*, 33(6), 461-69.
Steiner, C. M. (1974). *Scripts People Live: Transactional Analysis of Life Scripts*. New York: Bantam.
Stewart, I., and Joines, V. (1987). *TA Today: A New Introduction to Transactional Analysis*. Nottingham: Lifespace Publishing.
Visser, W., Matten, D., Pohl, M., and Tolhurst, N. (Eds.) (2007). *The A to Z of Corporate Social Responsibility*. London: Wiley.
Woollams, S., and Brown, M. (1979). *The Total Handbook of Transactional Analysis*. Englewood Cliffs, NJ: Prentice-Hall.

Index

A

ABS (Australian Bureau of Statistics), 25, 43–44
abuse, 91, 120
AC (abstract conceptualisation), 142–43
acceptor, 116
ACCI Small Business Survey, 25
accountability, 47, 68, 70
action learning, 139–41, 157
Action Learning Cycle, 140
activist, 143–44
adult ego state, 103–5
adult learners, 49, 132, 134–35, 137–38, 145
adult learning, 49, 62, 110, 124, 129–31, 134–38, 142, 155, 158
adult learning theories, 130
AE (active experimentation), 143
agenda, 34, 79, 156, 160
agility, 37–38, 58–59
alignment, 37
Allen, P., 55, 57
altruism, 65–66, 75, 82
andragogy, 136–37
anxiety, 13, 45, 60, 76, 108, 147, 152–53, 161–63
approach
  contractual, 102, 105
  holistic, 32, 135
  institutional, 66–67
  positivist, 63–64
  professional, 63, 83, 93, 154, 173
    progressive-humanist, 125, 131, 134–35, 144
  scientific, 63, 125, 131, 135
  traditional business, 39
APS (Australian Public Service), 69
APSC (Australian Public Service Commission), 69
aptitude, 100, 125, 132
Araujo, L., 126
area:
  blind, 96, 98, 101
  free, 96–97
  hidden, 96, 98–99, 101
  unknown, 96, 99, 101–2
arguments, 19, 108, 111, 127, 130, 134, 154, 168–69, 174, 176–77, 183
Asia, 23, 27
Aspinall, C., 126–27
assumptions, 48, 50–51, 68, 104, 122, 136, 138–39, 145, 163, 165, 174–76, 179
attitudes, 48, 54, 60, 65, 71–75, 86–87, 94–95, 99–100, 103, 115, 122, 125, 133, 138, 176
attributes, 52–53, 57, 74–75, 79, 153–54
Australasian region, 19, 23

203

Australia, 14, 20–25, 27, 29, 34, 43, 68–70, 82–83
Australian Council for International Development, 70
Australian economy, 19–20, 27, 44
Australian Institute of Management, 66, 70
Australians, 29, 34, 90, 118
authentic leadership theories, 148
authority, 46–47, 52, 54, 69, 120, 125, 152, 161
Avolio, B. J., 92, 153–54
awareness, 29, 63, 78, 90, 94, 96, 99, 102, 110–12, 114, 117–18, 120, 127, 131, 158, 164, 177–78, 182–83

B

Baer, R. A., 111–13
bands, 62–63, 163
Bandura, A., 133, 182
bank manager, 31, 39
banks, 21, 28
Bass, B. M., 149, 151, 153
behaviour, 35, 46, 48, 53, 55, 61, 65, 69, 71, 73, 81, 87, 90, 92, 99, 111, 115, 130–32, 151, 161, 164
  ethical, 55, 61
  human, 53, 131
  new, 132
  non-professional, 69
  of others, 73, 133
  responsible, 81
  unprofessional, 71
behavioural examples, 76–77
behavioural state, 105
behaviourists, 131–33
being, 105
beliefs, 46, 54, 80, 93, 99, 125, 131, 137–38, 145, 175

benchmarks, 76
Berne, E., 102–3, 106
Blanchard, K. H., 149, 151
Boulton, J., 55, 57
Brazil, 23, 33, 136
bridges, 29
Brookfield, Stephen, 131, 135, 138–39
Bryde, D., 33, 36
Buhovac, A. R., 148
building, 45
bullocky, 91
bullying, 86, 90, 151
Burns, R., 132, 136
business environment, 30
businesses, 15, 20–21, 25–26, 28–29, 36–37, 39, 43–44, 66, 163
business leadership, 124
business performance, 162

C

capabilities, 38, 53, 90, 99, 125, 154
carbon tax, 14–15, 25–26, 28, 31, 56
CASs (Complex adaptive systems), 52, 55, 57–61, 63
catalyst, 178, 180, 183
CE (concrete experience), 142–43
challenges, 14, 31–32, 38, 79, 81, 163, 166, 168
Chandler, A. D., 46
change, 14, 16, 19–20, 31, 36–38, 41, 46, 48, 53, 55–56, 58, 62, 68, 71, 73, 79, 85, 93–94, 104, 120, 124–30, 132–33, 138–40, 146, 149, 153, 156–57, 163–64, 168–81, 183
  constant, 68, 149, 170
  organisational, 38, 62, 126, 140, 174–76, 183
  process of, 126–27, 146, 168–69, 176–78

second-phase, 175
technological, 19–20, 31
child ego state, 103–5
childhood, 100, 102–3, 105, 138
children, 88, 103, 136, 155, 179
China, 21–23, 27, 34
Chinowsky, P., 164
Chisholme, H., 45, 56, 61–62, 127, 132–33, 161
chopper, 90
CIPD (Chartered Institute of Personnel and Development), 35–38, 40–41
climate, 13, 26, 31, 64, 99, 134, 148, 154, 159–60, 164, 169, 183
codes of conduct, 68–70, 81
commitment, 13, 32, 39, 45–46, 54, 75–76, 78, 82, 94, 102, 104, 125, 147, 155, 157, 172, 179–80
communications, 23, 95–96, 99, 102, 106
community, 21, 36, 44, 47, 58, 61, 67, 81–83, 86, 92, 127, 161, 171, 182
companies, 20, 161
comparative employee engagement databases, 38
compassion, 75, 79, 111
competence, 55, 61, 70, 129, 150, 155
competencies, 36, 52–54, 57, 67, 76, 140, 157, 164
competitive advantage, 36, 52–53, 82
complexity, 30, 53, 59, 73, 116, 152, 156–57, 174–76, 183
conceptualisation, 41, 45, 143, 174, 178
conceptual understanding, 174
conditions, 13, 19, 23, 25, 29, 35, 47, 56–57, 60, 111–12, 136–37, 139, 163, 168, 176
 changing environmental, 47, 57, 168
 changing socio-economic, 176
conferences, 14, 43

conflict, 58, 69–70, 83, 94, 120, 122, 126, 128, 149, 162, 169, 179–80
confusion, 13, 60, 139, 176
consequences, 13, 23, 29, 35, 39, 45, 50, 56, 65, 73, 77, 121, 171–74, 183
construction, 27–29, 36, 43–44, 136, 168
context, 15, 35, 41–42, 52, 61, 93, 106–7, 116, 124–27, 130, 132–36, 138, 141, 148, 154, 156, 177
 environmental, 93, 135
 social, 15, 127, 134, 138, 177
 socio-cultural, 135–36
contextual understanding, 146
contingency theories, 148–49, 151
continuous improvement, 41, 124–26, 128, 169, 176
contracting, 102, 105
contracts, 68, 105, 130
control, 46, 55, 58–59, 88, 104–5, 108, 117, 141, 145, 152, 162
conversations, 58, 158–60, 163–65, 167–69, 177
 meaningful, 158–65, 167–69, 177
co-operation, 34, 95–96, 116
Corbin, J., 64
costs, 22, 25, 30, 34, 39, 50, 83, 170
counselling, 71, 100, 111, 122, 175
countries, 20–23, 29, 34–35, 37–38
creativity, 41, 53, 56–57, 62–63, 121, 150, 153, 173, 175
crisis, 19, 22–25, 27–28, 30, 44, 56, 79, 118, 149, 153, 168, 171, 176
criticiser, 90
cultural change process, 168
culture, 42, 44–47, 54–55, 60, 64, 72, 82, 93, 98–99, 147, 162, 164, 169, 173, 176
 organisational, 46, 147, 164
Cunnington, B., 46, 48
customer complaints, 30, 39–40

customer service, 20–21, 54, 69, 128
cycle, 53, 100, 140, 142–44, 182

D

Daft, R. L., 53
decisions, 56, 60–61, 63, 80, 86–88, 92, 116, 119, 134, 137, 145, 152, 156, 162
delineate change processes, 175
Deming, W. E., 41
democrat, 119–20
demographics, 171
despot, 91–92, 119
destination, 49, 56, 169
development, 14–16, 26, 28, 30–36, 41, 43–44, 49, 52, 58, 61, 64, 66–68, 70, 74–76, 81, 83–84, 90, 93–95, 98, 100, 109–13, 115, 120, 122–24, 126–27, 129, 134–35, 139, 148–49, 151, 154–57, 162–63, 169, 172, 175, 177, 179–80
  individual, 157
  organisational, 156
  skill, 58, 76, 134, 148
development programmes, 123, 175
Dewey, John, 93, 135
Didonna, F., 109–10, 112
dignity, 16, 78, 90, 116, 119
disasters, 14, 24–25, 27–30
  natural, 14, 24–25, 27–29
disciplines, 32, 42, 48–49, 51, 170, 172
disclosure, 95, 97–99, 101–2
discontinuity, 175–76
discovery, 36, 167
discretion, 99–100
distress, 99, 112, 152–53
diversity, 56, 58, 60, 153, 157, 168
Dunphy, D. C., 176
duties, 45, 69

E

Ebie, S., 60
economic drivers, 19, 21
economic recovery, 14–15, 19, 24, 26–27
economies, 21–23, 27
education, 19, 24–25, 32, 34–35, 44, 53, 60, 66–67, 124, 135–36, 154–55, 182
effective modes, 107
egos, 89, 93
ego states, 85, 102–4, 106–7
egotist, 88–89
emergent thinking, 57–58, 63
emotional intelligence, 133, 150, 163
emotional variables, 61
emotions, 63, 95, 98–99, 108, 112–13, 116, 121–22, 139, 150
employee behaviour, 46
employee engagement, 38
employee expectations, 86
employee performance, 152
employees, 13–14, 16, 30, 37–39, 43–46, 49–50, 53–54, 56, 61, 63, 69, 73–74, 83, 86, 93, 97–102, 116, 122, 125–26, 128–30, 132–34, 139, 141, 145, 151–52, 159, 162–63, 165, 171–73, 176–82
empowerment, 46, 58, 128, 153
endocrine system, 73
energy, 27, 29–31, 33, 57, 95, 150, 161–62
engagement, 37–38, 83, 125–26, 135
environment, 13, 15, 19, 23–24, 26, 28–31, 33–34, 39, 46, 50–54, 56, 58–60, 62, 67, 72–74, 78–81, 94, 100, 109, 113, 117–18, 121, 127–28, 133, 137, 141, 150–51, 153, 156–58, 161, 163, 167, 170–71, 175–77, 182

changing, 54
competitive, 52–53
　external, 23–24, 50, 73, 109, 113, 117–18, 141, 151
　healthy workplace, 53
　natural, 28–29, 34
　work, 78, 80, 151
environmental instability, 176
Epstein, M. J., 148
equality, 56, 58, 60, 72, 120, 126
errors, 86, 116, 164, 167, 175
Estes, W. K., 132
evaluation, 36–38, 113
events, 23, 56, 58, 61, 66, 72–73, 103, 109, 132, 145–46, 162, 180
excellence, 67, 71, 75–76
expectations, 13, 15, 19–20, 25, 46, 55, 58, 62, 74, 76–77, 79–80, 86, 105, 107, 113, 116, 138, 152, 159, 162, 168, 174–75, 180–81
　unfulfilled, 174, 180
experiential learning, 32, 136, 141–42
experimentation, 54, 57, 143, 173, 175
expertise, 53, 58–59, 62, 67, 150

F

factors, 13–14, 19, 22, 41, 45, 56, 80, 100, 157, 175
　unknown, 100
failure, 22, 33–34, 49, 160, 164, 177
fairness, 72, 75, 80
fear, 55, 78–80, 99–100, 108, 126, 159, 161, 163–64
feedback, 20–21, 49, 56, 76, 87–88, 90, 95, 97–102, 115, 117–18, 126, 134, 163, 175, 178
　constructive, 49, 88, 90, 100, 118, 126
feelings, 46, 55, 72, 77–78, 87, 97, 99–100, 108–10, 112–14, 116, 118, 120–22, 133, 137, 151–53, 161, 163, 178, 181–82
Fiedler, F., 149, 151
Fincham, R., 153
first-phase change, 175
floods, 24, 27, 92
focus, 14–16, 19, 26, 28, 30, 34, 38–41, 44, 53–54, 70, 95, 108–10, 112, 114, 132, 154–55, 161, 164, 169, 174–76
forces, 44, 46, 87, 171–72
forecast, 27
framework, 32–33, 36, 41, 50, 59, 93, 106, 109–10, 135, 141–42, 169–70, 176, 182
freedom, 59, 72, 78, 90, 120, 126, 136
Freire, Paulo, 135–36
Freud, S., 88
Freudian perspective, 153
friendship, 87, 116
Fromm, E, 71
functions, 43, 45, 47, 74, 86, 88, 117

G

Gallup Consulting, 38
Gardner, W. L., 92, 133, 154
George, C., 33–34
Glaser, B. G., 64
global financial crisis, 19, 22, 24–25, 27–28, 30, 44, 56, 79, 149, 153, 171, 176
globalisation, 13, 22, 28, 45, 175
goal achievement, 54, 148
goal direction, 46
goal orientation, 46
goals, 45–47, 53, 72, 79–80, 82, 92, 114, 120, 137, 148–49, 151–52, 158–59, 166, 173
Goleman, D., 133, 150, 153

goods, 13, 21–22, 27, 39, 68
government, 13, 15, 19, 24, 26–27, 29, 31, 34, 56, 66, 82, 92, 154–55, 157, 162
group dynamics, 95, 161
group learning, 140
group norms, 164
growth, 20–21, 23, 27, 29, 34, 36, 60, 76, 93, 102, 113, 121, 128

H

happiness, 138–39
Hayes, S. C., 112, 143
health, 25, 34, 39, 44, 67, 72, 85–86, 110–11, 126, 139, 168
Hersey, P., 149, 151
Hick, S. F., 114
Higgins, D., 126–27
honesty, 16, 53, 64, 68, 70, 75–77, 99, 105, 159
Honey, Peter, 135, 143–44
Hulspas, L., 33
humanitarian, 119

I

ill-health, 152–53
IMF (International Monetary Fund), 22
implementation, 23, 50, 133–34, 145, 152
imports, 21, 28
improvement, 27, 38, 41–42, 60, 92, 113, 124–26, 128, 137, 140–41, 164, 169, 176
improvisation, 62–63
improvising, 57–58, 62
inability, 28, 50, 53, 79
individualist, 117
individuals, 50, 68, 95, 98, 126, 129, 138–39, 154–55, 159, 161, 176–77, 179–81

industries, 29, 38, 66, 122, 162
information, 14, 19, 38, 44, 60, 65, 69, 77, 86, 88–90, 95–100, 104–5, 117, 119, 128, 139, 142–43, 150, 156, 162, 165, 176
innovation, 24, 35, 46, 56–57, 60, 62, 162, 173
innovativeness, 53–54, 57
inspirationalist, 117
instrumental learning, 137
integrity, 53, 64, 68–70, 75, 77, 85–86, 89, 117, 121
  personal, 85–86, 89, 117
interconnectivity, 56–57
interpersonal behaviour, 161
interpersonal development, 126
interpersonal relationships, 94–95, 152, 179–81
interpersonal skills, 83, 121, 127, 150, 153, 177
interpersonal understanding, 95
intraconnectivity, 56–57
intrapersonal understanding, 128, 177
intuition, 62–63, 72, 121
irrationalist, 91
ISO (International Organization for Standardization), 81
ITW (income tax withholding), 43

J

Jämsä et al., 32
Johari quadrant, 97–99
Johari Window, 85, 95–97, 101–2, 123

K

Kabat-Zinn, J., 110–11
KLSI (learning style inventory), 143
know it all, 87

knowledge, 21, 32, 41, 49, 53–55, 61, 65, 67–68, 70–72, 74–76, 80, 83, 95–97, 100, 115, 118, 121, 126–28, 130, 135, 137, 139, 141–42, 155, 164, 167, 169, 177
  new, 100, 126–27, 169
  personal, 141
  practical, 67
knowledge development, 32, 67, 126
Knowles, Malcolm, 130, 134–37
Kolb, David, 131–33, 135, 140–44

L

labour, 13, 19, 21, 28, 31
Lagarde, C., 23
lawyers, 66, 81
leaders, 37, 52–53, 93, 147–55, 157, 176
  strategic, 52–53
  transactional, 152
  transformational, 152–53
leadership, 37, 46, 50, 52–53, 55, 57–58, 66, 93, 95, 98, 118, 121, 124–25, 128, 146–49, 151–57, 161–62, 164
  authentic, 153–54
  strategic, 52–53
  transformational, 152
leadership behaviours, 151
leadership capability, 155
leadership development, 58, 148, 154–57
leadership process, 155
leadership skills, 153, 155
leadership style, 50, 125, 151
leadership tasks, 57–58
leadership theories, 148–49, 151–52
learners, 49, 127, 130, 132, 134–38, 141, 143, 145
learning cycle, 140, 142–44
learning organisations, 41–42, 61

learning process, 50, 63, 124, 126–27, 129–30, 132–33, 136, 142, 145, 173–77
learning programme, 139, 145–46, 157, 159, 178
learning styles, 130, 135, 140, 143
Limerick, D., 46, 48
limitations, 32, 48, 51, 86, 90–91, 112, 116, 133, 135, 143, 153, 170, 177
linear regime, 143
Lombardo, M. M., 149–50
LSQ (Learning Style Questionnaire), 143–44
Luft, J., 95
Luthans, F., 92, 154
luxury, 21

M

Maliepaard, F., 33
management, 13, 22, 34–35, 40–41, 44–45, 47–50, 52, 54, 58, 62–63, 66, 68, 71, 79–80, 86, 92, 105, 117, 125–26, 130, 151–52, 156–57, 161–63, 169–70, 175–76, 181
management group, 161–63
management organisations, 68
management theories, 151
managers, 14, 16, 32, 36–37, 43, 47, 50, 53–55, 61–63, 66, 71, 92–93, 100–101, 122, 124, 129, 134, 159, 161–63, 170, 176
manipulator, 89
McCall, M. W., Jr., 149–50
McGregor, D., 93, 149
MDC (medical device companies), 161
measurement, 132, 137, 141, 143–45, 152
mechanism, 89, 139–40
meditation skill development, 115
medium businesses, 25

Meehan, J., 33, 36
meetings, 22, 160–62, 164–65
memories, 100, 108, 110, 112, 114, 171
mental models, 42, 48, 51–53, 55, 57, 63–64, 172
  new, 48, 52–53, 63–64
mentoring, 134, 157
metaprocess, 108, 114
methodologies, 177
Mezirow, Jack, 135, 137–39
military, 55
mind, 109–10, 121
mindfulness, 48–49, 58, 85, 108–15, 117, 120–23, 155, 181
  using, 110, 113, 122
mindfulness skills, 111
mining, 14, 20, 25, 27, 29, 44
Mirvis et al., 49
mistakes, 115–16, 119, 150, 164, 173
models, 35, 42, 48–49, 51–53, 55, 57, 63–64, 95, 127, 140, 143, 154, 156, 172, 175–77
Molenaar, K., 164
money, 43, 46–47, 68, 129, 168
motivation, 32, 83, 92, 95, 108, 114, 129, 150, 153–54
Mumford, Alan, 135, 137, 143–44
music, 62–63, 88, 104, 163
musicians, 62
mutual understanding, 99, 101
MYOB, 24

N

nations, 20, 149
nervous systems, 73
network, 66, 88, 148, 163, 168
networking, 58, 60, 79, 89, 115, 121, 169
Neuman, J. H., 152

O

OANDA, 24
occupations, 65, 67, 81, 122
OGC (Office of Government Commerce), 67
open area, 96–99, 101
openness, 70, 117, 126, 154, 159–60, 162
operating environment, 46, 59, 156
organisational effectiveness, 37, 54, 176
organisational effectiveness understandings, 54
organisational learning, 123, 176–77
organisational life, 58, 61, 125, 128, 156
organisational memory, 128, 164, 177
organisational norms, 67
organisational performance, 147, 172
organisational structure, 46, 129, 161, 169
organisational systems, 120
organisational values, 155
organisations, 13–14, 16, 32, 34, 37–38, 40–42, 44–45, 48, 50, 52, 55, 61, 66, 68–70, 76, 79, 81–83, 93, 125–26, 130–31, 134, 137, 139, 149, 154, 156, 160–62, 170, 175–76
  contemporary, 13, 34, 93, 149
  large, 38, 44, 52, 55, 61, 154, 156, 160–61, 170
owner, 15, 26, 31, 36, 41–42, 44–48, 53–56, 61–63, 86, 93, 98–99, 101, 112, 122, 129, 147, 157, 164, 171–72

P

Paparone, C. R., 55, 57, 59, 61–62
parent ego state, 103, 105
parents, 72, 103
Parker, G. M., 166
participants, 25, 83, 111–13, 143, 145–46, 161–62, 165
patients, 111–12, 168

patterns, 29, 59–60, 126, 175, 179
Pavlov, I. P., 131, 149
perceptions, 25, 35, 110, 112, 125, 178–79, 181
performance, 15, 19–20, 23, 25–26, 37, 39–41, 43, 49, 53–55, 58–59, 65–67, 71, 74, 76, 82, 86, 90, 95, 99–101, 105, 117, 122, 147, 151–53, 157, 162–63, 167–69, 172, 175, 177–79
performance management, 40, 49, 58, 71, 105, 152, 157, 169, 175
personality, 47, 65, 80, 88, 99, 117, 150, 153
personality traits, 47, 65
personal mastery, 42, 48–49, 123, 172
perspectives, 53, 68, 95–96, 145
Pirola-Merlo, A., 53
PLT (Practical Legal Training), 67
power, 22, 31, 45, 52, 69, 77, 91, 103, 110, 119–20, 128, 139, 152, 161, 173, 179
pragmatists, 143
principles, 33, 36, 55, 63, 65, 69–71, 73, 75, 77, 82, 155–56
  guiding, 70–71, 75
problems, 13–16, 28, 32, 50, 58–59, 86, 120, 122, 125–26, 151, 164, 170, 172, 175, 183
problem solving, 107, 120, 122, 126, 137, 141, 151, 172–73
processes, 36, 40, 45–46, 56, 63, 94, 110, 126–27, 130–34, 141, 145, 161, 164, 167, 173–77, 181
procurement, 24, 33, 35–36, 67–68
productivity, 71, 82, 92, 95, 99–101, 105, 122, 126, 137, 148, 164, 167–68, 172
products, 13, 21, 25, 28, 31, 36, 57, 66, 161–63
professional development, 67–68, 70, 74

professionalism, 41–42, 48, 64–65, 67–70, 74–75, 84–86, 95, 121, 123, 127–29, 135, 148, 154–57, 171, 183
professional responsibility, 75, 81
professionals, 37, 68, 122, 182
professions, 59, 65–67, 69, 79
profitability, 26, 30, 41, 162, 173
programmes, 14, 37, 65, 123, 129–30, 134, 136–37, 175
  adult-learning, 136
  change, 37
projects, 27, 141, 168
PSEC (professional sound equipment company), 163
punishment, 41, 76, 98, 108, 151, 163–65

Q

quadrants, 96, 100, 106, 142
  blind area, 96, 98, 101
  hidden area, 96, 98–99, 101
  open, 99
  open free area, 96–99, 101
  unknown area, 96, 99, 101–2
qualities, 48, 53, 68, 74–75, 84, 89, 95, 111, 115, 135, 148–51, 155, 183
Queensland, 14, 24–25, 27–29, 66–67, 92

R

races, 60
rational discourse, 137
rationalist, 119
Ravi Kanth, D., 28
realisation, 13, 31, 162, 181
recognition, 19, 36, 54, 66, 82, 85, 114, 118, 134, 149, 155, 172, 182
reconstructing relationships, 174, 179

reflectors, 143
relationship building, 57–58
relationships, 15, 21, 45–46, 58, 68, 75, 77–78, 82–83, 94–95, 103, 106, 111, 115, 120, 128, 139, 147–50, 153–55, 172–74, 177–82
religion, 60, 80
report, 23–25, 31, 35, 37–38
reputation, 36, 61, 69, 82, 89, 91, 119
research, 14, 16, 33, 38, 65–66, 82, 95, 110–11, 131, 151, 154, 156, 162
resources, 21, 33–34, 48, 55, 69, 82, 106, 130
respondents, 15, 20, 24, 38
responses, 31, 59, 73, 94, 106–7, 109, 122, 130
responsibility, 15, 36–37, 47, 54, 58–59, 61, 68, 70, 75–76, 81–83, 86, 92–93, 98, 115, 117, 126, 130, 148, 154–55, 157, 162, 164, 166–67, 169, 172, 178, 180–81
Revans, Reg, 135, 139–41
reward, 41, 54, 81–82, 98, 128, 149
Rhodes, P., 153
rights, 76, 78, 102, 116, 118, 120, 125, 165
risks, 24, 29, 38, 54, 59, 121
RO (reflective observation), 143
Rogers, Carl, 135–36
roles, 15, 26, 46–47, 58, 65, 74, 134, 149, 158, 166–67, 169, 172
rules, 69, 77, 80–81, 104, 107–8, 119, 126, 132, 151–52
Ryan, R. M., 110, 112, 114

S

SD (sustainable development), 30–33, 35–36, 81
second-phase change, 175
Segal, Z. V., 113

self, 72, 85, 88, 92, 95, 98–99, 104, 108, 112, 114–17, 161, 175
self-assured, 115–16
self-awareness, 48–49, 58, 83–85, 87, 89–95, 98, 102, 104, 108–9, 111–12, 114–15, 123, 127, 150, 154–55
  lack, 87, 89, 91
self-development, 14, 43, 135, 154, 157
self-discovery, 100, 121
self-management, 150
self-understanding, 85, 94–95, 104, 113, 117, 121, 180–82
Senge, P., 42, 48, 50, 123, 125, 165–66, 170, 172, 176
sensations, 112–13, 116, 122
sensemaking, 57–58, 60–61, 63
serendipity, 100, 167
service, 13, 17, 20–21, 29, 36, 39–40, 45, 54, 56, 69–71, 76, 80, 128, 162, 171, 183
shared purpose, 37, 149
shared vision, 42, 48–50, 95, 172
Sheehan, M. J., 20–22, 24, 28–29, 34, 47, 60, 62, 64, 66, 94, 126, 131–32, 145, 157, 176–77
shift, 28–29, 55, 128–29, 168
situations, 16, 63, 85–86, 90, 94, 104, 111, 118, 120, 122, 129, 134, 149, 151, 168–69, 180
skills, 15, 19, 26, 32, 35–36, 38, 41, 44, 49–50, 54, 58, 63, 67–68, 70–71, 74–75, 80, 83–84, 86–87, 90–91, 93, 95, 111–13, 121–23, 125, 127–29, 132, 134, 145, 150, 153–57, 163, 167, 177
  intrapersonal, 58, 86–87, 121
  new, 41, 48, 134, 145, 156–57
  problem-solving, 35, 129
skill set, 50, 71, 85–86, 112, 150

small businesses, 15, 20, 25–26, 44
SME (Small and Medium Enterprise), 16, 27, 30, 32–33, 35–37, 39–49, 51, 53–61, 68, 70–72, 75–76, 79, 81–84, 86, 91, 93, 95–97, 99–102, 105, 120–23, 125–29, 148–49, 154–57, 159, 164–66, 168–73, 176, 178–80, 182
  change, 174
  employees, 46, 54, 83, 98, 139, 165, 177–78, 181–82
  employers, 155
  managers, 47
  members, 60–61, 180
  owner, 15, 31, 41–42, 47, 53–55, 61, 63, 93, 98, 100, 112, 122
  professionalism, 74–75
  staff, 56, 114
  system, 57, 59
social actors, 127
social entity, 42, 45
social learning theory, 133–34
social responsibility, 75, 81–82
social structures, 180
society, 33, 60, 82, 86, 120, 154–55, 182
soft-skills development, 95
solutions, 50, 120, 162, 168, 170–72
  short-term, 50, 170–71
Stace, D. A., 176
staff, 14–16, 19, 21, 26, 35–36, 38, 40–41, 43–44, 47–48, 56, 58–59, 69–71, 74–75, 79–84, 92–94, 97, 112–14, 117–18, 122, 124, 128, 147–48, 152–53, 157–59, 161–63, 168–69, 173
staff development, 15, 26
staff member, 56, 69, 97, 113
staff skills, 19, 26
stakeholders, 14–15, 37, 75, 79, 82–83, 86, 125, 170

standards, 69–71, 81, 152
stimuli, 73, 106, 109, 114, 131
Stogdill, R. M., 149–50
Strauss, A. L., 64
strengths, 50, 63, 93, 116–17
stress, 105, 111
structure, 25, 42, 44–46, 48, 52, 55, 61–63, 70, 129, 132, 139, 161, 169, 176
suppliers, 14–15, 19, 28, 36, 40, 47, 65, 79, 82, 90–91, 94, 114, 116, 118, 120, 147–48, 169, 171, 179
supply chain, 36, 75–77, 171, 173
support, 13, 49, 54–55, 62, 66–67, 82, 89, 117–18, 126–27, 130, 132, 134, 149, 151–52, 164–65, 177, 181
supporter, 118
survival, 15, 26, 29, 55, 57, 83, 171, 175
sustainability, 29–37, 41, 148
Sustainable Organisation Performance, 37
systems, 19, 22, 34, 41–42, 45, 48, 50–52, 55–60, 63–64, 73, 76, 95, 120, 126, 128, 152–53, 169–73, 178
systems thinking, 42, 48, 50–51, 57, 95, 126, 169–73

T

TA (Transactional Analysis), 102, 105, 123
TBL (triple bottom line), 33–34
teachers, 72, 103, 135
team, 36, 42, 48, 50, 55, 61–62, 88, 95–96, 99, 116–17, 149, 153, 157–59, 161, 164–69, 172
team development, 95
team learning, 42, 48, 50, 62, 95, 157–59, 164–69, 172

team members, 149, 164, 167
team roles, 166
team understanding, 164
Teasdale, J. D., 113
temptation, 120, 171–72
tensions, 33–34, 50–51, 120, 128, 156
themes, 37, 39, 41, 67
theories, 62, 85, 102, 124–25, 127, 130–34, 142, 145, 148–52, 154–55, 157–58, 174–75, 183
  behaviourist, 131, 133, 142
  cognitive, 132–33, 142
  of organisational change, 174–75, 183
  situational, 148, 151
  trait, 148, 150
  transactional leadership, 148, 151
  transformational leadership, 148, 152
theorists, 131, 135, 143, 175
Thompson, P., 111, 132
thoughts, 72, 89, 108, 110–14, 116–18, 120–22, 166, 181–82
Toffler, A., 124
Toffler, H., 124
tolerance, 35, 88, 117, 168, 175, 181–82
tool, 37, 40, 46, 58, 76, 95, 102, 111, 124–25, 139, 145–46, 181
  developmental, 124
  information processing, 95
  performance management, 58
  soft skill development, 122
traits, 47, 65–66, 149–50
transactions, 102, 106, 149, 151–52
transformative learning, 137–38, 155
transparency, 68, 70, 75, 79, 154
travellers, 24
trust, 53, 58–59, 63–64, 99, 105, 121, 128, 148, 152, 154–55, 161–63, 172, 180
truth, 77, 87, 91, 137

TSC, 161–62
typologies, 85, 87, 109, 115

U

UK (United Kingdom), 27–28, 37, 67–68, 163
understanding, 13, 15–16, 27, 32, 36, 38, 41–42, 46, 48, 50, 54, 58–59, 63–64, 72–73, 83, 93, 95, 98–99, 101–5, 111, 114, 116–17, 121, 123–28, 130–31, 137–40, 145–46, 148–49, 153, 158–59, 161–62, 164–65, 167, 169–71, 174–83
Universal Declaration of Human Rights, 78
universities, 32, 34, 55, 154
US (United States), 22–24, 27, 161
utilisation, 36–37, 126

V

valuer, 118
values, 32–33, 36–37, 41, 46, 54, 58, 60–62, 65, 69–72, 74–75, 77, 80, 85–87, 92, 94–95, 99–100, 115, 122, 137–38, 153, 155, 175–76
value systems, 59, 178
vision, 37, 49–50, 74–75, 95, 152, 172, 177
voice, 87, 90, 115, 118–20, 163, 177
vulnerabilities, 24, 62, 99

W

weaknesses, 93–94
weather, 19, 21, 29, 56, 88
Weber, M., 149, 151
Western framework, 109–10
whinger, 88

workers, 28
workforce, 28, 35, 45, 58, 60, 128, 163
workplace, 14, 50, 53, 80, 86, 88, 90–91, 93, 99, 110, 119–20, 122, 126, 130, 132, 134, 137, 139–41, 151, 156–57, 159, 162, 177–79
world, 15, 21–23, 26, 29–30, 32, 48, 57, 61–62, 72, 78, 88–89, 119, 136, 138–39, 156, 161

Printed in Great Britain
by Amazon.co.uk, Ltd.,
Marston Gate.